# TOUGH
# AS
# THEY
# COME

TOUGH
AS
THEY
COME

# TOUGH
# AS
# THEY
# COME

## TRAVIS MILLS
### WITH MARCUS BROTHERTON

**CONVERGENT**
NEW YORK

CONVERGENT BOOKS is a registered trademark and its C colophon is a
trademark of Penguin Random House LLC.

Originally published in hardcover in the United States by
Convergent, an imprint of the Crown Publishing Group,
a division of Penguin Random House LLC, New York, in 2015.

Library of Congress Cataloging-in-Publication Data
Names: Mills, Travis, author. | Brotherton, Marcus, coauthor.
Title: Tough as they come / Travis Mills, Marcus Brotherton; foreword by
  Gary Sinise.
Description: New York : Convergent Books, 2015.
Identifiers: LCCN 2015022590 | ISBN 9781101904787 (hardback)
Subjects: LCSH: Mills, Travis. | Afghan War, 2001—Personal narratives,
  American. | United States. Army. Airborne Division, 82nd. | Disabled
  veterans—United States—Biography. | Amputees—United States—Biography.
  | Soldiers—United States—Biography. | BISAC: Autobiography / Military.
  | Religion / Christian Life / Inspirational.
Classification: LCC DS371.413 .M55 2015 | DDC 958.104/7—dc23 LC
Record available at http://lccn.loc.gov/2015022590

ISBN 978-1-101-90480-0
Ebook ISBN 978-1-101-90479-4

Printed in the United States of America

Book design by Lauren Dong
Cover design by Jessie Sayward Bright
Cover photograph by Victoria Johnson of Molly & Victoria Co.

10 9 8 7 6 5

First Paperback Edition

*To all my fallen brothers and sisters of the 82nd Airborne Division*

*Be strong and courageous. Do not be afraid; do not be discouraged, for the LORD your God will be with you wherever you go.*

JOSHUA 1:9

# AUTHOR'S NOTE

THESE DAYS I do a lot of public speaking, and there are two things I say to any audience right up front. I wanted to say those things to you as well.

The first is that I don't hold the value of my service in the military above anyone else's. I don't think I served better or harder or greater than any other soldier. I'm just thankful I was able to serve my country. If you were in the service or are serving now, no matter what your job is, I want to tell you I'm hugely thankful, personally. If you aren't a veteran, but you support our military service members, then thank you for that support as well. Sincerely, it means a lot to me.

Second, even though I've been wounded badly, I don't think the challenges in my life are any greater than anyone else's. Sometimes after people hear my story they say, "Man, I don't know if I could ever press forward like that, and overcome challenges like you have." But I say everybody faces challenges in life, big and small. My problems are no greater than yours. Simply put, yours are yours, mine are mine, and we're all in this together.

I've been fortunate to work through my situation and lead a

positive and fulfilling life again. I hope this book will motivate you if you need to get through a challenging situation. The key is that you've got to believe it's going to get better. Keep going. Keep persevering. You're going to get through tough times. Never give up. Never quit.

# CONTENTS

# FOREWORD

IN HIS BOOK *The Price of Their Blood: Profiles in Spirit*, wounded Vietnam war veteran and former U.S. Secretary of Veterans Affairs Jesse Brown writes, "For every life unraveled by military battle, there are a dozen tales of individuals who have managed to triumph over the harrowing experiences of war and ruin." After his service at the Veterans Administration, as executive director of the Disabled Veterans LIFE Memorial Foundation, Mr. Brown went on to create the American Veterans Disabled for Life Memorial in our nation's capital, the first and only memorial honoring disabled veterans. Jesse certainly lived these ideas himself, and this quote is etched on a glass panel as part of this tribute to injured U.S. service members from all wars.

These words perfectly describe my friend, United States Army Staff Sergeant, Travis Mills.

Serving with the 82nd Airborne in Afghanistan during his third tour of duty, while on patrol on April 10, 2012, Travis was critically injured when the blast from an improvised explosive device (IED) took portions of his legs and both arms. He is one of only five quadruple amputees from the wars in Iraq and Afghanistan to survive his injuries. One would think that losing both arms and both legs would slow a person down. But with Travis, it seems to be just the opposite. He truly is one of those individuals who have managed to triumph over the harrowing experiences of war and ruin.

I met this incredible young man shortly after he arrived at Walter Reed National Military Medical Center and, like everyone who meets Travis, I was immediately struck by his amazingly positive outlook, his humor, his confidence, and his sense of gratitude for having survived the blast. While I am sure he has had his more challenging, discouraging, and darker moments in private, in public he never fails to spread joy and light to everyone he meets, and I know that his love for his wife, Kelsey, and daughter, Chloe, and their love for him, are motivating factors for him to get up each day with a new attitude to look forward, not back, and to take on the world.

Like the amazing Jesse Brown and his lifelong devotion to fellow disabled veterans, Travis is working to use his means to take care of a new generation of service members injured in battle. Whether speaking on behalf of his own foundation and his effort to build a retreat to assist wounded service members and their families, or traveling to raise awareness and funding for other military charities, Travis is constantly serving and honoring the needs of his brothers and sisters in arms. Personally, I am inspired by this resilient warrior, am proud to know him, and honored that he is an ambassador of the Gary Sinise Foundation.

In the pages that follow, I know that you also will be inspired by Travis's story—a story of hope and resilience. It is a reminder that no matter what life may throw at us, as long as we "never give up, never quit," as Travis says, we can achieve anything we set our hearts and minds to. He is quite simply a great American and an example for us all.

*Gary Sinise*

# A 15-MINUTE HELICOPTER RIDE FROM KANDAHAR

*Early spring 2012*

NLY ONE BOY PLAYED WITH HIS KITE.

The rest of the kids in the village of Maiwand took the kites we'd given them and ripped them apart. They threw the shredded kites on the ground and spat on them. Then they went over to the boy who played with his kite and hit him and spit on him. The boy's lip swelled up and his nose turned bloody. They destroyed his kite too. When there were no more kites to destroy, the children glared in our direction, cursed, and shouted anti-American slogans. A few flung dirt clods. Those Afghan kids were the best dirt clod flingers I'd ever seen.

We shrugged off our chilly reception and adjusted our weapons. I checked to see that the security detail was all right near the perimeter of the village and reminded myself that this was only our first patrol in the area. You can't blame a kid for hating American soldiers when terrorists have spread lies about us throughout their region.

I knew the Taliban were bastards. They ruled by fear. They hated us, and they also hated schools, elections, women's rights, and freedom. They slaughtered civilians, scorched acres of fertile farmland, stopped United Nations food shipments from reaching starving people, and destroyed tens of thousands of homes.

The Taliban didn't even fight fairly. They were too chicken for that. They blended in among civilians and shot at us while they used their own schoolchildren for cover. They placed improvised explosive devices (IEDs) into the ground where anybody passing by could step on them—enemy, farmer, or child.

No, I thought, these kids in Maiwand weren't Taliban. They had no news, no TV, no iPods, no means of ever hearing anything different about us. No, they weren't to blame. I always kept in mind who the real enemy was.

Clouds hung low, and wind whipped cold at us from across the desert. After our failed attempt at kite diplomacy, we sat down with village elders and explained our purpose for being in the area. They gave us a warmer welcome. About thirty men gathered in a circle. The elders, shrouded in dark beards and flowing robes, nodded at us from underneath their turbans. No women were present, although once in a while a female figure would pass by in the distance. The figure would be covered in black from head to toe. No face. Only eyes.

We gathered out in the open in the middle of their town square, a primitive dirt crossroads in the middle of a cluster of mud huts. The lower-ranking soldiers set up a security detail and didn't join our circle. They kept their helmets on, their weapons ever ready. But the higher-ranking soldiers, the officers and most of the noncommissioned officers (NCOs), joined the circle. We took off our helmets, wanting the elders to begin to feel comfortable in our presence, and we sat on the dirt or took a knee while they squatted on their haunches, a style of sitting they're comfortable with. We were served scalding hot chai tea as a gesture of their hospitality. At that temperature, the tea would be safe to drink, yet we eyed the cups closely anyway, knowing what havoc a microscopic desert bug can wreak inside a gut. The elders listened intently when we spoke through an interpreter, and when we shut up they spoke passionately about their desire for freedom and security in their homeland.

We communicated to the elders that we were in their region to help the Afghan National Army (ANA) gain a presence in the area. Maiwand is only about a fifteen-minute Chinook helicopter ride away from Kandahar, the second-largest city in Afghanistan, and a city that once had been the Taliban's headquarters.

Ultimately, we wanted to push the Taliban out of the region and keep them from influencing the population. I knew the village elders were no strangers to American soldiers. As soon as our helicopters had touched down earlier the night before, the unit ahead of us had rotated out. We were just another spoke in the military wheel, and the elders nodded along with us and smiled and agreed that the Taliban were the bad guys. The elders didn't want them there either. They'd do whatever they could to help us, they said.

I hoped the elders weren't just telling us what we wanted to hear. This was my third deployment to Afghanistan, and I knew by now to be wary of even the most sincere-sounding agreements. A quiet circle of village elders might indeed be our friends, but they also could have a Taliban member secretly embedded in their circle. Or they might simply be playing it safe, declaring their allegiance to whatever military force was present at the time. I drained the last of my tea and stayed alert, always on my guard, always ready for an attack.

I was even wary of the ANA, the Afghan soldiers, who'd come

along with us on this mission. They stood near the circle, rifles in arms. They'd signed up to fight for their country and were our allies, our counterparts. During other deployments, Afghan soldiers had hiked along with us on almost every patrol we went on, and we'd helped train and equip them. By decree, we were on the same side.

Still, I feared getting shot in my sleep. Not by the ANA themselves. But, again, by whoever might be embedded within their ranks. Whenever we stayed outside our compound, the ANA slept only about a hundred yards away from us. My fear was that some dude would pop up suddenly in the dark of night and start killing U.S. soldiers. I'd long since learned that danger lurked around every corner in Afghanistan. I never knew for certain if we were safe.

The meeting with the elders seemed to go smoothly, so we headed back to the strongpoint to report to our higher-ups what we knew so far. It had been a good day. Nobody got hurt. Everybody came back alive. When we were about twenty yards away from the barbed-wire gate of our base, I jogged ahead of my guys, did an about-face with a big smile, held up my hands to high-five them all through the gate, and started singing one of my favorite marching cadences as loudly as I could:

> *When I was younger I always wanted to be,*
> *In the 82nd Airborne, knees to the breeze.*
> *Now that I'm here, I'm going to do it right,*
> *I'm gonna slip on down to a firefight.*
> *All the way Airborne, Airborne all the way.*
> *Drive it on, drive it on.*

The guys all grinned, hiked at a faster rate, and high-fived me back as they ripped through the gates into the strongpoint. They knew I was just performing my routine. By nature, I'm not an angry person. Not usually grumpy, moody, or upset. I love life, and the biggest reason I was on this deployment was because of a sense of solidarity with my guys.

My rank was staff sergeant. I was an NCO, part of the backbone of the army. Specifically, I was a weapons squad leader in 1st Platoon, Bravo Troop, 4/73rd Cavalry Squadron, 4th Brigade Combat Team, 82nd Airborne Division. It's a long title, I know. Basically I was a paratrooper and a combat infantry soldier. I was a frontline soldier in a war without front lines.

As an NCO, I worked for my men. My job was to take my men to Afghanistan, do the job, and bring them all home safely. My attitude was that my guys always came first. Always. They ate first, and if there was no food left, then I didn't eat. When we were tired, they slept first. When we were out in the hot sun, they drank water first. They carried lighter loads than me. That was the way I wanted it.

I'd known most of the men in my unit for about a year, but already we felt like brothers. Work in the army can be like that. The army is a moving machine—guys get plugged in and taken out all the time. But the brotherhood you feel in a combat unit such as mine is intense; it has no direct comparison in the civilian world. The closest I'd ever experienced to it before was the feeling I got on a football team in high school. But even that wasn't the same. The time you spend together in a combat troop is concentrated. It bonds men together because of the constant need to lay your life down for the sake of others. Because of the ever-present threat of bloodshed and death.

I wasn't even supposed to go on this third deployment. I was supposed to be stationed somewhere else. But I had my orders changed. If my guys were going, then there was no way they were going to go to Afghanistan without me. I'd promised my wife,

Kelsey, that this deployment would be my last. My plan was to knock out this time in Afghanistan, come home, and become a recruiter at Fort Bragg. Kelsey and I already owned a house near there. In time, I'd finish up my twenty years in the military, retire from the army, then become a schoolteacher and football coach all by the ripe old age of forty.

Those were my big goals. The plan seemed smooth. But why did I have a different feeling in my gut about this deployment? One I'd never had before?

Six weeks passed in Afghanistan. We went on patrols every day and got into a series of firefights. Fortunately, none of our men were wounded in combat during those first six weeks. We gritted our teeth and carried on. This was our job. This was what we signed up to do. A constant uneasiness hung in the air.

The morning of April 10, 2012, dawned bright. It was four days before my twenty-fifth birthday, and the sun hung low and hot in the eastern sky. Glancing about me, I saw the little villages that sat in the sand all around our strongpoint. Mountains squatted far in the distance. All looked calm. But there was a sly, almost unnoticeable breeze. It dried a man's sweat and kicked up a handful of dust on his skin. It felt like the type of day where anything could happen. Or hopefully nothing.

I brushed my teeth in bottled water, rinsed my face, and woke up my team leaders by heartily singing the 82nd Airborne song.

*Put on your boots, boots, boots and parachutes, chutes, chutes,*
*We're going up, up, up and coming down, down, down,*
*We're All American and proud to be,*
*for we're the soldiers of liberty,*

*Some fly their gliders to the enemy,*
*others are sky paratroopers.*
*We're All American and fight we will,*
*'til all the guns of the foe are still.*
*Airborne from skies of blue, we're coming through, Let's Go!*

Our strongpoint was triangular-shaped, 150 yards by 150 yards by 150 yards. Inside the triangle was a dining tent, mortar pits, a parking lot for vehicles, an operating office, ten tents for living quarters, and walled-off areas where you could shower by using bottled water. There was no running water. No outside power. We burned our own trash and feces. At the edge of each of the three vertices of the compound stood a huge guard tower. At this particular time, forty-six men lived in this stronghold, along with two women soldiers who had their own tent. Our deployment was a short one, set to last seven to nine months at most, and we'd probably be based out of the strongpoint for the entire deployment, although plans could always change.

We were taking the day off; no patrols were scheduled, so I let my other men doze a bit longer while my team leaders and I headed over to the chow tent for breakfast. A Unitized Group Ration (UGR) was being served. I was thankful. While a UGR wasn't as good as eating at IHOP, I knew there were days on deployment when a soldier doesn't eat at all. There were no complaints from me, particularly with my sausages and eggs smothered in hot sauce, salt, and pepper.

Days off when you're on deployment are nothing to write home about. Everybody on deployment has a computer with a hard drive stocked full of movies and TV shows. My favorite movies were *The Last of the Mohicans*, *Gladiator*, *300*, *Troy*, and *The Patriot*. I'd seen them all more times than I could count. I loved the crime drama *Sons of Anarchy*, about an outlaw motorcycle club, and I think I'd seen every episode of the sitcom *How I Met Your Mother* at least twice. If a guy had something—anything—then we watched it. I don't know what it was about *That '70s Show*, but it always made me laugh. My lieutenant was even sent a DVD of the show *Glee* once, and everybody mocked him for it, but we all watched it anyway. We were also lucky in our strongpoint to have three telephones and five computers with Internet access, so we were able to check email regularly and Skype home, which is what I did right after breakfast.

Because of the time difference, my morning was Kelsey's nighttime, and her familiar face popped up on the computer screen looking like she was just about ready for bed. My wife is beautiful. She has blondish-brown hair that falls a little past her shoulders, and I looked straight into her eyes. We usually didn't have long conversations over Skype like this. But we'd check in each day with each other just to say, "I love you, all's well." She held up our baby, Chloe, for me to see, and I kissed the tips of two fingers and touched them to the screen to say good night. Chloe cooed, grinned, and waved.

After that, I hit the gym. It's nothing to write home about either. We called it a prison gym. It's in the middle of the strongpoint and has bars, bells, and benches. Nothing fancy. At six foot three and 250 pounds, I liked to stay in shape. I never did cardio while on deployment, because when you're out all day on patrol, packing 150 pounds around in the hot sun, that's all the cardio you need. But every day I went through a basic weight routine of rolls, shrugs, backs, and presses. The sun was already hot, and I wished I was back at home heading down to the local air-conditioned Planet Fitness.

When you're hanging out with guys lifting weights, you tend

to shoot the bull in between reps. A favorite topic at the prison gym was what you'd eat for your first meal when you got home again. My favorite meal is steak, preferably wood-fired, with cheesecake for dessert. So we lifted, then talked about steak, then lifted some more. Then we talked about homemade mac and cheese. Then we discussed fried chicken and buttery corn on the cob in great detail. We concluded with a conversation about a frosty glass of beer along with a salty bag of potato chips. Somewhere in there we talked about a fresh slice of warm apple pie.

The rest of the day passed slowly. We threw around a football for a while, ate more military rations for lunch, and watched some crap on TV. We were always ready to go, even while on a day off. Our weapons were always cleaned and loaded. Our backpacks were always full. Our ammo was stocked and set. If an order came in, we could fully assemble as a platoon and head out the gate in under ten minutes.

Late in the afternoon, about 4:30 p.m., we received a tip from a local civilian informant. There were IEDs in the area, the informant suspected, and he asked us to come check it out. That meant our day off was officially over. The tip wasn't anything unusual, but we weren't nonchalant about it either. Each time we went out the gate, we were on high alert.

Specifically, I was responsible for two weapons teams of four men each. Whenever my teams got into a firefight, the responsibility ultimately fell to me. I told my men where to go and what to do. I told them to shoot or not to shoot. I made sure they stayed safe and came back alive.

Each of my teams carried what's called a 240 Bravo—the biggest dismount-and-carry machine gun the military has. It's a long, sinister gun that weighs about twenty-seven pounds. It can shoot at a rapid rate and hit a target a long distance away. You can mount a 240 Bravo on a vehicle if needed, or carry it around with you while patrolling. In addition to the guns, between both of my teams, we carried two thousand rounds of ammunition.

My senior team was composed of four soldiers: Specialist Cobia Farr, the assistant gunner; Private First Class Armando Plascencia, a designated squad marksman who carried a long-range rifle like a sniper would; Private First Class Eric Hunter, the gunner; and Private First Class Jon Harmon, the ammo bearer, who carried the rounds and also took rear security. This team could operate without me and had just come off a patrol, so that day I told them to stay back on base.

My junior team was composed of myself and three others: Private First Class Ryan Theriot (we called him "The Riot"), the assistant gunner; Private First Class Brandon Fessey, the ammo bearer; and Private First Class James Neff, our gunner. They were the younger guys, so I stuck with them.

When the call came, I suited up along with my junior team and buckled my Kevlar plate carrier vest around me. It clicked into place and I instantly felt tough and protected, like a gladiator with his sword unsheathed and his shield up. Along with the bulletproof plates, my vest also carried a small first-aid kit, a grenade pouch with ten of those inside, twelve ammo magazines, a camera, a bottle, a sunglass holder, pens and maps, and a radio hookup. I slapped on my kneepads, threw on eye protection, and rolled my gloves at the wrists and flexed my hands into fists. It's an internal signal that lets me know I'm ready for battle. It reminds me that I'm not looking for a fight, but if someone wants to fight me, then he's going down, not me.

I clipped my helmet into place and slung my weapon around me. In my backpack were more rounds of ammo, water, food, an extra T-shirt, baby powder to prevent chafing, and a little photo album I always carry of my family. Altogether, depending on what it had in it for any particular mission, my backpack added another 80 to 110 pounds onto my frame.

As I walked out of the gate past the guard tower, I pulled back the charging handle of my weapon and let it go. Every man did the same. That way, you're "cocked, locked, and ready to rock," and when you hear the round lock into place, you claim the dominant mind-set that nobody had better mess with you today.

*Absolutely* nobody.

WE HIKED ONLY about four hundred yards to the village. In addition to my weapons team, there were other squads along on the patrol, a total of twenty-eight soldiers. My lieutenant, Zachary Lewis, went to the left with the first and second squads, heading to meet with the village elders, while the rest of our men went with me around the village on the outside to offer support in case of an attack. Along with my gun team, I had my platoon sergeant and a medic, Sergeant Daniel Bateson, with my group. All looked calm. It seemed like just another day in Afghanistan. Another normal patrol.

We approached an abandoned ANA security post (two portable buildings), and stopped near the buildings to establish a security perimeter. I called for Fessey to bring the minesweeper. It's a wand that goes up and around his arm, and it looks like a metal detector a guy would use at the beach. If the minesweeper makes a noise, that means something's in the soil. If we hear a beep, then we mark the spot, go around it, and have the Explosive Ordnance Disposal (EOD) guys dig out and dispose of whatever's under there. Whenever we found an IED, we'd never mess with it ourselves. Mines can be unpredictable, and you want the experts to handle them. Some IEDs aren't even made of metal, just plastic and glass, which can sometimes fool a minesweeper. But even then, the minesweeper is designed to have ground-penetrating capability. It can usually detect if something's in the ground and it's not soil.

"Check this area" was the only order I gave.

Fessey walked up a path used by villagers and scanned all around the area. He went up and back, and all was clear. No beeps. There was no reason to question anything. Fessey finished his minesweeping duties and went to set up on the far flank.

I called Riot up to me and asked him where he thought we should put up the gun. I knew where it should go, but I wanted to let him decide, making sure he knew his stuff. He motioned to exactly where I thought we should put it, a good spot, and I said, "All right. Go get Neff and bring him up here." That was it. Riot left to go get Neff, and as he did, I set my backpack down. The backpack touching the dirt was all it took.

Such a simple act of war.

My world erupted.

I saw a flash of flame and heard a huge *ka-boom*. Hot jagged pieces of explosives ripped through me. I cartwheeled backward end over end, hit the ground, and slammed my face hard against the compacted earth. Instantly I felt my left eye starting to swell shut. I smelled burning flesh—my own. I tasted dirt, and I was wet with sweat and moisture like I'd just walked out of a hot shower.

Dirt fell everywhere through the air. It rained down and clung to my eyes, nose, and mouth. I don't remember rolling over, but I must have, because I glanced to the side and saw that my right arm was completely gone. I caught a glimpse of my left arm, covered in blood and tattered. The arm trembled as if it had a will of its own. I looked down and saw that my right leg was also gone. The stump looked like a piece of raw meat. The bottom of my left leg was still attached but held on by only a few strands of skin. I saw all this in a flash, an instant.

I felt confusion but no panic. My first thought was of my guys. I flopped my remaining arm toward the microphone clipped to my plate carrier and somehow managed to push the button. "I hit a bomb," I said. "I need help."

Bateson, my medic, rushed up to me along with Staff Sergeant Keith Hambright, our platoon sergeant. Only about thirty seconds had passed since the blast. Immediately they applied tourniquets to hold in whatever blood was still inside me.

"I'm not going to make it," I said. "Leave me and go save my guys."

"Shut up, Sergeant Mills," Bateson said. "Let me do my job."

I ignored Bateson and yelled my men's names like a roll call: "Fessey! Riot! Neff!" to see if they were okay. Two were hit, Fessey and Riot, and other medics were already caring for them. They were bleeding, but nothing was missing. They yelled back that they were going to be okay.

I calmed down.

More soldiers ran toward me. Sergeant Alex Voyce, another medic, wondered aloud where to best get IV access. There were no pulses to check except for my carotid artery. He quickly ripped open my vest, shaved a spot on my chest, and put an IV straight into my sternum. It hurt going in, and I must have howled, because he yelled at me that I was going to be fine. I yelled back, "Doc, shut up. I know." He and I both calmed down.

Someone stuck a Fentanyl pop in my mouth. It's a potent painkiller that releases as the pop dissolves. I downed the first one, spit out the stick, and asked for another.

"You won't need it," someone said.

I was still thinking that I was going to die. I didn't want to show fear. I didn't want to freak out. You never want to show fear around your men. "Let my family know I dealt with it without crying," I said.

"Tell them yourself," someone grunted. He was being encouraging, letting me know I wasn't dead yet.

I tried to see around me. I raised my head, wanting to get a visual of Fessey and Riot.

Someone shoved my head back down. "Lie still," commanded a voice.

My one eye was completely swollen shut. The other eye was blurry from dirt. I tried to raise my head again. Again I was pushed flat. My eyes were watering now, the dirt turning to mud. Time passed and I didn't know what was happening. I mumbled something, but there was no reply. Only the steady *whup whup whup* of a Blackhawk helicopter touching down nearby. Six men surrounded me, hefted me up, and carried me over. All told, it might have been ten minutes since the blast until the helicopter arrived.

Fessey and Riot were already inside the helicopter. Everything was foggy and noisy, and I couldn't make out my surroundings clearly. My two guys were on seats and I saw blood and bandages jumbled in their direction. Fessey had shrapnel in his face. Riot had shrapnel in his face, legs, and hand. Their images faded away. I focused on the *whup whup whup* of the rotors.

We were in the air, and the flight medics were taking care of me. Riot yelled in pain. I tried to look around. Someone needed to attend to Riot. Where were the medics? One of the medics was talking to the pilots up front. Riot was yelling again. I looked in Fessey's direction and told him to calm down. Fessey nodded. Riot stopped yelling, and I winked at him to let him know he was going to be okay. It was all I could think to do.

The flight medic was back in view. I could barely see him

through the goop in my eyes. He wore a green flight suit and a big Darth Vader helmet. I tried to speak. He gave me a quizzical look. I yelled as loudly as I could, "Take off your helmet!"

He took his helmet off.

"Give my guys water and tell them they're going to be okay!" I barked.

"Don't worry, I'll take care of them for you," he said. He was busy with some task on me that I couldn't see.

A moment went by, and I added, "I'm sorry."

"For what?" the medic asked.

"For making you take your helmet off."

He gave me a wry grin.

I realized he'd been doing his job all along. Doing it well. Both of the medics had. I just couldn't see all that was happening around me. My mind went in and out. I was coherent but fuzzy in spots.

In fifteen minutes, the helicopter landed in Kandahar.

Hospital staff rushed me straight to the operating table. "We're going to put you under now," came a voice from above me.

"I'm fine," I said. "Leave me alone."

The mask came over my face and I tried to push it away. I remember asking one question: "Am I ever going to see my baby girl again?"

# BORN IN A SMALL TOWN

THE NIGHT THEY FOUND OUT I WAS HIT, THE PEOPLE IN MY hometown of Vassar, Michigan, held a vigil for me. Community members formed a gigantic circle in the middle of the football field, the same field I'd run touchdowns on only a few years earlier. They lit candles in the dark and prayed that I would live.

Of course, I didn't know then about the candlelight vigil. I was in and out of sedation in an intensive-care unit half a world away. But it does me good today to know that a bunch of people from my hometown were rooting for my survival.

Even when I was stationed at Fort Bragg and lived in Fayetteville, North Carolina, I'd always pictured myself coming back someday to Michigan and living a full and rich life there, where my roots are. If you live in Vassar, you work your job, raise your family, and do whatever you need to do for your community and country. That kind of straightforward living appealed to me, to my core.

It also reflects the way of life for a lot of today's American military personnel. To understand a soldier's grounding in his hometown is to understand him, his values, and what he holds important. Ultimately, it helps one understand a country that values liberty so deeply it's willing to lay down the lives of its sons and daughters in the name of freedom.

Here's how this American soldier's journey began.

I was born on April 14, 1987, in Saginaw, Michigan. The town is not quite twenty miles away from Vassar, and I was born there only because Saginaw has a hospital and Vassar doesn't. It's in the part of the state they call the Lower Peninsula, which is shaped like a mitten. Where I lived is at the base of the thumb.

Vassar is not like Washington, D.C., Los Angeles, or New York City, places of far-reaching ambition. It's a town of about 2,800 people, a settlement of quiet permanence where you can feel the soil underneath your bare feet on a summer afternoon while talking to your neighbors over the backyard fence. I was the fun kid who lived at the end of your block. I was always big for my age, and for a lot of my boyhood years I had a big gap between my two front teeth. I liked to wear my hair shaved in a buzz cut, particularly in summers when it got hot. With that Opie Taylor kind of look, I fit in fine in small-town America.

It was against this backdrop that I learned early to lead with love and determination and courage and humor. I'm the middle child of three. My sister, Sarah, is two years older than I am, and my brother, Zachary, is two years younger. Sarah was tough and could hold her own against two brothers, but I always felt like the leader of my siblings in a protective sense. If anyone ever messed with my big sister or my little brother, then that person would have to answer to me. A kid tried to move my sister out of her bus seat once, and I didn't like that, so I moved the kid out of the way and gave the seat back to my sister. That was the last time the kid ever tried a stunt like that.

I could also be the leader when it came to mischief. Once I got in trouble because we had mashed potatoes for dinner, and when Dad went into the other room for something, I dumped a bunch of pepper into Sarah's mashed potatoes and laughed my fool head off. When Dad found out he got mad and gave me a spanking. I deserved it. That's the kind of guy I am—always wanting to have fun, even when pushing boundaries. You show me an unguarded plate of mashed potatoes, and I was gonna mess with it.

One fine summer day, Dad bought us squirt guns to use outside because it was so hot. Zach and I got into a squirt gun fight, and I won, but even after I'd won I kept squirting my brother in the face. He yelled at me to stop messing with him, but I wouldn't, so he picked up a lawn chair to throw at me. That's when Dad intervened. He broke our squirt guns in two and threw them in the trash. I think we'd had them a total of half an hour. I never gave up the fight, even in a squirt gun war.

Dad worked as a truck driver and maintenance engineer. Mom worked for a grocery store. Together they made okay money, and we always had what we needed. We weren't rich, but we weren't poor either. In addition to my parents' regular jobs, we owned and operated a twenty-acre hobby farm, so as a child, I learned how to clean out a barn, cut and stack firewood, tend a field, and grow food. On a farm, even a small farm, there are never enough hours in a day, and we were always outside working the fields doing something: plowing, fertilizing, planting, hoeing, weeding, or gathering in produce when the time came for it to be picked. We grew our own vegetables in a garden about half the size of a football field—corn, tomatoes, cucumbers, squash, onions, potatoes, and even a few watermelons. That was the best food I ever tasted, the kind that comes straight from your own backyard. I've always known it's not a bad feeling to be on the end of a hoe, sun beating down hot on your back, muscles aching.

My brother, sister, and I were given a lot of responsibility at a young age. One day, at age ten, I was driving a huge Case backhoe with a front loader around our property. Dad told me to go put it in the barn, but I didn't swing the huge vehicle wide enough. I hit the broad side of the building on its corner and nearly brought the whole barn down. I thought he'd make me get off it so he could do it right, but my dad just shook his head and told me to do it again until I learned. That was Dad's style. You were given a job to do, and you figured it out. When I joined the military, I turned into a pretty good shot with a rifle. But unless you're a sniper, even the best shooters will be slightly off target every now and again. I was always waiting for some joker to say I couldn't hit the broad side of a barn. I'd just smile and say that target had already been hit.

We went camping a lot as a family, sometimes in nearby campgrounds, sometimes up at Grandma and Grandpa's cabin at Higgins Lake, about two and a half hours north. It was nothing fancy. Just a two-bedroom cabin with a pull-out couch for the extra kid to sleep on. We went fishing and tubing, and on hot summer afternoons we walked the mile and a half to the store to buy Fun Dip or Charleston Chews. It was up camping that I be-came aware of my first—and pretty much only—fear in life.

Fish.

I hated 'em. I couldn't tell you exactly why. I don't mind eating fish today, and I never cared if they were out in the water splash-ing away having a grand old time by themselves. But if Grandpa put me on an inner tube behind a ski boat and went as hard as he could—then I would not fall off. Period. I could be sideways, upside down, hanging on by my fingertips with one hand—but I would not let go. Fear of fish glued me to that inner tube. If for some strange reason I did fly off, then I'd hit the water with a literal clenched fist. I'd go down punching the water. Kicking. Swinging. Any old snapping turtle in my vicinity was going to get a hard smack upside his head. Maybe I'd seen *Jaws* too many times. The thought of a huge aquatic monster swimming beneath me made me shudder. Even in a lake.

Mom put me in karate when I was six because I liked to watch Chuck Norris in *Walker, Texas Ranger* on TV. Mom took karate lessons right along with me, and I loved having her in class. Everyone learned a few basic moves, then we went to our first tournament, where we were told to spar off against each other. My first opponent was a girl with a black ponytail. She was about the same build and height as me. The referee blew the whistle and the girl shifted into attack mode, punching and kicking the stuffing out of me like I was a fish in Higgins Lake. I just stood there taking it without throwing a single punch. She scored all the points, and when the tournament was over my parents were like, "Why didn't you fight back?!"

"Because you told me never to hit a girl," I said, my face uncharacteristically glum.

My parents chuckled, and my mom said, "Well, it's okay to fight back in a karate tournament—even if your opponent is a girl. And if ever you find yourself in a fight, you just make sure you never lose—okay?"

I nodded, and the next round I turned into Jackie Chan. I won that match, and the next and the next. More tournaments came after that, and medals began to line up on my dresser at home. I kept going and never looked back. That year for my weight division I was state champ.

It wasn't all easy. In one of my first karate matches I got

kicked hard in the sternum and couldn't breathe. I gasped, pan-icked, and tried to suck in air. When my normal breathing didn't return immediately, I raised my hand and forfeited the match. My dad rushed over and said, "Travis, what are you doing? You never forfeit a match, no matter how hard you're hurting. You never quit—ever!"

I never quit again.

The military teaches you the same thing. When you're in basic training and doing push-ups by the hundreds, you feel like quitting. And some guys do. They pack their bags and go home. But I couldn't fathom that. Just because something's difficult, or you don't want to do something, that's no excuse for giving up— that's what my gut told me. When you're out in the Afghan desert eating sand and taking mortar fire, you can't quit until your job is done. You take whatever hardship comes your way, and you take it without complaining. I learned that principle early.

Dad never showed any pain. Once, we were working on a tractor, and I saw him slice his finger open deep. He didn't yell or quit the job. He just bandaged his finger and went back to work. If ever I got hurt as a kid, I tried to follow in my father's footsteps, suck up the pain, and continue on. After I was wounded by the IED blast and had to learn to walk all over again, lessons like that came back to me. The pain of rehab was intense, sure, but I wouldn't give up. It just wasn't in my blood.

In school, I loved recess best. That, and talking with my friends, and playing sports. Always sports. I was restless as a kid. I always needed to be running, jumping, moving, and I found it hard to sit still in a classroom. One of my earliest memories is of dribbling a basketball on the cement outside my parents' house. I kept dribbling, dribbling, dribbling, around my back, through my legs, switching hands. I wanted to get better, and the quest to excel became a pattern for whatever I did.

About the only sport I didn't play was T-ball. I thought it was a waste of time. But I played hardball, which I loved. I was fast and quick, good at outfield, but there was never enough action for me out there, so I soon switched to catcher. That way I could have my hands on the ball every play, always part of the action. Sometimes people think of the pitcher as the leader on a baseball field, but it's actually the catcher who makes things happen. He's got his eyes on everyone on the field, and he calls the pitches and defenses. It's the position for players who like action and want to work hard. That was me. I batted .450 my sophomore year, .500 my junior year, and .550 my senior year, and for a while considered a career in Major League Baseball. I had a number of offers to play college baseball, but I was more sold out to football, and the football offers were the ones I considered more seriously. I lettered throughout high school, and was captain of the football team my junior and senior years, but I never got a varsity jacket, since I needed to pay for it myself. I didn't think it was a good investment.

School administrators had something called Captain's Club, where you needed to go to three football camps, maintain a 3.2 GPA during football season, put in a specific number of hours in the weight room, and perform fifty hours of community service. I liked that. It was challenging and measurable. I made the Captain's Club all four years.

I loved the thought of financial independence and bought my own car in high school and paid for my own gas. My first car was a 1996 two-door Cutlass Supreme. Man, that was a nice car for a high school kid. It had leather seats and a sunroof, and while driving it around town I felt like the mayor of Vassar, the fresh prince of every good opportunity that small-town America held out to me.

■ ■ ■

VASSAR HIGH SCHOOL is home of the Vulcans, our mascot. I wore the football uniform with pride, with the same kind of pride that I later wore the uniform of the United States Army. Whenever I'd played sports as a kid and a teenager, I felt part of something larger, a camaraderie, a brotherhood. Football and the military always seemed to me to be related in that sense. As part of the legendary 82nd Airborne, I felt a connection to something beyond myself. Something larger. Something more important. Something that needed to get done.

Here's how my high school coach, Vince Leveille, described me back then:

*The first time I met Travis, he was in middle school at a track meet. I'd heard about him, so I went over to watch him. He won the shot put, which meant he was strong. Then he ran over to the 100-yard hurdles and won those, which meant he was fast. You don't see that combination a lot. I knew then that this kid was going to be special as an athlete.*

*In high school, he became a superstar, a three-sport athlete: baseball, basketball, and football. He was the leader on each team, and made First Team, All-Conference, in all three sports. With football, he was definitely the key cog in our team's wheel. We were the smallest school in our conference, and we got beat up for a lot of years. But his junior year, Travis and his friends got into weight lifting and power lifting and went to all the football camps. That year we won the conference championship and made the playoffs for the first time ever. Travis's work ethic motivated everybody. Everybody got stronger because Travis was their leader.*

*Other teams knew that if they had any chance of beating Vassar, then they needed to stop Travis Mills. I saw other teams gear their whole defense to stop him. We would either fake the ball to Travis (and then the other team would wrap their defense around him), or we'd just hand the ball to Travis and let him run.*

*Travis did everything on the football team. He was the fullback and the linebacker and the punter and the kicker. Without him, we wouldn't have won half the games we did. Our school's winning streak started with Travis's junior year. Since then, other classes have seen what can be accomplished by buying into the program, and our football program has turned around. We make the playoffs almost every year now. It all started with Travis.*

One of my most favorite games ever was the seventh game of my junior year. We were up against our biggest rivals from Frankenmuth, the next town over, a real David versus Goliath story. They were 6-0, familiar with winning, and this was their homecoming game, so their hearts were in it. We were 5-1. Nobody expected us to win. But if we won the game, then we'd lock in the conference championship and make the playoffs. The entire town of Vassar showed up to cheer us on.

It was a close game, back and forth, back and forth. It seemed like nobody could gain the advantage, although the other team sure looked like they would. Late in the game, I broke our opponents' line and ran for sixty yards. To this day Coach Leveille says that one run changed the whole dynamic of the game. It broke things wide open and knocked the wind out of the other team's sails. They realized they weren't going to win the game after all, and their play after that showed they were deflated. With the final minutes ticking, we had the ball and were ahead. We took a knee for the last two plays to run out the clock. The volume of the crowd was huge. Everybody was yelling *Vassar! Vassar!* The game was ours.

When it came to sports, the atmosphere around the town of Vassar was the same as in *Varsity Blues* or *Friday Night Lights*. Vassar thrived on football, and if you were a star player, then everybody knew you. My girlfriend at the time was from a different town, and once on her way over to see me, she got pulled over for speeding in a school zone.

"Where you going, Speed Racer?" the cop asked her. He opened his ticket book.

"I'm going over to see my boyfriend, Travis Mills," she said.

The cop stared for a moment, then closed his ticket book. "Just keep him out of trouble for football season," he said, and waved her on without another word.

In high school I worked as a bagger at the local supermarket, although I seldom actually bagged any groceries. I preferred the term "grocery packaging engineer" or perhaps "official store greeter." Townsfolk would approach me at all hours of my shift to talk about football. There was endless speculation about what we as a team were doing, about the upcoming challenges, about how this player or that player was faring, about which play to call and when, about which players we needed to watch out for on the rival teams. The store owner never once yelled at me to get back to bagging. He was just as interested in football as the rest of the town.

Coach Leveille was the assistant principal in addition to his duties as the coach, so his job was to ride our butts about behavior issues too. I never did anything really wrong in school, just nickel-and-dime shenanigans, but I was always highly social, far more interested in hanging out with friends than I was in my schoolwork. I could be a bit mischievous too, in a fairly harmless way, and we just did stupid stuff where I was known to be the instigator.

One time in ninth grade my buddies Erick and T. J. and I were in geometry class just before the start of the period, and the school must have served beans in the cafeteria for lunch, because our intestines were ripe with gas.

I tried to keep the pressure in at first, but I also recognized a golden opportunity for comedy. I slid out a fart that everybody could hear, and sure enough Erick started laughing, and while he was laughing he slid out one of his own. That made it doubly funny, and T. J. didn't want to be left behind, so he squeaked out a big brown roar that stunk like a rotten tortilla, and we all howled. The farting ice was broken, and our ever-present sense of competition kicked in. We each tried to fart the loudest and the longest. For several gleeful minutes it was a chorus of one juicy honker after another. The girls around us all held their noses and declared we were gross, but we were dishing up vengeance on the lunch gods and couldn't be stopped. When the bell rang to start the class, the teacher told us to shut up, but we were long past the point of no return. T. J. ripped a huge floater, and the teacher kicked him out in the hallway. I let out a duck call, and the teacher pointed to the door. I guess Erick didn't want to be left alone, because he laid a rumble of an egg and got tossed out behind us. There the three of us sat in the hallway, dead guilty for passing air biscuits.

Coach Leveille rounded the corner, his vice principal hat on too tight, and in a stern voice asked, "What are you boys doing out of class?"

"Uh . . . you don't want to know, sir," I answered. We tried to smother our snickers.

He looked straight at me. "What was it, Mills? Out with it."

*Out with it?* That was the wrong thing to say. We each let loose with the last of our gas.

Leveille let the stench clear then said, "I've got to write you up for this, you know." His voice was all business. "Now get back to class!"

Coach Leveille just laughs today when he tells that story. He was only doing his job.

MOM ALWAYS SAID I could talk myself out of trouble just as surely as I could talk myself into it. And I'd say it was that skill for running my mouth that brought me close to fistfights but also kept me out of most while growing up. I was a big, tall, muscular kid, and nobody messed with me for that reason alone. But I also found I could joke my way out of disagreements, and I liked to handle tense situations that way. Why fight when you can laugh?

One day in grade school I came home with a fat lip. Mom asked what happened. I explained how I didn't want to fight back because I was afraid of hurting the other guy. Mom said, "Travis, if you're getting beat up, then hit him back. Hit him hard enough so it won't be a problem again." So I did. And Mom was right—if you're going to be in any fight, whether a playground fistfight or a war in Afghanistan, then you need to do the job right. I hit the kid hard and concluded what had been started. It never was a problem again.

On the football field, I played as hard as I could, and if during a play I crushed a guy, then that's what I'd do. Once I hit a player so hard I knocked him clear off the field and into the benches. He was okay but a little shaky afterward. I went over to him and made sure he was okay. That's usually how I operated. If I flattened a guy, then I'd help him up afterward. I wasn't a scrapper on the field, even though I often felt like a marked man. Once, in the final seconds of a game we were winning, I cut through a bunch of players from the other team. A guy was at my ankles, and after the play was over, he grabbed my ankle and twisted it hard. When we both stood to our feet, I picked his face mask up and punched him in the chin. The referees broke us up. The game was over. So that was that. If you're going to play football, you need to get physical. Your opponents might be the greatest guys off the field, but when they're on the field they were trying to beat you, so I was trying to beat them, and if one of them hit me, then I'd hit 'em back.

The only thing close to a fight that I got into during high school happened the day I saw somebody cut ahead of my kid brother in the lunch line. I was a junior in high school and Zach was a freshman. The kid who cut ahead of Zach was a junior. With a smirk on his face, he put his hands on Zach, then said, "Senior cuts," and shoved him out of line.

I could see Zach getting mad, but he held himself back. My little brother played sports like I did and wasn't afraid of a fight. Even though the other guy was older and bigger than he was, Zach would have mopped the floor with him. But Zach was smart and didn't want to get kicked out of school.

Zach sat down to eat lunch, and then I saw another kid walk near his table and toss down a napkin as he passed. The other kid, a friend of the first, said, "Here's a napkin to keep you from crying." Something snapped inside me. Zach picked up a chair and looked like he was going to throw it. He reconsidered, dropped the chair, and pushed the kid. By the time the chair hit the ground, I was on the run.

I picked up the other kid by his collar and slammed him down on his back flat against the lunch table on top of the trays. Nobody was going to mess with my little brother! On the menu was chicken nuggets with mashed potatoes, and I ground the kid hard into the food. I was about to punch him in the face before a friend of mine pulled me off. My punishment was two days' suspension. The other kid got four.

Years later, after we were grown-ups, Zach and I ran into that same kid. He'd gotten into a lot of trouble later in life. I was getting ready for the paratroopers and was in great shape. We were in a store and the guy bumped into my little brother's shoulder as he passed by and sneered that he'd been "in the joint" and nobody better mess with him. I walked by the dude and bumped his shoulder so hard I just about knocked him over. He didn't like the feel of that, I could tell. But in the end, I decided a brawl wasn't worth it. Zach and I walked away. When it comes to a fight in civilian life, I've learned that's almost always the best course to take.

WHEN WE WERE kids, my mom took us to the Presbyterian church down the road every Sunday that I can remember for both Sunday school and the church service. I liked our pastor, John Becker, a lot, and I believed in God, and I learned some Bible stories. After I got a job in high school, the hours were such that I couldn't both work and go to church anymore. During the school year I worked at the store as a bagger, then each summer I'd go work at a farm during hay season. We'd work up to ninety hours a week, carrying hay bales and stacking them as fast as we could. There wasn't a lot of pay in it, but it kept a guy in shape.

We prayed as a team before each football game, and I'd pray on my own if there was something that I felt needed prayer. I'd never ask God to help me get my homework done—I considered prayers like that a waste of God's time. But my grandfather had triple-bypass surgery once, and I prayed for him to make it through—and he did.

My dad went to the Lutheran church when he was a kid, and as a grown-up, he prayed every night. We had a big family dinner every Sunday, and we prayed before dinner, and I believe in prayer today. I believe that faith can help a person along in life. I believe in the Bible, at least as it pertains to helping a person live his life better. I believe in right and wrong. When I got into the military, I took a Bible on every deployment I went on. The prayer that sometimes goes through my mind the loudest is the Lord's Prayer, perhaps the most famous of all prayers in Christianity. I can hear the words in my head during some of the toughest situations:

*Our Father, who art in heaven, hallowed be thy name.*
*Thy kingdom come.*
*Thy will be done on earth as it is in heaven.*
*Give us this day our daily bread, and forgive us our trespasses,*
*as we forgive those who trespass against us, and lead us not*
*into temptation, but deliver us from evil.*
*For thine is the kingdom, and the power, and the glory,*
*for ever and ever.*
*Amen.*

WHEN I WAS sixteen, I was six feet tall and 205 pounds.

At seventeen, I was six foot one inch and weighed 225.

By the time I went into the military at age nineteen I was six foot two and 235 pounds and still growing. I eventually grew to six foot three and 250 pounds, although I was up to 275 pounds when I was lifting three to four hours every day.

At my peak, I had a 22-inch biceps and a 64-inch chest. During my workouts I started my squats by loading 450 pounds on the bar, and I'd go up to 550 for a total of eleven sets of ten repetitions each. My whole body was rock solid—arms, legs, trunk, core. I could run the 40-yard dash in 4.5 seconds—fast enough to play professional football.

And that's exactly what I wanted to do, but I threw a wrench into the plan myself. You see, when it came to sports, I wanted to be the best. In baseball, I wanted to hit on any pitcher. In football, no one was going to outrun me or slow me down. In basketball, I was going to drive hard to the basket every time I got the ball into my hands. I was governed by a healthy sort of pride. My mom describes how I could naturally take command of a room full of people. I never just blended in or faded into the backdrop. I was a natural leader, and I led whatever I was doing.

But I made some mistakes too, and that affected my dream of playing professional sports. My senior year after football season was over, I let my grades slip, and I graduated in 2005 with a cumulative 2.7 GPA. Most colleges want you to have a 3.2 before they'll give you any athletic scholarships. I could have done better, and I should have done better. That closed some doors for me.

I know now that I didn't put enough effort into my grades. In spite of my strong work ethic in most things, I could often be found wandering the hallways when I should have been in class. Or I'd be at McDonald's with my friends when we should have been studying. If you're in school or college right now, I'm not going to be the old fat man who tells you to study harder because if you don't you're going to miss out on a bunch of stuff when you're older. I'll just say my mistake was that I didn't commit hard enough to the things that were important. I tried to find my way around the grades, rather than buckle down and do the work. That fact is embarrassing today, but at the time when I was in school, grades didn't seem important. Today my wife and I watch

*Jeopardy!* on TV and we get a ton of answers right. My mother-in-law says, "Travis, sometimes I forget you're a really smart guy."

More than anything, what I wanted to do was play professional football. But you don't go straight from high school to the NFL, and because of my grades, I knew I wasn't going to make it to one of the big universities so I could get my shot at that.

I hated the thought of trying something else only to come back to my hometown with my tail between my legs, not successful. I wanted to go somewhere and do something important, something where I could be the leader I'd always been. Ultimately I wanted to become a productive adult, a good citizen, a grown-up who could be trusted to get the job done—whatever that job was. It was my responsibility to figure this out.

But if I couldn't play professional sports, what was a guy like me going to do?

# TEN FEET TALL AND BULLETPROOF

FTER HIGH SCHOOL COMES COLLEGE—RIGHT? AT LEAST THAT'S what I figured. So right out of high school, I started attending Grand Rapids Community College. I wasn't sure exactly why I was there or what I wanted to study, but I thought I could get some general education while I figured it out. Some 32,000 students attended the college, taking into account all of its campuses, and there were no sports scholarships, but I tried out for the football team anyway and earned a spot. The college was about two and a half hours from home, so I moved southwest to Grand Rapids and got an apartment. It felt like what I was supposed to be doing. But my heart wasn't really in it.

In high school I'd been a starter both ways and was one of the best players on the team, but in college I was the new guy and needed to earn my stripes. Football season came and went. I did well but wasn't a standout player. When the season concluded, I decided to move back to Vassar and go to Delta community college, closer to home.

It wasn't a tough decision for me to make. Thanks to my time in Grand Rapids, I was now more than $9,000 in debt, which I thought was a ridiculous amount to pay for a quarter of school plus an apartment and food, particularly when I wasn't quite sure why I was at college in the first place. I couldn't quite figure out why college was designed the way it was. Like, I needed to take a PE class, so I took weight-lifting. But it didn't seem right to me to be forking out all that cash on a weight-lifting class when I lifted weights all the time on my own. Plus, I also lifted weights at football practice, so paying money for another time to lift weights was a waste of money. I took an art-appreciation class to fulfill a requirement—and I appreciate art—but what was I ever going to do with that? I could draw a stick figure, and that was as far as a guy like me would ever go in art.

After I moved home, I worked at a department store, but even then money was always tight, and the weight of my debt hung around my neck like a millstone. I went to Delta for half a semester, then withdrew from school completely. I concluded I just didn't have the academic drive to be throwing money away like I was. Going to college, ironically, felt irresponsible.

Just before I left college, I noticed some military recruiters on campus, and that option looked like it might be a better way to go. I could get a job and begin to pay off my bills. I talked to the recruiters, mulled over the idea of enlisting for about two weeks, then decided to join up. Joining the military felt like joining a sports team. With the military came camaraderie. The job itself took a lot of drive. I was an adrenaline junkie, and it seemed like a big adventure. I talked two buddies into joining with me. One backed out, but the other joined right away, got an E3 rank (private first class), and is still in the service to this day.

I didn't like the idea of being on a ship, so I dropped the possibility of the navy in my first cut. The air force didn't have much of a presence two of the three times I talked to the recruiters, so that option wasn't seriously in contention. I liked the idea of being some sort of combat infantry, so the marines appealed to me. But the army said I could basically pick my job once I got in, so that seemed to be the best choice, plus they offered me a $24,000 bonus to sign a four-year contract. I went back and talked to the marines, and the recruiter said, "Sorry, we can give you duty, honor, and respect but no bonus." So I joined the army, paid off my debts, and shipped out within two weeks.

Initially I planned to become an electrician within the military and get a journeyman's card so I'd be certified to work in that trade later on in civilian life too. The army said I could do that with them. Eventually I'd get my degree and become a public school history teacher and coach once I got out. But then the army asked me if I'd ever heard about the airborne infantry, and showed me a video of guys jumping out of planes. I'd never thought about becoming a paratrooper, but seeing that video was all it took. Being an electrician could wait. The airborne infantry was the route for me.

The Mills family wasn't any stranger to military life, but my parents still didn't like the idea much. My dad had been in the army for a few years in the 1970s. He took a diesel course, was stationed in Germany, and didn't see any combat, but he'd seen guys get hurt and knew how potentially dangerous serving in the military could be. My grandfather had been in the navy during the Korean War, and I had a cousin in the marines and another cousin in the air force. My mom understood it was a job, and a duty and responsibility, but she didn't want me getting too gung-ho about it or ever relishing the thought of going to war. My dad was also pretty concerned about me becoming a combat soldier, and he basically begged me not to go into the 82nd Airborne. He knew that with my personality I could never do an office job in the military, but he didn't want me being infantry either.

"Think, Travis," he said. "You could do something big in the military. You could fly helicopters."

"Dad," I said, "I think the 82nd Airborne *is* big."

About a week passed where my dad was angry that I'd joined, particularly that branch—and my mom didn't seem too happy about it either. But when they saw the joy on my face, they knew that I had the spark back, the same old spark I'd felt when I played football. My parents said they'd accept my decision and support me.

I WENT TO boot camp (basic training) at Fort Benning, Georgia. It proved a rude awakening to military life. A busload of us new recruits arrived there in the middle of the night. They took away our bags, clothes, cell phones, and whatever other "civilian" stuff we had on us, and basically kept us awake all the rest of that first night.

They shot vaccines into our arms, shaved our heads, and told us to put on uniforms. I'm allergic to penicillin, so they told me to wait while all the other guys got this one particular shot, I forget now which one. You get that shot in your butt, and you're supposed to relax your butt cheeks as you get it, or else it hurts more. But just to be a joker I told all the guys near me to brace for impact and clench their cheeks really hard when the needle went in. I didn't know these guys from Adam, but I noticed quite a few of them walking around sore the next few days. Yep, army life was going to suit a comedian like me just fine.

The next fourteen weeks were pretty much a blur. Our drill sergeants yelled in our faces. We ran everywhere we went. We did push-ups until our arms shook and our hands grew numb at the wrists. We learned how to march, and we stood perfectly still in formation until our feet hurt and our backs burned. The first time we went to eat lunch someone yelled, "Everybody gets cole-slaw." I don't like coleslaw, but I figured that's what you do when ordered (plus we were only given eight minutes to eat), so I put a scoop of slaw on my plate and chowed it down first to get it out of the way. I thought I'd seen the last of slaw for a while, but when we came back for dinner the drill sergeant saw me and yelled, "Mills, you big bastard, if you like coleslaw so much you get two scoops!" So two scoops of coleslaw showed up on my plate every day for the next two weeks. I'd made the mistake of drawing attention to myself, and the drill sergeant was just toying with me. I wasn't sure why, but I quickly figured out that nothing any of us recruits did was going to be right, so if I stopped trying to sort out logic from illogic, then everything in boot camp was going to be okay.

We learned how to rappel with ropes and shoot the standard M16A4 rifle. We learned the correct techniques for avoiding ambushes and IED attacks. We learned combat first aid, hand-to-hand combat techniques, how to fire a machine gun and a grenade launcher, and how to survive a gas attack. We learned how to read maps and navigate over unfamiliar terrain. We learned how to move as a convoy, and how to move when under direct fire.

We were always on the go, always moving, never taking a breather, never growing reflective. Basic training is designed to be physically and mentally exhausting, and it definitely achieves that goal. But millions of other Americans have been through it over the years and survived, so I figured if they could, then so could I. There were times during boot camp I grew so tired and angry and frustrated I didn't know whether to laugh or cry. I figured laughing was better, and that became my fallback response to crazy situations. Somewhere in the midst of boot camp, my nineteenth birthday came and went. I think a guy or two said "Happy Birthday" to me. We were too tired to do anything else, and besides—we couldn't get out of camp even if we'd wanted.

The boot camp portion of training lasted nine weeks of the first fourteen. After boot camp came three days of transition, then five more weeks of Advanced Individual Training (AIT), which was equally hard, although the training was more speci-fied to being in the infantry. At one point the thought of quitting tempted me. The thought flashed at me that maybe if I stopped drinking water, I'd grow severely dehydrated and get medically discharged. But that thought evaporated in an instant as my dad's words came back to me: "You never quit—ever!"

Particularly in the latter stages of training, I had to get my mind around what my job as an infantryman truly was about. That thought didn't make me laugh. It's drilled into every soldier that killing is definitely involved in the messy business of war. One of our cadences was a Q and A yell that went: "What makes green grass grow? Blood and guts, blood and guts makes the green grass grow!" And every time we went to dinner, we did a right turn and shouted in unison, "One shot, one kill! Kill we will!"

Even as I yelled as loudly as anyone, I wrestled with these concepts. I'd never thought of myself as any sort of killer, so this new way of thinking took some getting used to. Sure, I'd hunted and fished before. But killing an enemy in battle is entirely differ-ent. There's a quote that's sometimes attributed to writer George Orwell that says, "We sleep soundly in our beds because rough men stand ready in the night to visit violence on those who would do us harm." That's who I was being developed into—one of our country's "rough men." My new job was to protect and serve my country. And if that meant visiting violence on those who would do us harm, then I now needed to be ready to do that.

My wrestling with these ideas had actually begun back when the planes had slammed into the World Trade Center on 9/11, when I'd been a freshman in high school. Shocked by the news of the sudden attack and the massive casualties, all of the students were taken into the library to watch the historic footage on TV. At that young point in my life, I was still thinking about playing professional sports, not going into the military. But I remember feeling a ragged mix of emotions—anger, confusion, dismay—and wondering why anybody would want to do this to us. I was American. I understood we'd been attacked and that our country was now at war—and that when there's a war, somebody needs to have the courage and intestinal wherewithal to do the actual defending, fighting, and unavoidable killing that accompany military actions.

That would turn out to be me.

AFTER BASIC TRAINING and AIT were completed, I went down the street at Fort Benning to airborne school, where they teach you how to jump out of planes into combat situations. At first, you work from smaller heights and jump off towers, learning the correct techniques for jumping, falling, pulling the risers to maneuver the chute, and landing. In our third week, we did our first actual jumps out of planes.

For my first actual jump, I loaded up in a C-130 airplane along with sixty-three other guys. The plane took off and reached altitude. The command came: *stand up.* We stood up. Then came *hook up.* We took the cord that pulled out our chutes and hooked it over our heads to a steel cable that ran the length of the plane. We were ordered to *check equipment*, so we checked our equipment and the equipment of the guy ahead of us. We sounded off, one by one in a line, to indicate all was okay. The door to the plane opened. My knees shook and a long swallow went down my throat. The green light flashed on, and one by one the guys ahead of me exited the plane. Split seconds before I reached the door, two thoughts went through my head almost simultaneously. *This is crazy!* and *Why am I doing this?*

I jumped.

My parachute opened almost immediately. The shock of its opening slowed me down with a jolt. The float to the ground only took about two minutes. After I landed, I unhooked my parachute, then rolled over, unzipped my fly, and took the ceremonial tinkle. All the guys were doing it. Every dude who jumps out of a plane is pretty jazzed up, and by the time you hit the ground you've got to pee something fierce.

More jumps came after that. Most were without incident, except my third jump, which was supposed to be a daytime combat jump with full gear. On the way down I dropped my rucksack too slowly. You're supposed to release it when you come to the tree line, but when I released the pack, it stayed just ahead of me, and I landed on top of its metal frame. Ouch! I yelled in pain. The jumpmaster was already on the ground and yelled back at me, "Did you break something, Private Mills?" I said no. He glared at me and added, "Then shut up!" I shut up.

On a different jump, the wind shifted direction just before I hit the ground. I landed on my feet, then bounced on my butt, flew end over end, and hit my head. A kaleidoscope of colors and images swirled in front of my eyes. I figured I had a concussion, but if I admitted that then I'd need to sit out for a while and probably repeat part of my training. No way was I going to do that. Instead, I took three Advil that night and went to sleep. I had a jump scheduled the next day and didn't intend to miss it for anything.

Our fifth and final jump was a nighttime jump with full

equipment—a loaded rucksack and a rifle. I was nervous for this jump, full of adrenaline, and dove out of the plane like Superman. My left leg got caught in the risers and my parachute collapsed. I couldn't see the ground coming up at me because of the darkness, but by the rush of wind I knew I was streaming deadweight like an anvil from the sky. I popped my reserve chute out, but I'd popped it out at too low an altitude for it to fully deploy. Seconds before impact, I did the only thing I could think of: I reached up and yanked my foot out of the risers. My main chute caught a puff of air and I hit the ground with a thud. I lay there for a moment, taking stock of my surroundings. I could still breathe. Nothing appeared to be broken. I'd lived. I let out a war whoop of a yell, collected my chute, and went to rejoin the rest of my team.

On graduation day from airborne school, sometimes you receive your jump wings, and sometimes you get what's called your "blood wings." It's an old school tradition, officially prohibited, where the jumpmaster goes to pin your wings on your uniform, but instead of pinning your wings onto the cloth, he lines them up and punches them into your chest so the point goes into your flesh. Mine went into my collarbone. It was pretty painful, but I was happy and proud to have my wings. I was a full-fledged airborne infantryman now.

It's hard to describe that feeling fully. Confidence and capability (and undoubtedly arrogance) coursed through my veins. I felt like I could do anything. It's an old military slogan, but ask any new paratrooper, and he'll tell you the same thing—

We were all ten feet tall and bulletproof.

I GRADUATED FROM military training in August 2006 and went home for a week to see my family, then drove over to Fort Bragg in North Carolina to become part of the famed 82nd Airborne Division. Becoming part of the 82nd was something I chose. I could have gone to three other places—Louisiana, Alaska, or Italy. But I wanted to be part of the 82nd. The division fights longer, harder, and better than anyone else in the world, although that's just my humble opinion. We were the toughest outfit around, and we believed it thoroughly.

The 82nd Airborne Division has a proud history. Originally formed in 1917, the division has played a major role in almost every international skirmish since, including World War I, World War II, Vietnam, Grenada, Panama, the first Gulf War, Haiti, Bosnia, Kosovo, and the present-day global war on terror. The division also helped out during the search-and-rescue operations associated with Hurricane Andrew, Hurricane Katrina, and the destruction caused by the massive Haitian earthquake of 2010.

It's hard to describe the 82nd unless you've been part of it yourself. Our job as paratroopers is to jump out of airplanes with our rifles in our hands, ready to fight. Not every mission we'd go on would involve airdrops into hostile territory, but we were ready at a moment's notice to do this, and we could deploy anywhere in the world within eighteen hours. There were about 22,000 troops in the division when I joined—every soldier tough as steel. It takes a lot of courage to jump out of an airplane, assemble as a group, and continue a mission from there. We were trained to fight even if we were surrounded by the enemy, trained to keep our heads, to charge hard and get the job done.

Decades ago, the unit was given the nickname "All American," and I wore the famed shoulder patch that simply reads "AA." I felt proud to be part of that kind of tradition. The 82nd is a brotherhood and I love it. It's in my heart forever.

★ ★ ★

FOR FIVE MONTHS, my unit was built up while we were stationed at Fort Bragg. We knew deployment was on the horizon, but I wasn't worried. By contrast, I was having the time of my life. For reasons unknown to me—probably luck of the draw—I was put in an artillery battalion and attached to headquarters. Our commander, Lieutenant Colonel Scottie D. Custer, was heading overseas on deployment with us, and he wanted three guys put on his personal security detachment. One of them was me.

That meant that for my first five months in the 82nd, headquarters could use me any time they wanted. But a colonel doesn't really need a personal security detachment until he goes overseas. So in the meantime I mostly did odd jobs. I cut grass. I went and shook out the parachutes. I did more medical aid training. I was sent to the motor pool to help out the mechanics. Each day was something different, all light duty. A lot of days, the three of us on security detail would get up early and go for a run, then take a shower, eat breakfast, do an odd job or two, then play video games until lunch. After lunch we'd take a nap, do more odd jobs, and hang out until dinner.

Normally I look forward to a challenge, so I didn't want to spend the rest of my life biding time like this. But after all the rigors of the training I'd just been through, this was the closest to a vacation that the army ever gave to a man on duty. I'd hear horror stories from friends about how they tried to break into their units and got yelled at for days on end. Nothing like that ever happened to me. Nobody messed with the colonel's security detachment. We just did our jobs and flew under the radar, and altogether had a much better time of it than the privates who went elsewhere. The two guys on detail with me, Levi and K. C., were solid dudes from Columbus, Ohio, and the only hard part of the job was that I had to take smack from them about Ohio beating Michigan each year in college football.

Overall, I felt a growing sense of excitement combined with seriousness toward where we were headed and what we'd be doing. A lowly private isn't briefed on the bigger picture of any combat mission, but bit by bit I pieced together the strategy, at least as it was specific to the 82nd Airborne Division.

Personnel from the United States and its allied countries (the International Security Assistance Force, or ISAF) would be working in Afghanistan in the region around the city of Khost to help shore up the population's infrastructure. Part of that meant building new roads, schools, electrical grids, water systems, a modern municipal hospital, and a commercial airport. Having these in place would boost commerce and help the population trust their new, democratically elected government under Afghan president Hamid Karzai. Overall, it would make life better for the Afghan people.

To get all this stuff built, soldiers would be strategically placed throughout the area around Khost to maintain security and keep everything peaceful. That's where an infantryman like me came in. Ever since the old Taliban-controlled government had been toppled in December of 2001, the Taliban had been fighting to oust the new government and regain control of the country.

If the Taliban regained control, then they would once again keep their thumbs tightly pressed against the population like they did in Afghanistan from 1996 to 2001, when they were officially in power. Out of power, like they were at the time of my first deployment, the Taliban insurgency fought against civilians and troops who supported the democratically elected Afghan government. The Taliban insurgency also continued to grow and sell opium (a key ingredient in heroin) so they could buy weapons like they did before. They continued to intimidate the population around them (and anyone not sharing their views) by attacking offices, businesses, mosques, hospitals, and schools. They continued to recruit and train groups of terrorists who could go on to attack America and other countries and kill innocent people like they did before.

Sometimes the media portrayed the Taliban as mindless fanatics, but that wasn't the case for the group as a whole, for their movement, particularly as time went on. The Taliban were cunning and vicious fighters who strategically blended in with the general population and used a variety of guerrilla tactics such as ambushes, suicide bombings, IEDs, and vehicle-borne IEDs (VBIEDs) to accomplish their objectives. Many of the older Taliban soldiers were highly experienced—having fought against the Soviets in their war from 1979 to 1989. We didn't fear the Taliban, but a good soldier knows the potential force of his enemy, and we respected the lethal clout these savages could wield.

I wasn't sure if our presence as well-armed paratroopers of the 82nd would actually keep things peaceful around Khost, or if it would work a different way. Maybe the terrorists would see a fresh enemy and turn their attention on us. Maybe while they were busy fighting us, the work of building the infrastructure could get accomplished. It didn't matter. My job as an infantryman wasn't to build up the schools or roads. It was to support the soldier next to me so we could get the job done and all come home alive. For me, this meant protecting Lieutenant Colonel Scottie D. Custer.

Okay then, that's what I'd do. For my first deployment, I was going to be one small part of the greater force of ISAF, helping to fight the war against global terror. It felt a lot more purposeful to me than sitting in community college, worrying I was wasting money.

# GUNNER IN A HUMVEE

COULDN'T BELIEVE WHAT I'D JUST HEARD ON THE OTHER END OF the phone call.

"I'm so sorry," I said. "I'll tell everyone here." I hung up.

It was less than a week until I would be sent overseas, just after Christmas 2006. Our unit had received a block leave, and I'd gone home to Vassar to my parents' house. I was standing in our kitchen, and my mom was about five feet away from me doing the supper dishes. She paused when I hung up, gave me a steady stare, and asked, "Who was that?"

"Kerry needs to go home right away," I said. Kerry was my brother Zach's girlfriend. My mom seemed to know instinctively what was going on and what to do. Kerry went home. Zach went with her.

The phone call was news that Kerry's brother, Marine Corporal Chris Esckelson, had just been killed by a sniper in Iraq.

One shot went through the plates in his body armor and hit him in the heart.

We all knew the family. Chris's father had been my Little League coach for years. Chris's mother delivered our mail. Chris had played football for Vassar High School a few years ahead of me. When I was a freshman, he was a senior. He also played basketball, and was an outfielder and catcher in baseball. Same as I'd done.

After Kerry left, my mother broke down and began to cry. I felt like crying too, although I didn't know how. We were deeply saddened by the news and concerned for the Esckelson family. But I could tell there was something more to the feelings that came from Mom. She was concerned about me—about us as a family—about me staying alive in the combat zone I was heading to in a few short days.

My dad didn't talk about me leaving. Over the next few days we hung out and did whatever we normally did. The most he said during that time was "Be sure to keep your head down."

Then, the day before I left, Dad told me a story about when he went into the army. He'd taken washable paint and written a note to his parents in their shower stall where they were sure to see it. It said one short sentence of reassurance: "All will be fine."

Early the morning that I left, I took a washable marker and went into my parents' bathroom. Right above their faucets, where they were sure to see it, I wrote the same short message.

"All will be fine."

I was miles away from the house when my dad called. He told me he saw the note. I didn't say much, and he didn't say much. He told me he loved me. Then his voice became hoarse, and his words of support for me came out broken and choked.

★ ★ ★

My NEW HOME in eastern Afghanistan was at Forward Operating Base (FOB) Salerno, named in honor of a WWII operation by the same name. Some guys called the FOB "Rocket City," due to the large number of incoming rockets and mortar shells it had taken over the last few seasons, but I never used that nickname myself. My deployment began in January 2007, and I know now that as far as deployments go, my first deployment was as good as they ever get.

FOB Salerno was a large base, maybe ten football fields put together. It had a good flight line to bring in aircraft on the diagonal, plus a well-protected helicopter pad for horizontal take-offs and landings. The ground was thickly graveled, not muddy, and there was a walled dining facility (DFAC), and even an indoor gym. We always had hot meals, the menu rotated, and it was always good. Baked chicken. Spaghetti and meatballs. Cheeseburgers. Meat loaf. Burritos. O'Brien potatoes. Hot brown gravy. Fresh biscuits and bread, lots of bread. Some Fridays we even saw steak and shrimp. They had a pizza place on base as well as a laundry facility and a Post Exchange where you could buy toothpaste or a razor or whatever you needed. It was definitely a good setup by combat standards.

On our first day in-country, we ripped in and took over for the team who'd been there before us. We did inventory and signed a bunch of forms to confirm that all the stuff was there. Over the next few days we went out on patrol with the old team a few times, then they left and we moved in for good. Some of our guys were housed in tents, but I was billeted in a hard structure about as big as a dining room in an average-sized home. Ten guys total lived in there. We each had a cot, and that was about it. That was all we needed.

Lieutenant Colonel Scottie Custer was in his early forties. He wore a high and tight haircut and had slate blue eyes. He'd played hockey at West Point and was powerfully built. Soon after our arrival, my job on his security detail came into full swing. Each day he would travel to some different location, usually around the city of Khost, although sometimes out of town. He met with city officials and businessmen, political leaders, and heads of the area Afghan police and army forces, ever explaining and promoting the plan of a better Afghanistan and helping to implement the actions it took to achieve that goal.

To me, the plan looked like a solid way forward, although a private isn't paid to think such lofty thoughts. We were helping businesses grow, giving medical aid, mentoring the Afghan police and army, and handing out schoolbooks to children. By contrast, the Taliban just came in and cut off people's heads. Some days, we'd be out on a four-hour mission. Some days our missions took twelve hours. Some days we went out two or three times. We took a few overnight trips, sometimes for days at a time, but usually we were back each night at the FOB before dark. I always went with the colonel wherever he went. My job was just to jump in and go.

My specific task was to be the gunner in a Humvee, one of those larger four-wheel-drive vehicles that looks like a really big jeep. Fully armored, a Humvee weighs more than 12,000 pounds and costs about $140,000, but the weight and cost were about the last things on my mind. Cut in the top of our Humvee was a hole with a shallow, turret-like gun base mounted on top. My job was to man the machine gun in that turret. Below me rode the colonel in the shotgun seat and a driver. In our convoy, we also rode with a medic in the backseat, a hard-charger of a guy named Josh Buck whom I'd met back at Fort Bragg.

Josh was a good guy, twenty-one years old, who'd already been married for two or three years. His wife, Deanna, was pregnant with their first kid. He'd lived in Maine until he was thirteen, then moved to Texas when his dad got a job there. This was his first deployment too, so he was as confidently wide-eyed as the rest of us, although he'd been in the service a little longer than I had. He never failed to remind me of that particular fact. Josh had a good sense of humor, and back when we were in the States before we were deployed, he and Deanna had double-dated with me and my old girlfriend from high school days. The four of us went bowling and out to dinner at Smokey Bones, and I considered Josh a real friend. I always tried to get him to lift weights with me, and he always tried to get me to go running with him. We slept in the cots next to each other in our billeting area at night.

Three other Humvees accompanied the colonel's Humvee wherever he went. Whenever the colonel reached his destination for that day's particular mission, we all stopped and pulled security detail. The guys manning the guns stayed on the guns, ever on the lookout for danger. The rest of the guys made sure the colonel got where he needed to go. We were sort of like the Secret Service is to the president. A good day for us meant no action. We were always mindful that a high-ranking American officer in Afghanistan posed a big target for the Taliban. If action happened, we were prepared to defend the colonel to our deaths.

THE DAY WAS seasonally warm. Word was that the Taliban had pledged to severely up the number of suicide bombers in the region. They were pissed at us because they'd lost some conventional-style battles late in 2006, so I guess this was all they could think to do to get back at us: blow themselves up.

That day, the colonel needed to be in the city at the opening ceremony of a hospital. We drove him over in the Humvee, parked, and I stayed on the gun like I always did. The colonel went inside with several of our men around him. Something didn't seem right, but I couldn't put my finger on it. You've always got to be on edge, always ready for something to happen. You hope for the best but expect the worst. A bead of nervous sweat crept out from underneath my helmet and slithered down the side of my face.

The ceremony was held outside the hospital in a walled courtyard. I was on the other side of the wall from the colonel. My back was to the hospital, so I could keep a clear lookout for any potential threats approaching. The army teaches you to sense danger. You're taught to look for it. If a guy in the crowd appears nervous. If he's sweating or yelling or acting frantic or moving too quickly compared with the other people around him—these are all warning signs.

People were all around us, going every which way, most heading inside. I noticed a man in the crowd who seemed to move a hair quicker than everybody else. Maybe it was nothing. He just looked like any other Afghan dude—dark hair, bearded, wearing manjams, the pants that look like loose-fitting hospital scrubs. He reached the security personnel around the door and seemed to be arguing with them. From where I was positioned, it was hard to tell. My eyes stayed on the crowd. My finger remained motionless on the trigger of my machine gun.

I heard yelling inside. Some sort of scuffle. My orders were not to leave my post, and due to the rules of engagement I was not permitted to fire unless fired upon. I kept my eyes constantly scanning the terrain ahead of me. A minuscule tremor moved the air. Then without warning . . .

*Ka-BOOM!*

Behind me roared a huge explosion. People screamed and yelled. Dust flew everywhere. I stayed on the gun, my eyes frantically searching through the crowd. Everyone scattered. Rocks and rubble fell from the sky. Small chunks of the Afghan's body landed on the roof and hood of the Humvee.

No other shots were fired. What had happened, I learned later, was that the guy had walked nonchalantly up to the door into the courtyard, where he'd had a scuffle with one of the ANA soldiers. Then an American stopped the guy, and the guy grabbed the American's gun. The American grabbed it back and kicked the guy over backward, which is when the guy pulled out his detonator and blew himself up. It was a smaller bomb with probably a five-meter kill radius and a twenty-five-meter wound radius, similar to the blast of a grenade.

My team leader was right there and saw it happen. He had pieces of the guy's skin on his helmet, little bits of charred hair and skin on his uniform. My LT's hand got hit with shrapnel, and he needed surgery on it. A few other people were hurt, but nobody died except the suicide bomber. The colonel was safe.

I stayed outside the compound manning my gun during the entire incident, like I'd been ordered to do. My first thought was *Oh wow, this stuff is really real. It's not training anymore.* I wasn't scared. I didn't crap my pants or shake in my boots or anything like that—that's not the kind of guy I am. It was just a reminder to be ready to go at all times.

OTHER THAN THAT incident, my entire first deployment was pretty relaxed in tone, although busy in pace, and plenty of days contained tense moments. I didn't fire my weapon once the entire first fifteen months I was in-country. I received my combat infantry badge for my role in the action with the suicide bomber. I couldn't believe it. I hadn't done anything except stay on my gun. Of course, I made up for it in subsequent deployments. Basically, that bit of staying put was my first official introduction to war.

As a gunner, I was always up, always scanning my sector, always making sure we were seen and being vigilant. All the other gunners were this way too. The 82nd came in strong, and we weren't messed with much because of that strength. If somebody wanted to fight, we were ready. And sometimes a show of force can be just as effective as actual force.

I know now that the Taliban is an extremely patient pack of wolves. If a unit such as the 82nd comes in, they can tell the unit is tough, so what they'll do is maybe test them a few times to confirm their hunches, then simply wait for the unit to leave and for the next one to arrive, hoping the next unit will be softer.

In spite of our toughness as a unit, we had our tender moments too, if that's what you'd call them. One day we were out doing a humanitarian aid drop where we took bags of rice and beans to the civilians in the area around Khost. When the food was distributed to the adults, a few of us started handing out school supplies, pencils and notebooks, to the children.

A little group gathered around me. The boys shoved their way to the front, while the girls stood near the back. The girls wore head coverings, but their faces were open, and they were smiley and cute. The boys were mostly all smiles too, but they were tougher, meaner. If ever I gave a girl something nice, a boy would take it from her. I did this a couple of times with the same results, then called over an interpreter and told him to tell the boys to let the girls have nice things too.

It couldn't have been more than two minutes after that, I gave a little girl a nice booklet and a pencil set, and a boy ran up to her, socked her in the jaw, and took away all her things. So I ran after the boy, picked him up and swung him over my head, then set him down and took the stuff he'd just stolen, and gave it back to the girl. The interpreter ran up to the boy and kicked him in the butt. I told the interpreter to tell the children that we'd be coming back the next day, and if the girls didn't have their stuff then, there'd be hell to pay. We weren't coming back the next day, but the kids didn't know that.

Working with the local children came with its own share of problems. One of the neighborhood boys who lived near the base always threw rocks at the colonel's Humvee whenever we left the FOB. I got smart and bought a little slingshot off another kid for a buck, and the next time the rock-throwing kid went into action I jumped out and pegged him in the butt with a pebble as he ran away. You'd undoubtedly get in trouble for doing that in America, but as I'd already seen, the culture was different in Afghanistan. If a kid mouthed off at us, the Afghan interpreters we worked with would have no problem slapping a kid in the face. I'm not saying that was right. I'm just saying that's how it went down.

After six months in Afghanistan, I was promoted to the rank of E4 (specialist) and was moved to the "truck commander" position in the security detail. I loved this. It meant I was off the top of the vehicle now and inside the truck in the "shotgun" seat. In this position I was put in control of the Humvee. I was the one on the radio, and whenever we pulled into an area, I gave the orders for how the truck should be set up. If we got into combat, I was in charge about when to shoot or not.

One night back on base I was walking around camp in the pitch dark, heading over to the phones to call my parents. I stepped off a wooden walkway, tripped and fell, and my head butted a concrete wall. My nose and chin were scraped up, and I had a cut on my forehead that oozed a bit of blood, but nothing major. I went and called my parents, then took a clean T-shirt and held it to my face to staunch the bleeding. As the youngest guy in my billeting, I didn't want to make a big deal about the fall, because I knew the other guys were sure to give me a hard time about it. It was my only injury during my first deployment.

The next morning, when I went to pull the T-shirt off my face, the blood had dried and the shirt was stuck fast. Hoo boy, I was sure to never hear the end of this. Josh eased the T-shirt off my face and cleaned away the gravel and cement that were still there from the night before. He bandaged it up the best he could. Then he laughed at me.

I would have thought less of him if he didn't. From then on, I was known as the guy who walked into a wall. A little joke like that can go a long way in the army, particularly if there's nothing better to do than pick on a guy. I heard it all. I was called a moron and an idiot and plenty of other things that aren't friendly enough to print. They joked that walking into a wall caused an improvement to my face. They speculated that I shouldn't go out at night without my mama holding my hand. Height-wise, I towered over the guys I billeted with, and I could have beaten them all up if I'd wanted. But sometimes you just need to take the crap that comes your way to show it doesn't bother you.

Besides, I had far better things to think about besides taking insults. Christmas 2007 was coming up, and I was set to rotate home to the States for two weeks for some R&R. After that, I'd come back to Afghanistan for three more months and then come home to the States for good along with my unit when our deployment was finished.

During my two weeks of R&R at Christmas, I was set to meet somebody, and I was looking forward to that meeting a lot. Her name was Kelsey Buck, and she wanted to meet me too. We'd been talking by Skype for some time already, and it felt like I already knew her. But I couldn't wait to meet her in person. I felt like one lucky man for sure.

# 5

# CRAZY LITTLE THING CALLED LOVE

**I**T STARTED WHEN JOSH BUCK WENT BACK TO THE STATES IN SEP-tember 2007 to be there for the birth of his daughter, Reagan. While Josh was home, his eighteen-year-old sister, Kelsey, started looking at his MySpace page on his computer. (Yep, that was back when MySpace was cool.) Kelsey informed Josh that she'd contacted one of the guys in his unit back in Afghanistan, and that she'd received a reply.

"Which one?" Josh asked Kelsey. He wasn't smiling.

"The one with the blue eyes and the huge arms," Kelsey said. (Yep, that's word for word what she told him.)

"I still don't know who you're talking about," Josh said.

"You know him. His name is Travis. Travis Mills."

"Travis Mills?" Josh couldn't believe it. "Of all the guys you could have picked to talk to. That guy's an idiot. He tripped over his own feet while walking to the phone."

Kelsey wasn't deterred. Neither was I. This girl was the real deal—I could see that right away. Kelsey was very good-looking. She smiled a lot, and I loved talking with her. I didn't meet any women in person where I was in Afghanistan, so the opportunity for female contact, even by Skype, was always welcome. Kelsey and I weren't romantic at first or anything like that. Our talks just felt fun, like the start of a new relationship. When Josh came back to Afghanistan and rejoined the unit he wasn't happy with me at all.

"Hey—you didn't ask my permission to talk to my sister," he said to me, eyeball to eyeball.

"I didn't know I needed to," I answered, my glance never wavering.

I thought he was about ready to explode. "Look—if you treat my sister wrong, then we're going to need to fight."

"Okay," I said. I could've killed him in a fight, but I knew he was just being protective of his sister. "I won't treat her wrong. You've got my word on that."

Kelsey and I kept talking, and talking, and talking, and it got to be that whenever I wasn't on patrol, I was talking to her. Conversations with Kelsey made me feel the happiest I'd ever felt in Afghanistan. We talked about everything and nothing and anything in between. Movies. Favorite foods. What my day was like. What her day was like. Pretty soon, I knew there was something special about her. Something lasting.

The time for my leave home arrived. I've always been a fly-by-the-seat-of-my-pants type of guy, and although I was looking forward to seeing my parents and brother and sister when I came home, I also felt like going on a real vacation, preferably to somewhere warm and near the ocean. Michigan in December wasn't going to cut it. When I was seventeen, I'd been to Mexico for spring break with some friends and loved it there, so I found some plane tickets and a hotel at a resort—then, on a whim, I

Skyped Kelsey and asked her to go with me. And to my surprise, Kelsey said sure, why not.

I mean, you might be looking for something deep and romantic here, like I'd met my soulmate and I sensed our destinies and was already planning our futures together, but nope, my request wasn't deep. Going to Mexico was all about being crazy and wild and impulsive, and her enthusiasm for the adventure only made me like her all the more. We hadn't even met in person yet, and here we were planning a weeklong vacation together. Her saying yes meant she was fun-loving and spontaneous just like me, and I knew we were going to have a great time. If she would have turned cold and said, "Nah, a trip to Mexico doesn't sound like a very good time to me," then who knows what would have ever happened between us. Girls of the world, take heed: if a soldier you like invites you to Mexico on a whim, you should go. Actually, that's not true. Not all soldiers out there are the cream of the crop like this guy.

I FLEW HOME to spend Christmas with my parents. They were both happy to see me, and Mom was teary eyed when she met me at the airport. My grandparents were with us for Christmas. My sister had brought home her boyfriend, so they and my little brother and I all hung out together. We had a party on Christmas Eve, and all my friends from high school days came over. I missed my buddies from the unit, but it felt so good again to be near family and my hometown friends.

Then the time came for me to fly to Texas to meet Kelsey. The day before I left, I realized I didn't have a passport, which I'd need to get into Mexico. Dad drove me over to Chicago, and the passport folks were kind enough to fast-track it for me in one day. Neither of my parents was exactly happy about me going to

Mexico with a girl I'd never met in person, but they figured I was an adult and could make my own decisions.

There was an additional problem. I knew I should have asked Kelsey's parents first if it was okay for her to go, and I knew that would never be easy to do—not earlier and certainly not now that we'd already made plans. Put yourself in my situation talking to her father. "Uh, sir, I realize you don't know me and all. And, uh, I realize your daughter doesn't really know me yet either. But I promise I'm not a serial killer. Really. Cross my heart."

I flew into Dallas. Kelsey told me later she was pretty nervous to meet me for the first time. She got to the airport a couple hours early and paced around, wondering what she had gotten herself into.

We met at the baggage claim area. She remembers exactly what I wore: Doc Martens, jeans, a blue striped shirt, my Detroit hat on backward, and earrings in both ears. I also wore a bunch of cologne, which I thought was impressive. Kelsey didn't. She picked me right out of the crowd. We gave each other a big hug and I cracked a few jokes, and it felt right away like we'd known each other forever.

I can't remember exactly what she wore that day, but I remember specifically thinking she was beautiful. I think it was jeans and boots and some great-looking sweater-shirt thing. We kissed each other at the airport too, and it didn't feel awkward at all, then we hopped in her dad's truck, went to the mall for a bit, then to meet her parents, Craig and Tammy, for dinner.

Kelsey told me all this stuff on the way over about how her dad was a vicious hockey player known for beating guys up, but it wasn't like that at all. We met them at a Mexican restaurant—La Hacienda was the name. Josh had phoned in the meantime and told Craig and Tammy that I was actually an okay guy, despite how he'd warned Kelsey earlier about me, and that had helped win them over. It was a bit awkward meeting them at first, but not bad. We talked sports and stuff, and everything was smooth.

I met Kelsey's sister, Kaitlin, and thought she was cool. And after, we went to Kelsey's parents' house, and a bunch of her friends came over and met me.

The next morning Kelsey and I flew onto the island of Cozumel in Mexico. Everywhere we looked we saw palm trees and white sandy beaches and resorts lining the ocean. The sun was out. A breeze from off the ocean kept everything cool and bright, and it didn't feel weird being together so quickly. We just hit it off right away.

The next few days were solid fun. We swam with dolphins and went snorkeling and souvenir shopping and cliff jumping. We went zip-lining through Mayan ruins and dancing at night. We went out for lunch each day, and met another couple and had dinner together in a group. The legal drinking age is eighteen in Mexico, so with Kelsey being that age and me being twenty, we could both order drinks with dinner and feel okay about it. Neither of us is a big drinker, but we ordered the type of silly fruity cocktails that you can only get away with ordering when you're on vacation, like Bahama Mamas and Miami Vices. We were soon both sunburned, but neither of us minded. It felt great to be with her. We laughed the whole time we were together.

I can be super outgoing, and I soon saw that Kelsey was more introverted. She might speak ten words where I'd speak fifty. But opposites are known to sometimes attract. I got a little worried when she told me once that she could sometimes get annoyed with people if she spent too much time with them, but I grinned with relief when she added that she didn't feel that way with me. I wasn't looking to rush into anything serious or get married, but Kelsey was exactly what I was looking for, even without me knowing I was looking for anything. She was kind and caring and spontaneous and fun. She had a lot of trust in me, and I loved being with her. Somewhere during that trip—and I couldn't even tell you when—I knew I was falling in love with her.

We spent New Year's Eve in Mexico at this great little restaurant that looked more like a house someone had fixed up really nice. Kelsey and I ordered rich red wine and charbroiled steaks. That steak was the best I'd ever eaten, or maybe the company I was with made it taste so good. Kelsey and I sat outside the restaurant in the warm evening air, and there were manicured gardens as far as we could see, a really well-kept landscape. As the last moments of the old year ebbed away and the new year took its place, restaurant staff lit fireworks in the courtyard. Kelsey and I looked up into the nighttime sky with the colors exploding high over our heads, and I knew she was the one. It wasn't even an aha moment. I just knew.

When our time in Mexico was over, we flew back to Texas for a day to hang out with her family some more, then flew to Michigan so she could meet my family. It was a two-leg flight from Dallas to Atlanta to Michigan, and we'd forgotten about the time change and hadn't reset our watches, so we missed the second leg of our flight and were stranded in Atlanta for twelve hours. We just chuckled and took a train downtown and went shopping together, then caught the next flight out late that night.

We spent a week in Michigan together. My parents loved her right away. Kelsey and I went skiing—she's a great skier, better than I was, and afterward we both got tattoos. I got one on my back that said "Mills," and she got a Celtic tree of life design on her ribs. All my friends from home met her and liked her right away.

The time came for us to leave each other. Kelsey was headed back to Texas to finish up the year at community college, and I was headed back to Afghanistan. We said our goodbyes and I told her, "I love you." Almost at the same time, she said, "I love you" back. For a moment we just stopped right there and smiled at each other. Then we were talking about our future together. Things were getting serious, really serious, and I liked that a lot. Kelsey said she did too.

Kelsey flew back home, and I flew to Atlanta to connect with another flight that would take me overseas. In Atlanta, I was un-expectedly delayed for one more day. I was missing Kelsey some-thing fierce already, so I called her and asked her to turn around and meet me in Atlanta for a few more hours together. I bought her another plane ticket, and she flew straight back.

That was pretty incredible right there. I mean, you don't turn your travel plans around like that for just anybody. I think that's when we both articulated to the other person that we'd be to-gether forever.

In Atlanta, we said our goodbyes for the second time. She flew back to Dallas again, and I flew back to Afghanistan. I went straight to Zales.com, bought her an engagement ring, and had it shipped to Dallas. I asked her mom to pick it up then hide it from Kelsey until the moment could be right. The next time I Skyped with Kelsey, I told her I loved her and wanted to marry her. She was all smiles, and so was I. Near the computer on her desk sat her dad's hat. I told her to look underneath the hat. Inside was the box with my ring for her.

I said simply yet sincerely, "Kelsey, I love you. I want to be with you forever. Will you marry me?"

She nodded, then smiled again, one of those deep, deep smiles where she closed her eyes. And there was that type of shining wetness in her eyes when she opened them. Same as there was in mine.

"Yes," she whispered. "Yes, yes, yes."

✦ ✦ ✦

KELSEY'S MOM HAD always told Kelsey to marry someone who made her laugh. And I definitely made Kelsey laugh. She knew I was for real, and that I loved her with all my might. Nothing would keep us apart.

The army, however, didn't see things quite that way.

The moment I got back to FOB Salerno, I was told to report to my commander immediately. The person who told me let it slip that it was rumored all over base that I was in trouble for something big, but he couldn't say for what exactly. I went to the office and waited and waited. Eventually the story came out.

When I'd been in Mexico, I'd been dumb enough to post pictures of the trip on my MySpace page, which was set to "public." The whole world could see those pictures—including my sergeant major and battalion commander. I wore earrings and had grown a small chinstrap beard while away from Afghanistan, and these were apparently infractions of regular military appearance, even while on vacation. When Kelsey and I had hung out with that other couple, there were pictures of us and them taken on the dance floor. One picture made it look like I was dancing with the other guy, even though I wasn't.

This was in the era of the official U.S. military policy called "don't ask, don't tell," which prohibited gays and lesbians from openly serving in the military, but allowed them as long as they didn't reveal their sexual orientation. With my colorful holiday clothes, my earrings, my ultra-cool chinstrap beard, and my apparent dancing with another dude, the story was that some higher-up corporate paper pushers felt I had edged too close to the "don't ask, don't tell" button. The paperwork was presented to me in black and white, signed, dated, and stamped. An Article 15: nonjudicial punishment. It was official. I was in big trouble.

This was serious. An Article 15 meant I'd broken the rules of the Uniform Code of Military Justice. I wouldn't go to jail, but

I'd be disciplined somehow and likely stripped of my rank, which meant a cut in pay. Not to mention the incident would be in my records file forever, which could affect any future promotions I might get as well as my future army career. Man oh man, my stomach was in knots. How could I be so stupid? The future had been looking so bright with Kelsey, and now all this.

Hour after hour passed, and I awaited my fate. Four hours. Eight hours. Twelve hours. I was a nervous wreck. They made me sit in a conference room while more paperwork was filled out. Then they let me out of the room for a while to take a couple of deep breaths. I went back to my billet, to the cot where I'd normally stayed. They were already storing some old rusty gun mounts on my cot, like I wasn't even in the army anymore. I was sure to get shipped somewhere else thanks to my demotion. Then they took me to the sergeant major's room and had me answer a slew of personal questions about my sexual orientation. In the room along with me for part of the time was my team leader, my LT, the colonel—and a bunch of other NCOs and officers I'd thought I'd known well. I thought we were all part of the army brotherhood. We were all on the same side together, weren't we? Twelve men in all. Their voices were all stern. No one was smiling.

Finally the verdict was passed. One of the NCOs ripped off my rank and threw the patch on the ground. He reassigned me to another platoon. He told me to go stand in the hallway.

I did.

While out there, I thought I heard a chuckle.

I did. I definitely heard a chuckle. And then another. And another. Then an all-out gut-busting chorus of laughter.

The door opened wide.

"Mills, get in here," someone said. I walked in, my face still ashen. My sergeant major was grinning ear to ear. "Corporal Mills," he said. "You've just been punked."

Punked?!

It was all a joke.

A huge, elaborate twelve-hour joke, the kind of joke only your friends in the army can pull on you. They were all howling by now, rolling around, falling over themselves, all laughing hard at me. I was still shaking in my boots. This was the best joke they'd played in years, and they all did it because they loved me and cared for me and considered me a brother and friend.

Slowly the blood came back into my face and I croaked out one small chuckle. Before long I was laughing along with them, and threatening payback big time—even to the officers, although I said this cloaked in a barrage of "sirs." Hey—I was just glad it was all over.

When I walked outside, forty soldiers were waiting. They all pointed and cheered, whistled, and bust a gut. Everybody in the whole command center had been in on it. I called them all names. I threatened payback. It was game on. Never, for the rest of their days, would any of them be safe.


It took a while before Josh fully accepted that his sister and I were getting married. He wasn't angry or furious or not my friend anymore. He didn't even have any strong words with me. But I could tell something was wrong.

Normally, he and I spent a lot of our days together, both when we were on security detail and when we were just hanging out. But I guess a number of the guys had been giving him crap about me dating his sister, and now that Kelsey and I were engaged, the crap went through the roof. Poor Josh got it from all angles. We argued about a few inconsequential things and he even swung at me once, as only army guys can do, and hit me in the shoulder. But I wouldn't fight back. Not with Josh. Not then. He was going to be my brother-in-law whether he wanted to be or not. Eventually he got over it and welcomed me into his family. Family is everything to me, and I could tell it was the same with him.

The deployment continued, pranks notwithstanding. We still went out on daily patrols. There were still threats and rumors of threats.

One day we went out to a district center (sometimes called a Point of Origin site) with the ANP, the Afghan police. The center was basically a four-building compound in the middle of nowhere with a wall around it. The ANP had been getting mortared at the district center, and they wanted us to check things out. Sure enough, as darkness began to fall, mortars began to scream in and explode near the base. We calculated where the mortars were coming from, then got orders to go out the next night and check things out.

The next night we rolled out in our Humvees in blackout conditions with our lights off. When we got to the base of the hill where the mortars were being shot at us from, we hiked up the hill. It was nearing midnight, and before we reached the top, we got orders that the mission was over. We shrugged, hiked back down, got into our trucks, and headed back to the FOB.

When I got back, I started making a plate of food. It was rice and beans and meat, sort of a weird stew thing that I'd thrown together. I'd just got it heated up and was sprinkling on the salt and pepper, when more mortars started falling. We were in our FOB now, not out near the district center, and we'd been mortared before at the FOB, but these were falling really close to us. I could hear the whistle and the boom as each fell. The compound shook.

I ran to the trucks and jumped on my gun, prepared to shoot back if the order came. The mortars died down pretty soon after that. I sat for a while, then we heard the incident was all clear. That was it. As I headed back to my stew, I wondered if Kelsey knew what her fiancé actually did for a living. I wasn't going to tell her about incidents like this, because I didn't want to worry her. But getting mortared twice in two different locations in two days did give me pause for thought. Kelsey wasn't marrying an insurance salesman or a dentist. She was marrying a combat soldier, no stranger to taking mortar fire.

Shortly after the mortar incident, we had a bad day for our battalion. A dump truck full of explosives rammed into one of our district centers and killed three of our men. I didn't know the men well, but I was tasked with taking one of the bodies back to Bagram Airfield in southeast Afghanistan, in preparation for transport home to the States. It was a sobering assignment.

Altogether in our brigade we had close to 3,500 soldiers. On my first deployment, 18 were killed and 200 were wounded. It hurts to lose anybody, but those numbers are considered relatively light for fifteen months of being shot at in a combat zone. I was pretty sure Kelsey knew the dangers of being married to a man like me, but still I had to wonder. Nobody could anticipate a soldier's future, and anything could happen.

Anything.

OUR UNIT CAME home for good in the spring.

I was so excited to see Kelsey again. I returned to the States at night on April 13, 2008. The following day was my twenty-first birthday. Kelsey had turned nineteen by then. She came to meet me right away, and she was still sure she wanted to marry me. I was still sure I wanted to marry her. Our wedding was set for June 21, 2008, in Texas. We planned for a big wedding with all of our family members there, along with a lot of great friends.

The day of the wedding was Texas hot, and we lined up in front of a minister on the front porch of this beautiful historic mansion in Dallas—the Bingham House. Kelsey came around the corner of the house on the arm of her father. She looked absolutely stunning in a white strapless dress. At one point in the service, Kelsey had a vial of white sand, and I had some green sand, and together we both poured our sand into a glass vase to symbolize unity. Kelsey was my wife, and I was her husband, to have and to hold from that day forward, for better or worse, for richer or poorer, in sickness and in health, until death parted us. We spoke those vows seriously.

Following the ceremony, we held a reception with a lot of music and dancing and laughter. That night we went to a hotel while all our friends went back to my in-laws' house for another party.

Three days after our wedding, Kelsey moved from Texas to Fort Bragg. I had ten days' leave total. We found an apartment, moved in together, and got settled into our new life. We got our tax refunds back and bought a futon and some other furniture, nothing much. One of the very first things we did was go together to get a yellow Lab.

We named our dog Buddy, and the three of us felt right at home.

SHORTLY AFTER OUR wedding, I was promoted to E5 (sergeant), which meant more responsibility and a bit more money. Another deployment was coming up, but it wasn't for another fifteen months or so, and that seemed like a long way off still.

From moment one, Kelsey and I got along well in our married life together. There wasn't a lot to disagree about. We liked each other really well. My career was set, at least for the time being, so that wasn't a question. We had enough money to pay all our bills. Sure, we were young, but plenty of people in the military get married young. You're not trying to figure out your major in college or anything. You just want to get on with life.

We talked about Kelsey getting a job, but we could manage without the added income, and I really didn't want her to. It was a selfish wish on my part, but in the best of ways. Anytime I wasn't working, I wanted to see her. If she was working at another job, then I knew there'd always be conflicting schedules. I wanted us to be able to spend every free moment together. For now she agreed.

We made friends with our neighbors like married people do, and had barbecues and get-togethers and game nights. Josh and Deanna and their baby Reagan lived nearby, so Kelsey was never homesick for family. Buddy proved to be a great dog, friendly and protective, and I was glad he was around to be with Kelsey whenever I couldn't be there.

Orders came through, and I wasn't with headquarters anymore. I was switched to Charlie Troop, 4/73rd Cavalry. That meant I was still infantry, still in the 82nd Division, just not pulling security detail for the colonel anymore. I was fine with that decision.

As the time came nearer for my second deployment, I worried some about Kelsey being taken care of if something ever happened to me. We knew my second deployment wasn't going to be as easy as the first. Our unit was set to go to the worst region of Afghanistan, and I was sure to fire my weapon this time.

But all of that could be put on hold for now. We had a good life mapped out, Kelsey and me. This was our time of honeymooning. Our season of jubilee. When we looked ahead, we saw only hope. And when it came to our small family, we were certain the best was yet to come.

# 6

# FIREFIGHTS WITH THE TALIBAN

**THE FORM LOOKED STRAIGHTFORWARD.**

I wrote my name, rank, serial number, unit name, and date of birth at the top, then scanned the rest, filling in answers as I went. I'd filled one out before at the start of my first deployment too, but something felt different about filling out the form now that I was married.

The question of which song I wanted to be played at my funeral was easy. I'd thought of that before and had already picked it out—"American Soldier" by Toby Keith. I liked the way the song talked about how a soldier stands ready when a wolf growls at the door. I wrote down that I wanted to be buried along with my wedding ring and a picture of my family. I wanted to be buried in Michigan, so my parents could look after the grave. I figured Kelsey would remarry for sure, so I didn't want to saddle her with another responsibility. I didn't want a military funeral. It seemed too formal for me.

A few more blank spaces stared at me from the form, but I

didn't give much consideration to the rest of the details. I signed the paper at the bottom, glanced at my signature for a moment and considered how oddly vulnerable it looked on this particular page, then went on with the next form.

I didn't plan on dying. No one does. Every soldier fills out these forms prior to deployment. You need to think these things through in advance. You need to get all your paperwork in line in case something bad happens.

It's just a formality, I told myself. That's all.

THE CLOSER WE got to deploying, the more our training ramped up. On my first deployment, I'd been a private. My only job was to take orders. On this second deployment I was a sergeant and a team leader. Now I was not only taking orders but giving orders too. I was responsible for where guys got positioned, for what happened if a man went down, for how much ammo we used and at what rates of fire. Lives were on the line like they'd always been, but now I was responsible for those lives.

Some of that new responsibility was just funny. Once on a Friday night, I was on duty in the barracks. I didn't live in the barracks then, but I was the CQ for that night (stands for "in charge of quarters"), which meant I was responsible for the building and everybody there. Upward of three hundred guys lived in the barracks. An older private had been out drinking, and along about nine o'clock, he staggered back to the barracks and ran into me. He was a big dude, muscled, thirty-two years old, and I asked him a few questions and he got lippy.

"Tell ya what," he slurred at last. "I'll wrestle you."

"You don't want to wrestle me," I said. But right at that minute he reached over and tapped the side of my nose. He wasn't being aggressive. He did it just to irritate me.

"Come on, Mills," he said again. "Wrestle me."

So we got into it. We were ground fighting, nothing major, just arm bars and choke holds. I tapped him out three or four times, and he knew he was beat but wouldn't take no for an answer. The last time he came at me, he came hard. I put some pressure on him. He hit the ground and chipped his tooth. I felt bad about that, even though he was the instigator. So I got him safely to his room and showed him to his bunk, then I went over to the store on base and bought him a thirty-pack of Pabst Blue Ribbon to say sorry.

"Aw, thanks, dude," he said when he saw the beer. "This is awesome."

I told him to have a good night. It was all part of the job.

As part of the ramp-up, my unit went on a month-long training exercise at Fort Polk, Louisiana, held at the army's Joint Readiness Training Center (JRTC). We practiced the jobs we'd be doing overseas by doing mock-up scenarios first stateside. One day we hiked to an area that looked like an Afghan village and held a run-through of a key leader engagement (KLE), where our leaders met with village leaders. We were schooled on cultural sensitivities and how to work with interpreters, how to find the fine line between pressing Afghan leaders for more information and holding back, letting the realities of a working relationship occur naturally.

A fake IED went off during one of the exercises, so we jumped to respond to the blast. This meant holding a security perimeter while stabilizing the wounded and calling in helicopters to evacuate the casualties. The blood was fake, but the situation was as realistic as our trainers could design it. I tried to take it all in and do what needed to be done.

We talked about IEDs a lot. The enemy had concluded that it took too much firepower to fight coalition troops directly, so the

IED had become their weapon of choice in this war, and IEDs were responsible for some two-thirds of all coalition soldiers killed or wounded. Two-thirds! Strange, you fight a war these days and most armies have got all these huge weapons—tanks, bombs, fighter planes, warships, machine guns, missile launchers, and even access to nukes—yet something as small as an IED has become one of the most lethal and destructive weapons of modern warfare.

The IED is a relatively simple weapon, but when it came to making and positioning IEDs, the Taliban were getting smarter all the time. IEDs could be planted anywhere—the limb of a tree, the ground, under or beside a roadway, inside an empty soda can that looked like trash. An IED was triggered by someone stepping on it or driving over it, or sometimes by remote trigger. An IED could explode immediately if it was set to do so. Sometimes it would be delayed. That way, the soldier who triggered it would be twenty feet ahead of the blast, but the poor guy behind him would be blown up instead.

The strength of an IED varied. An IED might be designed to take out one person. It might take out an armored Humvee. IEDs would usually be filled with rocks, nails, shards of glass, ball bearings, nuts and bolts, or hard plastic. The blast itself could wound a man, but usually wounds were caused by flying debris: picture the blades of a thousand small running lawn mowers coming off and flying through the air. Sometimes an IED would be linked to other IEDs and trigger a chain reaction of blasts to take out a larger number of people. I took a lot of mental notes on IEDs, letting the Taliban's vicious tactics soak in, trying to file it all away in my brain for future reference.

A lot of information came at us right away, but we were used to it. And if we didn't get it right the first time, we practiced an exercise or procedure over again until we got it down cold. We all knew enough to take this training serious—dead serious. One disadvantage we faced from a strategy perspective was that we were going overseas for only a year at a time. By contrast, the Taliban had home turf advantage in Afghanistan. They were constantly fighting this war, and had more time to perfect their hiding spots, strategies, and specific combat techniques.

After the field exercises were completed at JRTC, we went back to Fort Bragg for more training. These felt like fairly routine days, although an uneasiness hung in the air. I remember hanging out several times with another sergeant named Tyler Juden. He was a sniper with the 82nd, and we watched a number of UFC fight nights together on TV. We had a lot in common. He was about a year older than I was and almost as big, one of the most physically fit guys I'd ever met. He'd played football in high school and run track. He wanted to become a teacher after he got out of the army. We had the basis for a long-term friendship. He struck me as passionate about the things he loved most: his friends, his family, and his country.

I hoped Tyler's dreams would all get realized one day. He had the patience, dedication, and high level of smarts necessary to make a great teacher, I thought.

Inwardly, I wished him well. I did. I wish I had told him that outwardly, but you don't think of these things when you're just sitting around watching the fights on TV. You just don't.


WHEN THE TIME came for deployment, Kelsey and I put all our stuff in storage in Fayetteville. She made plans to go back to Texas while I was overseas so she could live with her parents, attend college, and work. She enrolled in Collin County Community College to get more of her general education and found a job in a ski and outdoor shop. (Even folks in Texas like to get away to the mountains to ski every now and again.)

On our last evening in Fayetteville, I walked outside our apartment and said goodbye to our dog, Buddy. He sniffed around at my ankles, wagged his tail, and licked my face as I bent down to ruffle the fur around his neck. Neighbors and family members were outside at that time too, all saying goodbye. When all the goodbyes were said, I hopped in our car along with Kelsey and drove to the post. Kelsey hung out with me as long as time would allow. Then it was time for the soldiers to load up the buses and go to the airfield. I gave Kelsey a hug and a kiss and promised I'd be home soon for R&R. I hated the thought of leaving her, but we both understood this was the job I'd signed up for.

As a team leader, part of my job was to make sure all my guys were ready to go. Three soldiers were under me. Specialist Brian Schwartz was a rifleman. We simply called him "Schwartz," and he was a tough fighter out of Chicago who always seemed to get caught doing the wrong thing. PFC Jerred Pender was a year older than I was and had done more time in college first. We called him Pender or JP. He had brown hair and a skinny face with a pointed nose, and if ever in a fight, he'd go down swinging, never giving up. PFC Michael Hubbard manned our machine gun (called the squad automatic weapon, or SAW). He was out of Tennessee and always laughing, always up for anything. I was considered a rifleman in the team as well, but unlike the other guys, I had a 203 grenade launcher on the end of my M4 rifle in case I wanted to unleash that on the enemy.

Josh Buck and I weren't together on this deployment, but were in the same brigade, which meant we were both deployed at the same time although he'd be stationed elsewhere in the country. If luck held out, we'd see each other from time to time over there.

He found me right before we boarded the planes, and we offered each other a few final words of encouragement before leaving, giving each other solid slaps on the back.

It was the end of August 2009 and we flew overseas on a chartered commercial 747. We didn't carry bullets while flying, but we had our rifles and other weapons on our person in the planes with us. We flew into Germany, where our plane was de-iced and refueled, then continued on to Manas Air Base in Kyrgyzstan, where the U.S. military kept a military transit center. We deplaned in Manas and stayed for a few days while we were processed. Each leg of the flight seemed to give me a deeper sense of purpose and drive home our training. Next we boarded a C-17 military plane for the trip to Kandahar, and from there flew in a Chinook helicopter to the city of Herat in the west, the third-largest city in Afghanistan. This was it.

On my second deployment, as a sergeant and team leader, I was a low man on the totem pole as far as the army's leadership is concerned, but still in a strategic and vital position to engage the enemy and do the fighting. A sergeant is a noncommissioned officer, usually referred to as an NCO or noncom. When it comes to executing a mission, the NCOs are the guys the lieutenants and other officers look to and rely upon to get the job done. The NCOs have long been considered the backbone of the military. NCOs do it all.

From my position on up, the organization goes like this:

- Two teams make up a squad (about nine guys total), and it's usually commanded by a sergeant or a staff sergeant. I'd be made a squad leader later on my second deployment, but I'm getting ahead of myself.
- Four squads make up a platoon (about forty guys total), and it's usually commanded by a lieutenant.

- Four platoons make up a company (about 150 to 300 guys, depending on the specialty of the platoon), and it's usually commanded by a captain.
- Roughly four companies make a battalion (about 1,000 soldiers), and it's usually commanded by a lieutenant colonel.
- Roughly four battalions make a brigade (about 3,000 to 5,000 soldiers), and it's usually commanded by a colonel.
- Roughly four brigades make up a division (about 10,000 to 15,000 soldiers), and it's usually commanded by a major general.

When we first got to Herat we were stationed at FOB Stone (also called Camp Stone) just south of the city. It was a fairly large FOB, similar to the one I'd stayed at during my first deployment. FOB Stone had a bunch of tents and hard-sided structures. I tried once to describe to Kelsey what it was like at FOB Stone, but words failed me. It's just sort of a big empty canvas of brown, like an artist had painted his background and not added any color yet. Everything was various shades of tan out in the desert. The dirt was tan-colored. The dust was tan-colored. The low-lying mountains in the distances were tan-colored. We weren't at this base long enough so that it ever felt like home, and the first two weeks were nothing to write home about. We took over security from the departing unit, learned what we needed to, and guarded the gate. Then it was time to move on.

Before we moved, though, we received some sudden news— and it was bad. They put us in formation and told us what had happened to a part of our battalion that had been stationed at a different FOB about two hours down the road.

Tyler Juden, my friend the sniper who'd watched fights on TV with me back stateside, had volunteered to be part of a convoy that had been ambushed while out on patrol. The first vehicle in the convoy had been hit by a roadside bomb and was disabled. When the convoy ground to a halt, the enemy opened up on it with small arms fire and rocket-propelled grenades. Our men took heavy fire.

Our guys needed to get the disabled vehicle out of the way, and while they worked toward this objective, Tyler sprinted up to a high site on a nearby hill and fired through some five to seven magazines of ammo, protecting his soldiers below.

When the disabled truck was finally cleared, Tyler sprinted back to the truck. But the enemy had specifically targeted him. An RPG flew in, and he was hit. They rushed him back to the hospital at the FOB, but it was too late. Tyler died on the operating table.

Fury rose up inside of me. I wanted to find whatever Taliban savages did this to Tyler and shoot them in the face. Tyler was always cautious. He took his job extremely seriously and never made mistakes. There was no reason for him to die. He described to me once how he believed his job as a sniper ultimately saved innocent lives. He was putting into practice what he knew to be true. He was helping the world, not hindering it, and he'd been trained to be one of the rough men who stands ready in the night, prepared to do his duty, prepared to visit violence on those who would do us harm.

Tyler's death hit far too close to home—and we'd only just arrived.


ROADS CAN BE exceedingly vulnerable places in Afghanistan, particularly if a road passes between two mountains. Convoys are particularly susceptible to ambushes from both sides of the road. To win a fight, you need to have the best vantage point, and whoever has the higher ground near the roadway holds the most advantage.

Our platoon and another platoon were sent to a region up north to guard a section of roadway between two mountains a ways past FOB Todd. Another FOB was being built some eight to ten hours up the road from where we were stationed. That meant we were put in the "choke point" between the two FOBs. Our job was to make sure military convoys and civilian traffic weren't shot up by the Taliban as the traffic went through these mountains. My platoon was on the east side of the road. The other platoon took the west side.

All the civilians who lived in the region seemed to have moved out. Everywhere we looked in areas that had been settled, all we saw were ghost town remains. The region was featureless aside from the tan dirt everywhere and the mountains in the distance. When we first pulled in to the spot where we were assigned to set up, I looked around and saw no buildings, dining facilities, tents, outhouses, or showers. *Okay*, I thought, *this is it*. We set up security, then I pulled out my gear and started setting up a makeshift camp, and the other guys did so also. We sprawled in the sand and ate our MREs (Meals, Ready-to-Eat) and swigged from water bottles. Boring hours passed, although the what-ifs always hung in the air. We dug a hole in the ground for our crap. When night fell, we rolled out our sleeping bags and crawled inside.

Night after night it was the same: I lay there looking up at the stars and finally drifted off to sleep. Day after day, we went on patrols and carefully watched as trucks went past on the road below us, twenty to forty a day, although some days only a few. After several days a military convoy stopped and resupplied us, and I realized that meant we'd be here for a while. When it happened again, and then again, I understood we'd be out here for a long, long time.

So we just dug in and did our job. Nobody messed with us. We locked down the area and did our patrols and established a strong presence. The first week passed without incident. We ate our MREs and hiked around the place and took no showers. The second week was the same.

Somewhere about that time I drove down the road in a convoy of two trucks to get some more mortars. The supply sergeant was taking his sweet time, and his getting what we needed took maybe twenty-five minutes longer than expected. It wasn't a lot of wasted time, but something was still burning inside me, triggered by the death of my friend Tyler, and small inconveniences seemed larger than they actually were. I groused about the wait and punched the side of one of the trucks in frustration.

It was a stupid thing to do. Out of character for me. Nobody cared if I was frustrated, and I never wanted my men to see me lose it like this. In the process of hitting the truck, I ripped a scab off my hand, and it started to bleed. I took my wedding ring off and sat it on the front of the truck. The medic came over and patched me up. It was a good thing I didn't break my hand. We finally got our mortars dialed in, jumped in the trucks, and headed up the road again. Only then did I realize I'd never picked up my wedding ring. In my mind I saw it slide off and slip into the sand as we drove away. My heart sank. That ring was gone.

I chastised myself for being so stupid. As often as I could for our remaining time on top of that mountain, whenever I had a free moment, I took a metal detector and walked up and down that road, searching for my ring. Time after time I tried. But the ring proved a bright and shiny needle in a haystack, and I never did find it. I kept telling myself it was just an object, it wasn't Kelsey, and the ring could be replaced. But the loss of it unnerved me. It felt too personal. We had a satellite phone for a few days, and when I was able to call home and tell Kelsey about it, she said "Oh sheesh." I promised that when I came home in May for R&R, I'd get a new ring the day I got back.

While we had that phone, I called home and found out that both my grandmother and my uncle Brian had died of cancer while I'd been gone. Grandma was older, but Brian was middle-aged and went well before his time. My parents could have contacted the Red Cross, who would have found out a way to get in touch with me. But there was nothing I could do now other than grieve where I was. It made sense to stay put. Still, it was sad not to be able to be with my family for those important times, and another reminder of part of the sacrifice made by people in the military. On other deployments, I missed my sister's wedding and also my brother's wedding, where I was set to be best man. When you're away for up to fifteen months at a time, it's next to impossible for family members to plan their lives around you. Nor would I ever ask them to. The key was to stay upbeat and focused. Afghanistan can get you down if you start letting it, but I wouldn't let a deployment beat me like that.

Another week passed on top of the mountain, and another, and another. One afternoon I was hiking around on patrol and calculated that it was day forty-seven on this particular mission. Forty-seven days without taking a shower. Forty-seven days of living in the dirt. I became convinced that the outback of Afghanistan had a mind of its own. It wanted to get us. It might do it by harshness of climate, filth, or sheer boredom. But rest assured, it was playing the game to win.

An average day on the mountain meant waking up with the first light of dawn and crawling out of my sleeping bag, shivering. Each new day felt like the day at the end of a long camping trip, and my teeth would be furry and I'd brush them right away using bottled water. I shaved my face every few days or so. You don't want to shave every day for risk of nicks, which on dirty skin can become havens for germs and even for MRSA, the antibiotic-resistant staph bacterium that can cause dangerous, deadly infections. After shaving (or not), I'd grab a spool of toilet paper and my miniature shovel (called an entrenching tool), and trudge down the hill about fifty meters where I'd dig a hole and drop trow. I'd always face down the hill in the general direction of our supply sergeant and wave, because I figured he might be out with a pair of binoculars, and the thought of him surveying the hillside and spotting another dude dropping a deuce was hilarious. Then I'd spade over my hole and trudge back up the mountain to eat an MRE for breakfast.

We ate the same meals no matter if it was breakfast, lunch, or dinner. The army offers twenty-four types of MREs, but each larger box of supplies has twelve kinds only, so depending on what boxes came on our pallet, we were almost always limited to twelve choices. It could've been a lot worse, but after a few weeks of eating the same twelve MREs, they all tasted the same. There was chicken with noodles, which came with M&M's; a veggie omelet, which came with Skittles; chicken tortellini; beef stew; chili and macaroni—that was always a popular one. Some MREs came with a built-in heater, sort of like a hand warmer, so you could eat your meal hot. Some guys always ate their MREs cold, but if I had time I morphed into an MRE chef and tried to make the best meal I could.

After breakfast, we'd have a meeting to discuss what we were going to do for the day, what kind of mission we'd be going on. Then we packed up our gear and headed out on our mission. Usually that meant hiking all day in the hot sun. My back grew sore, and my muscles got tight. I felt hot spots on my feet, and sometimes they broke open and blistered. I ordered myself to keep going, and silently consoled myself that it was all going to be over soon.

An NCO won't grumble out loud, not if he's a good leader. He'll make light of the situation. Or he'll grumble indirectly. Like, I might start a conversation with the guy next to me by saying, "Man, I wish I could grab a cheeseburger right now." That will be code for saying, "This sucks," and he and I will both know it. But it might also prove an interesting conversation, so when we'd come back for the night, we'd pick up the same topic and talk about cheeseburgers again.

We had jobs to do at night. We might burn our trash, or clean our weapons, or pull a shift of guard duty, and then we'd talk about nothing again, and then we'd talk about nothing some more. We talked about nothing until we exhausted the very essence of nothingness. Life in the Afghan outback was the military version of *Seinfeld*, an endless show about nothing. We played ridiculous word games to pass the time. We discussed minuscule details of baseball games we'd played as kids. I might get into a debate with my guys about where the best cheeseburger in America could be found. We would've had the debate before, but it would be good to have it again, because it's a topic everybody had a strong opinion about. One dude would say Five Guys. Another would insist Red Robin. I'd insist it was from my parents' backyard barbecue, and I'd do this not because I hated Red Robin or Five Guys, but because it was the truth and also just to keep the conversation going longer because we were all so bored.

Going so long without taking a shower came with its share of complications. Guys got trench foot from their feet being wet and sweaty and not taking care of them properly. I got strange rashes in intimate areas, and it wasn't uncommon for a guy to mutter about his balls sticking to his leg when he hiked. Every dude got chafed up pretty badly in his bodily crevices, and a common complaint was that a guy had "swass," slang for "sweaty ass." My armpits hurt. I sweated so much that the salt got trapped in my skin and my back broke out in a raised bubbly rash. This happened to other guys too. The only solution is to get your ID card and have another dude scrape your back hard until the salt crystals pop out. It's a brutal procedure and feels like getting cut with a razor blade, but it's all part of the fun.

When you go for that long without a shower, you get a sticky and gross feeling at first. But then your body adapts with its oils and whatnot and after a while you don't feel so sticky anymore, although you still feel gross. You just feel like you've got a film all over you. If you want, you could still put on deodorant every day, but after a while everything sort of blends together, so you learn to accept that you smell like crap.

We did our best to wipe down with baby wipes, but only so much could be done. We took water bottles and cut holes in them with our knives and tried to spray them over us, but that made for a pretty poor substitute. We learned that it took about five days to get comfortable with our grossness. A week tops. Definitely not more than ten days. So, once we were comfortable, why bother with any sort of shower? We'd just need to get comfortable with being dirty and gross and sticky all over again.

One day toward the end of our time on the mountain, I was looking forward to a particular afternoon snack I'd gotten in the habit of concocting. One of the MREs came with vegetable crackers with jalapeño cheddar cheese spread that came from a tube. It sounds gross, but if you spread the cheese on just right, then let it sit in the sun for a few minutes, everything gets warm and gooey like it's straight out of the oven.

Time came for my snack. I fixed up a cracker and let it sit to get warm. Just then the wind picked up and blew my cracker up and onto the ground. Fortunately, it landed cheese side up. Unfortunately, it landed on a pile of goat turd. I'd totally been looking forward to this snack all day. I examined the goat turd more closely. The turd looked dried enough, not juicy. I picked up the cracker, brushed off the bottom a little bit, and popped it in my mouth.

"Not today, Afghanistan," I said. "You're not going to beat me today."

We lived on top of the mountain for fifty days straight, then our mission in that location was done. We were sent to the region of Robat Sangi-ye Bala, back over near the city of Herat, although this time we were about two hours north of FOB Stone. Winter set in. The weather turned freezing, with a forecast of snow.

WHEN WE ARRIVED back in Robat, we set up our tents in a snowstorm. About six inches fell the first day, just enough to cover a man's boots and make his feet wet. The area we were in was similarly featureless—mountains in the distance, similar paved road, similar tan-colored dirt, dust, rocks, and mud hut villages down the road. Our base was in a walled compound, although the building inside the compound wasn't yet completed. Again, there were no showers anywhere. This time we built a makeshift bathroom out of a long board with three buckets underneath. At least we had that.

We were closer to a village compared to the first time we were here, and we'd long since learned that it could be tough in Afghanistan to know where the line fell between civilian and the enemy. The Taliban didn't work "with" the population so much as they forced people into complying with their way of doing business. For instance, whenever IEDs were planted, the local population typically knew where they were. Sometimes they shared this information with us, sometimes not. Once, a farmer told us that he would make sure none of his goats ever stepped on an IED, because if they did, the Taliban would come around and demand that he pay for the lost explosives. That's the kind of survivalist mentality that had set in.

About as soon as we got set up in Robat, the local chief from the ANP came over to meet with our LT and our platoon sergeant. The police chief had once been a member of the Taliban himself, but as far as we could discern, he'd switched over and was now fighting for the good guys. He was a tall, muscular dude with a full beard and a big stomach. He was pleasant for the most part, almost jolly, not angry or spiteful, and seemed eager to cooperate. I never did catch his name, but he looked sort of like an Afghan version of the late actor James Gandolfini, the guy known for his role as Tony Soprano.

The police chief told us he knew all the bad guys in the area. He'd received some intel telling him that later that night a cadre of the region's most wanted Taliban members would be traveling down a wadi (dry riverbed) on motorcycles. They'd be coming from a meeting of their leaders and operatives and would drive right where we could get them, he explained.

Our leaders decided to check it out. These particular Taliban members were marked for "capture or kill" and they were known for previously placing roadside bombs that had killed American and British troops.

We locked and loaded, jumped into our trucks, and drove to a spot near the location that the police chief had indicated. I was a truck commander of a Humvee with a big .50-caliber gun on top. Pender drove. Schwartz stood ready as gunner. Hubbard manned the SAW. We shut the trucks off, set up a security perimeter about 150 yards from the wadi, settled in, and watched. After that it became a waiting game. Night fell, and we put on our night-vision goggles to get a better view. With the goggles on, everything looked a different tint of green. About twenty-six of our men were on this mission. The ANP brought a bunch of their men too.

About two in the morning I first heard the roar and sputter of approaching motorcycle engines. Dust lay in the night air, and instantly through my goggles I saw a group of bearded men round a curve and head down the wadi toward us. They weren't traveling very fast, and the motorcycles they rode weren't very big, probably Hondas or Suzukis, maybe 250cc at the most, typical of what the Taliban use. The police chief and his men ran into the wadi, waving their weapons and shouting, attempting to stop the motorcycles and arrest the Taliban. I didn't know if that was part of the plan our commanders had agreed to or not. Right away, the Taliban screeched to a stop and started shooting at the ANP. Bullets crackled all around us. We got the word from higher command to engage, and I yelled to my men, "Fire." We shot our rifles, and Schwartz let loose with several staccato bursts of the machine gun. *Rat-a-tat-tat. Rat-a-tat-tat. Rat-a-tat-tat.*

This was my first large-scale firefight of any kind. It hit me with a wham that this wasn't merely a training exercise anymore. This was the real deal. My adrenaline rose and with it a surge of energy. But I also felt calm, as if all my training had kicked in at once, and I just did what I was trained to do. I honestly wasn't afraid. I took aim and fired at the bad guys, and they fired at me, and it didn't faze me to think I might kill somebody when he wanted to kill me first.

I saw several Taliban members get hit and fall. More fell. And more. The last few who were left turned around and took off up the wadi. We got word not to give chase, because wadis are great choke points for potential enemy ambushes.

When the shooting died down completely, we approached close enough to see the bodies of the enemy soldiers I'd just helped kill. It was a surreal feeling, but I reminded myself that this is what soldiers are built to do. We received reports later that three of the men killed were top Taliban leaders in the region.

We also received another report, although this one came about a week later. The same police chief who'd given us the intel got word to go check out a house. He went out with his driver and six of his men. When they arrived at the house, the driver and the police chief got out and began to walk forward. Without warning, their vehicle blew up, killing the rest of the chief's men inside. The driver had parked on top of a remotely detonated IED.

Immediately, the police chief was surrounded by armed gunmen. They came from inside the house. It turned out the Taliban were exacting their revenge on the chief for tipping us off. Yet another indication of how the Taliban did business in Afghanistan. The driver, they let escape. He'd been in on the plan and had been paid the equivalent of $3,000 USD for betraying his chief.

The police chief, they made walk forward until he was clear of the wreckage of his vehicle. The Taliban made him take off his shoes, part of the Islamic cleansing ritual. Before they enter a place of worship, they want to leave the dust and dirt of the world at the door. They told him to kneel and pray. He did. After he prayed, they shot him in the back of his head at close range. The full-bearded police chief slumped over dead.

We were about a kilometer away on the other side of a hill and heard the bomb go off. We were sent to investigate. Blood was all over by the time we got there. We picked up body parts and loaded them into body bags. Other members of the ANP came out and policed the scene pretty well. The dead were all other members of the ANP, not civilians or American soldiers.

I picked up an arm and a leg. A couple of our guys picked up a torso or two. A foot here and there. A hand with some fingers still on the end. When a bomb goes off like that, there are a lot of body parts you never find.

I'd picked up dead bodies by then, and I felt desensitized to the experience. You just pick up what you need to, and you're done with it. No one throws up like the movies often show. Not by that point in the war anyway.

We handed over the bags to the ANP and left to go fill out the paperwork. It was a grisly day, and I was sorry that the Afghan police chief and his men had paid the ultimate price for helping their country become free.

ALTOGETHER, WE LIVED at Robat for three months. Once the snow melted, living conditions were okay, but not great. We weren't being shot at. I could heat up water, get a semblance of a hot meal, get some sleep. I missed the relative luxury of my first deployment, but I felt more like I was doing my actual job as a combat soldier this time. For the record, I took four showers total during the year of my second deployment. Yep, four.

One day about six weeks into our time at Robat, we drove some two hours into the country on a regular patrol, like we often did, and went to a village to talk to the elders. We made it a point to talk to everyone we could. Our meeting with the elders lasted about three hours that day. We had tea with them, learned what we could, and communicated what we could to them. Everything seemed to go okay, but we noticed there was nobody of military age anywhere in the village. One of our guys cracked a raw joke that it was a good day to get ambushed.

On the way back, I was in the lead truck in the convoy. Altogether, we had four American vehicles and four ANP vehicles, small Toyota Hilux trucks. We got about two miles away from the village when we started taking fire from the nearby mountain-sides. AK rounds hit all around us with a sharp *plink, plink, plink*. A dry riverbed lay to one side of the road, and a hill was in front of us, so it was hard for our gunner to see up to where he needed to. The vehicles in the middle, the ANP trucks, were targeted the most by the enemy gunners, because they were nowhere as secure as ours. A steady hail of bullets continued to pound around us.

We scrambled out of our Humvees, set up our weapons in an instant, and fired back into the hillsides. A squad maneuvered around to one side to outflank the enemies. I got my Mark 19 grenade launcher into the fight, fired, then yelled at my guys to stay there and man the guns. I ran back to the Humvee behind and drove it forward enough to where the gunner could see up the hill and engage the enemy. Then I ran back to my truck and continued to fire.

One of the ANP guys with us wore a brightly colored vest—fluorescent green with two silver stripes. Earlier in the day I'd heard someone joke that if we were in a firefight, he'd make an easy target. He was just so easy to see. Once we actually got into the firefight, the joke was no longer funny, because sure enough the guy got hit. We called in a helicopter evac for him. The firefight was so heavy that they couldn't land the helicopters at first. So we fired back enough to quell the enemy firing long enough to evac the guy.

Up on the hillside, we could see a Taliban dude firing at us. A couple of our guys hiked up and flanked him. By the time they reached him, he was lying on his stomach and he'd stopped firing. They told him to surrender and get up, but he pulled out his AK-47 and shot at them. His shots went wild. They peppered him hard and he was done. When the rest of the fight was all over, our men brought him back to where we were. It's a bit of a tricky situation, dealing with a body like that. You don't just want to leave a body out in the open—even an enemy. We're not pulling trailers with our vehicles, so you can't use what you don't have to transport a body. You don't want a bloody body in the back of your closed truck. So I did the only thing I could think of. I strapped him to the hood of a Humvee like a deer.

I realize that might go over bad in the public eye, but these are the improvisations you're forced to make in combat situations. We needed to take the body back to the authorities so they could notify the family, and we had more on our minds at the moment than how to handle a dead enemy body. We got word from intel that the Taliban were setting up another ambush, this one even bigger, up the road, ready for us. We were prepared to fight again, but word came to get out of there instead. So we figured out a different route back to the base at Robat.

It took about two hours to drive back. The ANP stayed with us. It was dark when we arrived, and we pulled the dead body off the hood, took him to the police station, and headed back to our compound. The next morning in the light I saw that the hood was covered in blood where the body had been. We washed off the hood, refit our ammo, and got prepared to go out on another patrol. For an infantryman, just another day at work.

I remember that day thinking about how we'd been in the country for less than six months, and my second deployment had quickly proved to be very different from my first. We were in the thick of the battle here, and I felt a long, long way from my two-bedroom apartment back at Fort Bragg, North Carolina, and my beautiful wife, Kelsey.

On top of that, we were only halfway done, and although my men and I didn't know it just then, more heavy combat would be right around the corner.

# ROOFTOP GRENADES

**A**SIDE FROM PUNCHING OUT A TRUCK AND LOSING MY WEDDING
ring, I felt like I steadily matured as a leader on this deployment. Others noticed this too. About three months into deployment, while we were still up on the mountain, one of our sergeants got frostbite and needed to be evacuated. I took over for him then as acting squad leader. When he recovered and came back, he was sent to a different platoon. They gave me his job permanently as a squad leader when we were back in Robat, which meant I now led two teams.

On the second team, my guys were Sergeant John Barton, a solid blond-haired fighter from West Virginia who'd crossed over from the army's maintenance department; PFC Wyatt Sorenson, a great fighter and an all-around great guy; Specialist Jon Sy, a solid rifleman and a real workhorse; PFC Raycroft, a good fighter—we always called him by his last name only; I'm not sure if anyone ever knew his first—and PFC Anthony Russell, a tall guy from the South. He was a young kid, mischievous, who needed to be kept out of trouble.

They were all good guys. Solid warriors ready to go to battle at a moment's notice. With a team like this, I was going to adjust to my new job just fine.

EARLY MORNING ON Valentine's Day, 2010, we got a call that the ANP had cornered a bunch of Taliban fighters in a building about two hours down the road. They wanted us to come and help flush them out.

We loaded fourteen of our men into four Humvees and headed up to the area under fire. The weather was calm that morning, sunny, still wintry cold although the snow had melted. My biggest goal that day, besides doing my job well, was to get home in time to call Kelsey for Valentine's Day and tell her I loved her. *No problem*, I thought. It was supposed to be a five-hour mission total. Two hours up, one hour to clear the building, two hours back. If everything went according to plan, I'd have lots of time.

Of course, this was Afghanistan. Time was relative.

We arrived at the site, parked our vehicles about 150 yards away from the compound, and assessed the situation. The building the Taliban fighters were holed up in was a large mud-and-brick structure with two rooflines and two chimneys. A little wall about five feet tall surrounded part of the building. A fence to keep animals at bay sat to the left. No lights were shining out from openings of the house, I guessed, because there was no electricity inside. Sporadically, the bad guys inside fired their weapons through the house's window holes.

Afghan soldiers and police crouched behind their vehicles with their rifles and pistols drawn. There were about 150 other soldiers total besides us. They hunkered down behind their trucks, far enough away so they couldn't get picked off by the bullets coming toward them.

Since it already appeared that the Afghan officials couldn't get the Taliban fighters to surrender and come out peacefully, the simplest solution to end the standoff was to do a bomb drop on the premises. Just fly a jet over the top and drop a GPS-guided bomb on the fighters (called a Joint Direct Attack Munition, or JDAM). We got on the radio and asked for a jet, but for whatever reason, we couldn't clear the ordnance. We tried this twice, but it wouldn't happen. I never found out why, but it's not a squad leader's job to ask. We just needed to figure out another way.

The Taliban inside the house had surmised that we'd arrived too, and occasionally they were now shooting at us. One of our guys manned the .50-cal and shot back sporadically. But nothing was moving, and all this took time—about three hours total so far at the compound—so we decided we needed to go down to the house with our interpreter and end the standoff ourselves.

Right before we did this, four of the Afghan soldiers decided to get a jump on things. They snuck down and tried to get inside the building. The Taliban dudes inside opened up, and one of the ANA guys dropped flat in the yard. The firing stopped. For a moment, I thought he was dead. But he jumped back up and sprinted for cover. Smart man. He'd only pretended to be hurt, hoping they'd stop shooting at him long enough so he could get away. The rest of the Afghan soldiers hightailed it back to cover too.

The Taliban opened up fire again, this time at everybody and everything they could see, and we shot back toward the house too. Right then I heard a scuffle down at the compound. We stopped firing. A full-size horse jumped out of the window and ran up the hill to safety. Yep—a horse. Animals are often kept inside houses during winter nights to keep them warm. But this was surprising since the day wasn't very cold. It was a large window, maybe four feet across. The horse made it out unharmed.

The gunner of a different team of ours was tasked with carving out the door to the house. After he blasted around the frame for a while, the door caved in as intended, and everything went silent in the house.

We took a six-man team and two of our Humvees and drove closer to the compound to clear the building. I was in the lead. Our trucks stopped about fifty meters away. Using our interpreter, we called out to them a variety of messages: "Put the guns down. You're outnumbered. Come out, this can all be over. We're not going to kill you if you surrender."

With the last sentence still in the air, gunfire erupted. Bullets whizzed toward us. The Taliban fighters shot out of every possible hole in the house. We ducked for cover. My team looked at me, and I looked at them. I decided we'd had enough.

We laid down some suppressing fire, and with bullets still flying in both directions, I circled the compound on foot, approached the structure from the back where it was built into the side of a hill, and climbed up on the roof. The building's frame was strong enough for me to stand on top. You'd be surprised what these buildings can hold—they're stronger than you think. The Taliban below heard me, I was sure, and my adrenaline was pumping, but I wasn't afraid I'd get hit. They fired up at me, but their bullets weren't penetrating through the thick walls or roof. All they could do was shoot up at me through the two chimney holes. Funny—I was planning the same tactic, only the fire from me would go down the chimney, not up.

From the firing pattern below, I could tell that the Taliban were in different rooms in the house. I crouched near the first chimney and listened. The gun below me sounded like this: *boom, boom, boom, boom, kechunk*—and hearing that last sound was my cue. It meant the fighter below paused to reload. I pulled a pin on an M-67 grenade, counted to three, and threw it down the chimney hole. A grenade blows up on the four count. *Kaboom!* This one found its mark. The house shuddered from the compression of the explosion.

I ran across the roof to the next chimney, pulled out another grenade, and listened for the fighter below to pause his shooting. He did. I pulled the pin, counted to three, and dropped it in the hole. I didn't even hear the grenade hitting the ground first before it exploded. *Kaboom!*

After the second explosion, no firing came from inside the building. I jumped off the roof, circled around, and ran back to our team. We enlisted the interpreter again to call out, "We're coming in. Come out with your hands up. We can end this right now."

This time, whatever Taliban fighters were left decided our plan sounded good. The ones who weren't hurt must have been low on ammo by now, and the two grenades I'd thrown in had slowed the group's enthusiasm considerably. Three men came walking out with their hands up.

Before we could make a move, the ANP and ANA charged at the three Taliban members and tore into them like an angry mob. The Afghan authorities swung at the Taliban, hitting them, ripping their clothes, pulling their hair, punching their faces. *Welcome to one of those tricky ethical situations*, I thought. We weren't going to pick a fight with our allies, the ANP and ANA. So if that's how the Afghan authorities wanted to handle the arrest of these surrendering men, then we had to just stand by. I didn't understand what was being said through all the commotion, particularly because the shouting was in a different language, but I could guess at the general theme, that the Afghans were expressing a pile of anger. *Hey Taliban—how's this for payback?! By the way, thanks for ruining our country for so many years!*

Two other Taliban members were still inside the house. Both were alive, wounded from the grenade blasts, and both needed to be carried out. According to the Geneva Convention, we're supposed to administer medical aid on prisoners, even if moments before their weapons were silenced they had been shooting at us and wanting us to die. So our medics started working on the wounded fighters to get them stabilized. One Taliban had a big chunk gone from his head and was wheezing. He wasn't going to last very long. The other fighter was bleeding and had some holes in him. He looked like he would make it okay.

We switched on our tactical lights, a bright white light on the end of our rifles, and combed through the building to make sure no one else was hiding inside. The interior was dusty and dark. The floors were made of dirt, and there was no furniture. We found some weapons and threw them out. A few old bedrolls. The house had been abandoned by its original owners. All of them except the horse, I guess.

The Afghan authorities loaded up the three prisoners on one of their vehicles, and the two wounded fighters on another. The wounded fighters were put on stretchers and placed in the back of the truck. Both trucks took off quickly and headed up a hill.

It sounds crazy now, but this is how it happened—as one of the trucks went up the hill, it hit a rock and bounced, and one of the wounded fighters skidded off the back of the truck and toppled onto the road.

Both trucks screeched to a halt, and a bunch of Afghan officials jumped out and argued with one another. They loaded up the wounded Taliban again, strapped him down tight, and took off in a roar of dust and exhaust.

■ ■ ■

THE SHADOWS WERE lengthening and a chill hung in the air. Evening was coming quickly. I glanced at my watch again. We loaded ourselves back into our four Humvees. Our drivers hit the ignitions for us to get out of there, but one of the Humvees wouldn't start. We climbed out and investigated.

It turned out the vehicle had an oil leak, and as it had sat on an incline on the hill, all the oil had leaked out of the engine. We hooked a towline to this Humvee and attached it to another Humvee and pulled it up the hill and onto the road. The Humvee without oil was dead for now, which meant we'd need to tow it back to the compound.

All in all, as challenging as the day had been, the mission was a success. We'd done what was asked of us, and none of our guys had been hurt in the process. That meant a good day. Clearing the house had taken longer than expected, and now with this setback, we were going to be slowed even further. That wasn't good. We'd now been at this operation for fourteen hours. But if all else went off without incident, I would still make it back in time to call Kelsey.

About an hour down the road, however, word came over the radio that the tow vehicle itself was driving funny, pushing dirt, basically not driving at all. We stopped and investigated again. Turned out the second vehicle had a busted tie rod. It had probably been damaged while navigating the bumpy trail down to the compound. We shut that vehicle down and looked at our options.

With the tie rod in that condition, the vehicle wasn't going anywhere and couldn't be pulled by another Humvee. We certainly couldn't abandon a vehicle of that size and head back to the compound without it. So our only option was to get on the radio and call for one of the huge six-by-six hydraulic military tow trucks to come and get it—and that would take time to reach us. Probably an additional four hours.

That meant we needed to sit tight. It would be a long wait.

Darkness fell. I knew that a roadway in Afghanistan is one of the worst places to be stranded. We were off the main highway on a road less traveled; nothing about it felt safe. We were stuck in the middle of nowhere. We pulled security and waited for the tow truck to arrive.

There wasn't much traffic. The moon rose through a hazy black sky and we could see a little in the pale light the moon provided. Every now and then the headlights of an approaching vehicle would spotlight us and we knew the driver could see us, then the vehicle would slow down and pass by. I tensed whenever I saw an approaching vehicle. Anybody could be inside, and I was always thinking "suicide bomber" in the back of my mind. But I told myself to relax and not freak out. If anything did happen, we had a lot of firepower with us still, and if the bad guys ripped into us, then we could always shoot back. They were tough, but we were tougher.

We are trained to look for patterns on the road, but there was no rhyme or reason to the traffic or the people who passed. One truck that passed was a semi-trailer probably making a late delivery. One car looked to be filled with a family heading back from a trip. Another car contained two businessmen intent on some destination. They didn't mess with us, and we didn't mess with them.

Standing in the dark on a lonely open road in the middle of Afghanistan, a thought flashed at me. I mulled it over and put it out of my mind, but it returned and I mulled it over some more. Call it an epiphany, if you will. All the delays in this mission were frustrating, that was true. I could have grumbled or yelled or punched the side of a truck, like I'd done before. But none of that was going to help the situation any, so there was no point getting upset or mad. I couldn't control a jet not arriving. I couldn't control our truck breaking down. I couldn't control a tie rod getting bent. I couldn't control any of the delays we'd had. There was nothing for me to do except take a deep breath and wait. The thought came at me again, and I held it in my mind this time.

*Things can always be worse.*

It was a good motto to live by in Afghanistan. We could be getting shot at. It could be snowing. We could be cold and wet. We could be locked away in a Taliban prison somewhere. We could be dead.

With that new perspective, I started to laugh, right there on the side of the road. It felt like I was back in basic training, during those times when I'd been so exhausted and frustrated that I could only cry or laugh. Laughing was my default then. It would become my default again.

*Things can always be worse.*

Our tow truck arrived after midnight. We hooked up the broken Humvee and lifted the front end off the ground so it would tow, climbed into the remaining vehicles, and got our convoy on the road and going again.

We didn't want to leave the tow truck by itself, out of our convoy, and it was slow going for him. So we all took it easy with our speed, trying to keep a sharp lookout for trouble in the dark. At 3 a.m. we arrived back at base. The mission had taken more than eighteen hours total. I grabbed some food and made a beeline for the satellite phone. Valentine's Day was over for me, and I hadn't yet made the one phone call that mattered so much. But there was the good news. Depending where you are in the country, Afghanistan is some eleven and a half hours ahead of America. Although it was now February 15 for me, it was still February 14 for Kelsey. I punched in the numbers and soon heard the ringing of Kelsey's phone. She picked up and I wished my wife a happy Valentine's Day. Earlier, I'd contacted a flower shop in her area and had a dozen roses delivered to the house.

"I love you and can't wait to see you again," I said. I never told her much about what was happening on our missions, and I didn't tell her about this crazy day. She didn't need to worry.

"I love you too, Travis," she said. "I'm so glad I married you."

"I'm glad I married you too," I said.

We didn't talk long. Just enough to communicate the important things. Sleep came quickly to me that night, and I dreamt of being back in America, back in the arms of the woman I loved.

THE NEXT MORNING I needed to discipline one of my men. This was Pender, the guy a year older than I was. This particular aspect of being a squad leader was new to me, but it came with the territory.

When we had been at that compound, he'd been ordered to stay with the truck to monitor the radio. But when the wounded Taliban fighter had been carried out of the house, Pender had jumped off our Humvee and rushed to help. That sounded noble, but for him it was actually the wrong thing to do. There were other medics present, and they could do the job. He wanted to get in on the action, and he'd left the radio unmanned during an intense situation. He'd disobeyed a direct order.

Pender was a good friend and a good soldier, and I didn't want to take his rank away, but disobeying an order was disobeying an order. I took him aside and walked him through the situation. He was upset at me for taking him to task, but I couldn't let it go by unnoticed. I decided to let him keep his rank, but as a punishment I told him he'd need to burn the camp's poop for a month. He wasn't happy about that, so I framed it another way.

"I'm doing you a favor," I said. "This is the army, and you can't just do your own damn thing. It's for your own safety."

We had a few heated words, then I realized I just needed to step up and be the leader the situation called for. I ordered him to stand at Parade Rest (this is a position of attention where your hands are interlocked behind you at the small of your back, your face and eyes are straight and looking forward). I got in his face, and ran through the situation again at full volume, shouting in his face what he needed to do.

After that, he understood what I meant.

He and I joke about that experience today. We're still good friends, and disciplining him didn't undermine our chance at ongoing friendship. I was doing my job, and after time went by and he cooled off, he respected me for that.

I WISHED EVERY problem we faced in Afghanistan could be dealt with so smoothly. Our commanding officer liked how we'd handled the rooftop situation, and we'd developed a reputation as an uncompromising unit that could get things done. Word came to shut Robat down. We were being sent elsewhere.

Up in northwestern Afghanistan in the area of Bala Murghab (commonly called BMG), a bunch of our guys were having a tough time of it. The fighting was intense and they were getting hit hard nearly every day. That's where our commanding officer planned to send us.

The enemy up at BMG was said to be well trained and well equipped. We'd be outnumbered. And we'd undoubtedly find ourselves in situations we never imagined. One thing was for certain: anybody who went up there was going to get shot at.

*Okay then*, I thought, *that's where we'll go next.*

# HEAVY FIREFIGHTS
# IN BMG

S WE FLEW UP TO BMG IN A CH-47 CHINOOK MILITARY TRANS-
port helicopter, I glanced at my watch and felt a surge of
adrenaline. We'd nearly reached our destination.

BMG is just below the Afghan border with Turkmenistan. It's
a Taliban stronghold. I wasn't scared. Just pumped. It felt like we
were on the brink of another purposeful adventure, one that I
wanted to begin now. That's the feeling I believe most soldiers
have en route to any mission. Even if the territory is hostile, like
this destination was, you just think, *Let's go up and get it done.*

Talking's hard inside a helicopter because of the noise. My
squad rechecked their weapons and kept watch out the window.
The scenery below us varied little. The same brown mountainous
high desert snaked along underneath us, and sparse foliage dotted
the land. The murky, fast-flowing Murghab River wound its way
through the valleys, and I caught glimpses of the river from time

to time. All we could hear was the smooth and steady *whup whup whup* of the powerful twin-rotor blades over our heads.

I thought about that river. Earlier in November, while the unit we were set to replace was in the midst of constant firefights, they'd received an airdrop of some supplies. But the airdrop wasn't on target, and some of the supplies splashed into the river. Two of our men from the 82nd, Sergeant Benjamin Sherman and Sergeant Brandon Islip, sprinted out to retrieve the supplies. They took fire, and the bank near the river gave way. One soldier fell into the water. He floundered due to his heavy gear. The other soldier jumped in to save him. The current was so strong that they were both swept away. A search began for the bodies, but intense fighting broke out during the first days of the search. Sergeant Sherman's body was found six days later, and Sergeant Islip's body was found three and a half weeks later.

I didn't know these men personally, but I knew their names, and any soldier in the 82nd is a brother to me. I remember praying for their families. I hardly ever prayed while on deployment, and I couldn't exactly tell you why that was the case. I kept my Bible on me. I felt safe with it on me, and I read it now and then. But prayer for specific things was more something that I left in God's hands. He was ruling the universe. Not me. He had it figured out, and I figured it was wise to leave that to him.

If anything, the deaths of Sherman and Islip fueled my resolve. BMG was described to us as a "Taliban vacation spot" where well-trained insurgents infested the region. I resolved that would all change with us in the area.

The problem of BMG was that the bulk of the coalition forces' efforts was focused on larger cities, so for quite a while the Taliban had felt safe and largely ignored up there. To compound problems, the ANA and ANP weren't known for cooperating with each other in the BMG area. Drug and smuggling routes ran up and down the valley corridor, and governmental mistrust spiked high throughout the remote region. The combination of these problems meant our job was twofold: to protect the local population in BMG by holding territory already taken from the Taliban; and to take territory away from the Taliban if we saw opportunities for advancement. Neither would be easy.

Picture BMG as a flat valley between two mountain ranges. It's brown and rocky, not green and lush. Sprinkled through this valley are dozens of small villages and settlements. Most locals are subsistence farmers or herdsmen, or they run some sort of small business. If you're high enough in a helicopter, you can see a patchwork of fields from the aircraft. The main road up to BMG is a two-lane track made of combined tar and gravel that runs from south to north.

If I'd heard the number correctly, some fifteen coalition combat outposts were spread thin up and down the BMG corridor. Most of the outposts were American-run, although some Italian troops were in the area too. If the locals lived near a security outpost, then they were usually safe from the Taliban. Although nothing was guaranteed.

What we knew for sure was this: if anyone—locals or American soldiers—ventured too far away from the perimeters of influence that the outposts provided, then BMG was said to be as dangerous as the blood-filled streets described in *Black Hawk Down*.

OUR CHINOOK LANDED without taking any fire, and we took a truck north the rest of the way to our first security post, nick-named Corvette. Twin mountain peaks ringed the post. Earlier units had nicknamed the mountains Jack and Daniels, and the three ridges around the post were nicknamed Bud Light, Miller

Lite, and Coors Light. The nicknames had stuck, and that's how they actually read on our maps.

The post itself was just three mud buildings surrounded by an eight-foot-tall mud wall. Conditions at Corvette were spartan. Dirt floors. No electricity. No running water. No toilets or showers. The Taliban had originally manned the post, but such as it was, it was ours now. We established security and went out almost immediately to talk to the locals. We wanted to get a feel for the place and show our presence.

The architecture in rural Afghanistan is basically the same throughout the country, repeated over and over and over again. Villages are made up of square mud huts, mud walls, dirt roads with ditches on the other side for wastewater. All windows are open. None of the buildings have electricity or running water.

Honestly, I don't remember the name of the village nearest to Corvette—and we referred to geographical landmarks by the names we'd given them anyway, more so than the actual towns. During the day we saw Afghan men out in the open but never saw any women on the roads. If we ever saw women in the early morning or dusk, their faces were always covered and they steered clear of us. There were a bunch of kids around as we set up at Corvette, but they mostly kept to themselves. On other deployments, kids would come running up to us and shake our hands. We would give them school supplies or engage in contests to see who could throw a rock the farthest. But I'd purposely chosen not to interact with the kids much on this deployment. I'd done it more on my first deployment, but after a while, I concluded it might prove dangerous for the kids. If I was in the middle of something mission-related and a kid came running up to me for a high five, then there was no way I could guarantee his safety.

This is sad to say, but there was also no way initially to know if a local kid was hostile toward us or not. The Taliban were experts at spreading lies about us and making up all sorts of stories about how we were there to ruin Afghanistan and steal children away and crap like that. Some local kids regarded us as heroes. Others had swallowed the Taliban propaganda wholeheartedly and were convinced we were the bogeyman. Although this never happened in any of the combat action I saw, the Taliban had no problem using a kid as a shield in a firefight. They'd stoop so low as to use a kid as a suicide bomber too. You never knew.

Outside the post at Corvette, most of the local men nodded to us as they walked by. Or they'd say a cautious hello from where they sat beside the side of the road. It's kinda weird; when resting, most of the men squat on their haunches like a baseball catcher with their butt off the ground—and they can sit like that for hours. I tried it, but it killed me after about five minutes. The local men do it from the time they're kids, so they're good at it. It's basically sitting down without a chair. The men kept to themselves, but we knew they'd interact with us more at key leader meetings. Our goal was to develop partnerships with them and let them know we were there to help them out.

Right when we'd arrived in BMG, we'd learned that our post's security perimeter ended at a four-way intersection at the far end of a nearby town. The intersection was north of us, about a quarter mile away from Corvette's security perimeter. If we crossed over that imaginary line, the word was we'd get shot at. The town itself wasn't much to look at: just a few businesses and houses with fields behind them. Same mud huts. Same mud walls. Locals frequented the town during the day. We made a mental note to stay clear of the line for now. But in the back of my mind I had a hunch that we'd need to cross it soon.

Our first two weeks at Corvette passed without incident. We were constantly on guard. Sure enough, we went out several times to test the security perimeter and got shot at a few times, but it wasn't much. It felt like the Taliban were waiting for us to make the first big move—not just crossing the line but crossing it for good.

My only injury came from a fistfight. We took antenna cable, nylon rope, and engineer tape and set up a makeshift volleyball net at the compound to help kill the time between patrols. Any game I play, I play to win, and the intensity of this game was right up there with the best. I leaped up in a jump meant to spike the ball down over the net, but I pulled my hand back too fast and the knuckle of my right hand caught me in the eye socket. I plowed into my own face so hard that my world went black, I took three steps, and passed out. The fistfight was with myself!

When I came to, medics were bent over me. Everyone made fun of me for a long time for that little escapade. They called me Twinkletoes and said I had a glass jaw. I knew it wasn't the case. It was just a hard, unlucky shot. Once in high school football, I'd taken a blow to the head but kept playing anyway and finished the game. Afterward, Mom took me to the doctor and it turned out I'd been playing with a concussion. I knew my jaw wasn't glass.

We could only kill so much time at Corvette. The area was proving secure, so I knew the next step would be to take the fight to the insurgency. Our orders came through: move on up the road a mile for a day. The idea was to make a bigger show of moving past the imaginary line at the crossroads to test the Taliban's resolve. I felt fine about that. We weren't in BMG to play volleyball. We were there to kick their butts.


THE COMPOUND UP the road was nicknamed Impala. Marines had taken this post earlier, but one of their guys had been shot in the head and died, so we knew the Taliban wanted the post back. The marines had left without another coalition troop coming in to the post, so we weren't entirely sure if the Taliban had retaken it yet or not. Our commander told us to pack for a twenty-four-hour reconnaissance mission. Our job was to go up there, see what was going on, and then come back and report.

We needed to use maximum speed and force on our side, so aside from our weapons, we packed light for the mission. For me, that meant carrying an extra undershirt and a pair of socks, two MREs, four bottles of water, my weapons, armor, and some extra ammo. No blankets or sleeping bag. I always carried my little photo album—pictures of Kelsey and my mom and dad, brother and sister. Altogether, this light load of gear still meant adding an extra fifty pounds on my person.

We took off at 2 a.m. Rain poured down from the night sky, and we were soaked before we'd hiked a hundred yards. The roadway was too heavily littered with IEDs to trust, so we headed cross country and hiked beside the river. It was going to be a cold, wet night.

Before long, we reached the compound's exterior. All was quiet, but silence could mean anything. We approached the building in tactical formation, slipped inside, and ensured each room was clear. The post was empty, but the Taliban had been there recently—we could tell by a bunch of sleeping mats on the floor and a mess of discarded needles and spoons. Lots of enemy soldiers do their fighting while hopped up on heroin. The Taliban were sure to come back. We set up our guns on three different rooftops, filled sandbags for extra cover, and waited for them to return.

Playing the waiting game was always ominous. We knew that shots could come from anywhere. We just didn't know where. The region was infested with Taliban. Our intel had already confirmed that. The Taliban might fire upon us from the surrounding hillsides, from the neighboring village, from behind trees and walls, from rooftops, ditches, or culverts. They'd move quickly too, fire and run, fire and run, so it would be hard to know exactly where shots were coming from.

Back at Corvette, we knew the area behind us, south and to the east, was secured. But the area north and west of us—where we'd just moved to at Impala—was all Taliban turf. Just up the road from Impala about a thousand meters was another little unnamed village. Same mud huts. Same mud walls. Word was this village was all Taliban.

Just before dawn, the rain stopped and the wind picked up. A shadow moved in the night. It might have been from a branch that swayed in the wind. Or from a piece of garbage that blew down the road. My heart pumped steadily, although my blood pressure spiked from adrenaline. Just before first light, a single rider on a moped puttered down the road. The rider glanced our direction once, twice, three times. Then he was gone. A moped rider might be only that—a moped rider. But he might be a Taliban scout, someone doing reconnaissance work of his own.

The eastern sky grew pink through the haze. The sun was just about up. All was quiet in the compound. Then—*Crack!* A bullet whizzed in and thudded into the compound's rooftop. *Crack!* came another. This one aimed right for us. *Crack, crack, crack!* More bullets blasted in. We lined up the enemy in our sights as best we could and unleashed with our rifles. Sergeant Christopher Bunnell popped the Javelin up onto his shoulder. The Javelin is a sophisticated, expensive, heat-seeking rocket launcher that gets the job done. Three Taliban fighters popped up on a rooftop, fired at us, then ducked for cover. Two more Taliban came up to join the fight. Bunnell's missile found its target, exploded, and took out all five.

Bullets continued to crackle all around us. Fire seemed to be coming at us from every direction. We kept firing and firing, letting them have it, laying waste to their positions, holding our ground. They kept firing back, enraged, wanting us dead and gone. Bunnell shot another Javelin, and another, and another, and another. I shot my M4 rifle and took turns on the .50-caliber machine gun. We wanted to send the Taliban a message: *We're here now; this is us. If you want us dead, then just try.* We fought nonstop for five hours.

By EARLY AFTERNOON the shooting was quiet. I counted, and we'd ended up shooting eleven of the Javelins. On a mission like this, the enemy was positioned far enough away that they'd come collect their own bodies, so we didn't worry about that. Our job was to stay put. We spent the rest of the day filling sandbags and putting in fighting pits. Word came in, and our mission was now officially extended to three days total at Impala.

Before the sun set, I checked around and saw that our food and water were running low. We weren't going to make it three days on what we had left. Someone needed to hike back to Corvette and get more supplies. It wouldn't be easy. Given the morning's firefight, there was no telling who'd still be out there to shoot at whoever went to do the task. I pointed to Raycroft and Sorenson and told them to follow me.

When the cover of darkness fell, the three of us headed out on the hike back to the first compound. Again, we didn't want to walk down the main road out of fear of IEDs, so we hiked back through the trails beside the river. We tried to move as fast as we could. We hiked through farm fields and along dirt paths. We had our night-vision goggles on and didn't see anyone around, which didn't mean much as the Taliban could be hiding anywhere. Our destination was a four-way intersection near Corvette where Sergeant Potts was meeting us with a Humvee and supplies.

Our destination was about a kilometer away, but it seemed longer because of nightfall and the tension of the unknown. Soon enough we located the platoon sergeant at the Humvee and collected as many MREs and water bottles as we could carry. The MREs, I loaded into the rucksacks of Sorenson and Raycroft. They were thickly muscled guys but smaller in stature than I was, so I wanted them carrying the relatively lighter loads. The water, I packed into a rucksack and swung that up over my shoulders. It added another 150 pounds onto the gear I already carried.

We set off again, heading north, sticking to the trails and varying them so as not to retrace our steps exactly. I felt top-heavy and wobbly and was careful to place each foot firmly on the ground.

About halfway into the trip, we switched course and followed a trail that traversed the side of a farmer's field. We hadn't walked this way before. At the end of the field was a plowed berm. I stepped up over the berm but stepped too slowly and fell backward into the soft soil, landing on my rucksack. I felt like an idiot as I kicked my arms and legs like an overturned turtle on its shell, but I was too heavy from the added weight to get up. Raycroft and Sorenson grabbed my arms and yanked. I took a few steps, wobbled, and stumbled again on the tilled ground, this time falling forward. It's harder to discern depth perception with night-vision goggles on. I hit something hard, and my goggles cracked against the bridge of my nose, making it bleed. I got up and kept going.

We made it back to Impala safely. The rest of the guys were happy to have the resupply. It was nearing midnight, and we'd been up since before 2 a.m. the night before. Security was tight, so I told my guys to get some sleep. As teams, we slept in shifts, two guys up and two guys down. Sorenson and I stayed awake for the first shift. None of us had any blankets, and the night was freezing again, although luckily not raining this time. The guys who were trying to get some sleep spooned each other, huddling together for body warmth. They were shivering hard, and before they drifted off, Sorenson and I had a good laugh about it.

"Just you wait till it's your turn, Sergeant Mills," PFC Russell said to me.

He was right. A couple hours later when the time came for Sorenson and me to lie down, the floor and air were so cold it felt like lying in a big dirty refrigerator. Sorenson lay down about three feet away from me because I'd told him to keep his distance. I shivered and wrapped my arms around my shoulders for warmth. This was not going to work. But I needed to think through my next move carefully before saying anything.

See, there's something you need to know about army pants. They're made in the traditional style to go up high and around your belly button. But none of the guys ever wear them like that because they're not comfortable that way. Almost everybody wears them low and around their waist, and some guys wear them so low that it's easy to rip your crotch as you're crawling through a field or whatever. That's what had happened to Sorenson. He'd ripped his pants during our movement to the compound. He never wore any underwear either. Almost none of the guys do, because you're so grimy and sweaty all the time, it's easy to chafe. Sorenson's man junk was just lying out in the open. He didn't care. It was a big joke to him. And this was the guy I was supposed to spoon with as we shivered?! No thanks! But after a few minutes of lying on the freezing floor, I changed my mind.

"Sorenson!" I barked. "Get over here. But I've got to be behind you. There's no way I want your dick hanging out on me."

Sorenson laughed and edged back against my body. All the guys laughed. We were still freezing, but at least we managed to get a bit of sleep.

* * *

THE FOLLOWING DAY we didn't get shot at very much. We worked in shifts and continued to build up the compound with sandbags, continually strengthening our fighting positions. The rest of our unit came up in Humvees—about twenty-one guys total, and my squad drove back in a Humvee to get the rest of our gear and then came back up to Impala. We turned over Corvette, the lower security post, to the ANA and let them man it.

Back at Impala, our unit worked as a team. About fifty feet in front of the compound, we drove poles into the ground and strung up coils of concertina wire—that type of razor-sharp barbed wire you see on top of prison fences. We laid a few mines and marked their positions confidentially so they could be located and dug out later. No one was going to cross that line and come into our compound now. That night we slept in shifts, then went right back to work the next day. About midafternoon we took a few more shots from the Taliban, and we fired back a few times. When the fighting was over, we went back to digging.

We understood that Impala was now the most northern point in the series of outposts. We were deep in Taliban territory, the farthest security outpost up the road in BMG. Our mission was changed again. Specifically, it was to hold the ground around Impala and work with the ANA and the locals in the region. And our mission at Impala was now to last indefinitely. Word was we'd spend the rest of our deployment exactly where we were. We had almost six more months to go.


FROM THAT POINT on, each day included another firefight.

Each night we slept in shifts.

When we weren't shooting, we were digging, lifting, shoveling to strengthen our position. If our orders were to stay at Impala, then we weren't going to quit. This had become trench warfare, and we were prepared and determined to last.

We noticed how difficult it was to see to the right from where we were located in the compound and knew we needed to get to higher ground. So we sent seven of our guys to go climb the hill called Coors Light, dig in, and improve the sight line on our right flank.

Our guys climbed the hill, started digging, and took fire almost immediately. We shot back. Eventually the shooting died down, and our guys went back to digging. That first day the pit they dug was eight feet deep, a good enough trench for us to guard the right flank. The next day we kept going. Eventually, our trench system became complex. Days passed, and turned into weeks. It rained off and on, and the nights were often wet and cold. We rotated guys up the mountain and back to the compound, but some guys decided they liked it better up on Coors Light and wanted to spend all their time there. Eventually, we hewed three huge fighting pits, plus a living area, a crapping area, and a storage area—all out of the rocky Afghan mountainside.

The compound below the hill was nothing to write home about. It was surrounded by an eight-foot-high mud wall. When you walked through the entrance of the compound into the breezeway, maybe fifteen meters, there were some trees and a building to the left and a building to the right that we turned into our headquarters and living quarters. A little garden was there, and growing in it were some sort of vegetables, onions, tomato plants. Nearby was a peach tree. The peaches in the compound weren't ripe now, but they would be by the time we left.

Inside the buildings we positioned green sleeping cots and our gear. We brought up a few metal army chairs and used a few MRE boxes to sit on. There was no furniture in the compound

from when the Taliban used it. We brought up a diesel genera-
tor so we could run radios and lights and plug in our laptops.
An outhouse was already built, but it had no seat, just a squat
hole. We took a steel chair, cut a hole in the middle of the seat,
and taped padding around the sides. Someone found a bunch of
old magazines the army had lying around—*Motor Trend, Popular
Mechanics*—stuff like that. The magazines were at least six years
old, but they made the outhouse really homey. I tell ya, with an
outhouse like that, we were really living.

One day near dinnertime, I spotted a guy in the distance with
an AK-47 on his back and binoculars in his hand. Pender was
with me. We were on guard on the rooftop of one of the buildings in the compound. The other guys were below us munching
on MREs. We knew what we needed to do. Whenever we shoot
an enemy fighter under these circumstances, we need to get permission first. So I checked with our platoon sergeant to get it
cleared. Word came back that we were good to go. Pender had
his M14 with him—it's the standard-issue long-range rifle, and
he started shooting before I could get my Mark 19 automatic grenade launcher ready. The Taliban dropped from Pender's shots
and Pender yelled, "I got him!" But just then the fighter hopped
up again and started sprinting for cover. He'd only been playing
possum. By then I had my Mark 19 ready, and I dropped the Taliban with one shot.

It turned out the enemy fighter hadn't been alone. Shots
started whizzing in from three directions at once. Pender yelled
that he'd spot for me, which meant he'd call out positions for me
to fire the Mark 19 as accurately as possible. The ammo for a
Mark 19 is belt-fed and comes out of a slit-shaped canister, similar
to how the ammo for a machine gun is fed. Earlier, Pender had
grabbed an ammo canister without checking its contents. While
firing, I looked down into that can and noticed the rounds were

backward. Earlier, the rounds had gotten rusty from all the rain we'd had. So we'd taken them out and scrubbed them up, but the private who had reloaded them had loaded them backward. So right in the middle of that firefight, Pender and I needed to stop and clear the gun. It was an easy fix and didn't take long, but I knew Pender and I were both going to take crap for it from the rest of the guys. They'd razz us by saying, "You jammed the gun up." Stuff like that's funny to an infantryman. You have to be there to get the humor. I don't remember now the specifics of the ribbing they gave us, but if there was ever a chance to give another dude a hard time, rest assured, the guys took it.

For some time, that's how our days went. Fighting and digging, fighting and digging. Typically we woke up to hear the Islamic call to prayer. It was piped all over from loudspeakers set up in town. We took a leak, ate an MRE, downed a bottle of water, and brushed our teeth. After that, the fighting would start. If someone took a shot at us, we shot back. Most days we fought until the sun sank. Then we ate another MRE, had another bottle of water, and lay down to sleep in shifts. That was our routine.

AFTER TWO AND a half months at Impala, I guess the Taliban realized we were there to stay, so they quit fighting us so intensely. They didn't stop altogether, but from then on the action was sporadic. It wasn't daily anymore, but just enough to keep us on our toes. Each day we went out on patrol. Sometimes we got shot at, but many days were quiet. We didn't have much contact with the locals in this area. If they walked by the compound we'd say hi, and usually they'd say hi in return. But it was really difficult in this region to know who was friend and who was foe. We'd arrived in BMG in March. Winter turned into spring, and spring turned into summer. The weather turned hot.

In April, I celebrated my twenty-third birthday. I ate an extra MRE that day. Birthdays are never a big deal when you're on deployment—and that was fine with me. The military was my home away from home, and it was good to be with my men. On my birthday, I thought back to a few months earlier when I'd re-enlisted in the army for another four years. We'd been at Robat then, and guys were joking that reenlisting was a bad idea, but I didn't care. The military was more than my job. It was the place I belonged.

To reenlist, I knew I'd need to raise my right hand and swear to defend the Constitution of the United States—and I valued that. But when you reenlist on deployment and you're out in a compound in the dirt and muck, the tone is more relaxed. I wrote "I 'heart' boobs" on my palm so that my guys could see it when I raised my hand. I wasn't a squad leader then, only a team leader, and the guys all got a good laugh at that. Anything to keep it light.

Late-spring and summer days in Afghanistan can be miserable—I'm talking 115 degrees Fahrenheit, even sitting way up on a mountainside. On those days, if we weren't fighting or digging or patrolling, Hubbard and I would sit out in the compound in our PT shorts and flip-flops and dump bottles of water over our heads, chests, and shorts, and then time how long it took to become completely dry. Ten minutes wasn't unusual.

At night, the buildings grew so hot that we dragged our cots into the interior courtyard to see if we could find a breeze. We slept out under the night sky, and the stars looked the same as in America, only clearer because we were so far away from any city. Up on the mountain, the moon could be so bright it lit up the sky almost like the sun.

Boredom set in, and we went back to talking about everything and nothing. We talked about food. We reminisced about the past. We talked about career plans, and a couple of guys wanted to stay in the military and go into Special Forces. Hubbard wanted to get back to snowboarding. Jon Sy talked about going to college in California. Pender was from Oxford, Michigan, and had attended Michigan State University for a while. I was a big fan of the University of Michigan (go Blue!), so he and I spent endless hours debating the old rivalry of Wolverines versus Spartans and the merits of each football team.

Pender and I were good friends. He was probably my best friend on this deployment, which is funny considering he was the guy I'd needed to discipline once earlier on. But he'd hung out at my house quite a bit before we left, and he knew Kelsey, and he was simply a great guy all around. Hubbard was a good friend too. All the guys were. We were all good ol' boys at heart, just-get-it-done type of guys, upbeat dudes making the best of a crappy situation. We were always willing to fight and willing to do the work that needed to get done. I don't remember anyone ever complaining.

Guys would rotate home on leave every so often, and after the fighting died down at Impala, I had ten days' leave. It was a bit of a pecking order in terms of who could go first, but rank wasn't the final say by any means. Say, a guy had a wedding anniversary coming up, then that would take precedence over a guy who just wanted to go home and shoot the bull with his friends. If there was ever a conflict between two dates, then the guys would hash it out and come to an agreement.

On the morning I was set to go, Sergeant John Barton tripped over a random piece of metal stuck in the ground in the compound. He started digging around. The rest of us joined him. We discovered we had positioned our sleeping cots on triple-stacked Taliban mines that were wired to blow. Sleeping on IEDs—how's that for a thought?! The only reason the bombs hadn't blown was because they'd been in the ground too long and their batteries were dead.

The days leading up to me going home felt like I was just killing time. I couldn't wait to get home and see my family again. At Impala, we weren't doing as many patrols by then, so a lot of days we'd just go through inventory, clean and polish the gear, and do nothing and everything to help pass the time.

Finally the date arrived. I left BMG in May and caught a series of connecting flights home to America. I gave Kelsey a huge kiss at the airport in Dallas and when I got back to the house I gave our dog Buddy a big hug. It felt great to be back, but it also felt surreal—and this was the strange part of this leave time. I didn't quite know what to do with myself. At home, I could take a hot shower anytime I wanted. I could sit around on the couch and play video games. I could drink a beer and eat a cheeseburger outside on the back porch. Nobody was shooting at me. Nobody stunk. Nobody was sleeping on triple-stacked IEDs.

Kelsey was finishing up the semester with college and work, so I bought a truck, and we drove up to Michigan to see my parents. We had a few bright and happy days with them, then it was soon time to go, just like that. I hugged my parents, gave Kelsey a big kiss, and flew out of Detroit to head back overseas to BMG.

It felt oddly good to be back to Afghanistan. The feeling is difficult to explain. In America, when I'd hung around with some friends in Dallas and got reacquainted with some of my buddies from high school back in Michigan, I'd seen firsthand how most of the people my age lived. If a dude was twenty-two or twenty-three like me, he was usually finishing up college or hanging out trying to find an internship or entry-level job. He might be living in his parents' basement, trying to scrape together enough money to move out. Or maybe he was partying hard on weekends, or maybe still in a frat. He was almost always short on money. Almost always wondering what to do with his future. Not that there was anything wrong with any of that. A guy's gotta do what a guy's gotta do.

But by contrast, at my age in the military, I led people in combat. I controlled firefights. I handled hundreds of thousands of dollars' worth of equipment. I made decisions that affected whether people would live or die. It felt real.

On a personal level, I made decent money. I was married. I had a good credit score. I was thinking of buying a house soon.

It felt good to be trusted with this much responsibility. I was proud of my drive and sense of accomplishment. I was already a man.

MY BROTHER-IN-LAW JOSH Buck was stationed at FOB Todd, a few miles away, and I saw him a few times on this deployment. He ran the aid station at FOB Todd, and was on the resupply route for a number of other posts, so if the trucks were coming up to Impala he'd sometimes catch a ride up and see me. That was always good, a real change of pace. For a while there, we saw each other almost once a week. We didn't solve the world's problems, we just BS'd back and forth, but it helped lighten things up and felt like a home connection.

It felt strange to be sitting in the midst of hostile territory with so little to do. The last few weeks at Impala, most of the time we were bored. We occupied ourselves with the usual shenanigans, despite the still-tense environment around us. A guy would be sleeping and we'd put shaving cream on his face. A guy would go to take a piss and we'd come up behind him and grab his ass like a joker or shake his shoulders so his stream would go cockeyed. Middle school stuff. We may have been wiser than our years, but our humor wasn't. We threw rocks and dirt clumps at nothing in particular. We talked about the food we were going to eat when we got home. Sergeant Andrew Gutierrez went out with a few of our guys and got into a pretty good firefight one day. When he got back to the compound he said, "Man, that was close." But that was the only serious firefight for our unit during those last few weeks.

The ANA guys living down the road at Corvette made us some food with fresh tomatoes and peppers. They liked us fine and we worked side by side nearly every day, so we trusted them. Yet we had learned by then that we played Russian roulette whenever we ate local food. I'd eaten it before with mixed results. But with only two weeks to go in-country, I decided to take another chance. A couple of guys joined me. We got dysentery so bad we constantly sprinted to the can. We just laughed about it. That's the way we rolled.

AT THE END of August 2010, our unit was rotated home for good. Our brigade as a whole had 45 soldiers killed in action and about 300 wounded. I was sad about that, but we hadn't lost anybody specifically from our platoon, so that was an accomplishment. When the helicopter took off, we heard the rotary wash above us. We lifted off from BMG, and everybody inside let out a loud cheer.

We'd lived in BMG for six months. Six stinking months. Part of me wanted to stay right where we were, because I knew the job wasn't finished. But I was excited to go home, to see my wife, drive my own vehicle, and eat my own food. High on my mind was a stop at Jersey Mike's sub shop. I couldn't wait to get my hands on a Big Kahuna Cheese Steak. Grilled onions and peppers plus mushrooms, jalapeños, and extra cheese. It's not called the Big Kahuna for nothing.

We flew back to FOB Stone to the south of the city of Herat where we'd begun our deployment. This was the larger FOB, and I took a hot shower there, washed my clothes, and ate a hot meal. After that, my job was just to police my guys and make sure they didn't do anything stupid before they got home. We played pickup basketball and went for runs. After three or four days, we flew to Kyrgyzstan, then to Ireland, and then back home to America, where they had pizza and beer waiting for us at Fort Bragg.

I figured the Taliban had concluded we were too tough for them, so they'd eased up on us and were waiting for the next unit to rotate in. Our colonel had sources among the locals, and he discovered that the Taliban had called us "unrelenting savage dogs that kept fighting and fighting." I felt fine when I heard that. You've got to be cocky to be part of the 82nd. Even your enemies respect you.

Sure enough, a team of light infantry soldiers from the army's 4th Infantry Division took over for us, and the area heated up again quickly. We received the report soon. In their first ten days in BMG, four men from the 4th were either killed or wounded.

Do I regret anything that happened in BMG?

Only that I didn't kill more Taliban while I was there.

# OUR FIRST HOME TOGETHER

**K**ELSEY PICKED ME UP FROM THE BASE AT FORT BRAGG WHEN I returned home from deployment, and she needed to drive, because I didn't know the way home.

In July 2010, while I was still in BMG, Kelsey had bought us a house. Her season of staying at her parents' place in Texas was finished, and she knew we would need a place to live once I got home and we were both at the base again. When I returned in August, I hadn't yet seen my own house except in pictures.

From the base, our home was about half an hour away. We drove into the small town of Raeford, North Carolina, and headed toward our subdivision and I thought about what I knew so far about our house. It was a three-bedroom, two-bath basic starter-level home, about 1,800 square feet, on a cul-de-sac and a quiet street. There was a nice deck out back and a fenced-in back-yard for the dog to play in. The yard was landscaped with shrubs and red cedar mulch. That was about all I knew.

The streets looked a little familiar. Josh and Deanna Buck and their family lived about a quarter of a mile away. I had to hand it to my wife. *Amazing* was the word that came to mind. I was so proud of her—I mean, it isn't easy to buy a house. While I was overseas, Kelsey had run down various choices of places to live, which I could see on a laptop screen at Impala. But in the end, she picked out the place herself, worked with a real estate agent to negotiate the deal, secured the loan, signed the mountain of paperwork that accompanies house buying, and moved our stuff in. She was twenty-one and I was twenty-three, and we were homeowners. It felt amazing to be able to make those kinds of big purchases at our young age. I felt secure knowing I could trust my wife to make them for our family.

"We're almost here," Kelsey said. "Close your eyes."

I shut my eyes and took a deep breath. Thoughts of why we'd taken this plunge of house buying ran through my mind. When I'd reenlisted, I reenlisted for stabilization, so I could stay in the 82nd. After deployment ended, I was guaranteed three months at home for integration, then another twelve months at Fort Bragg, then another deployment (which meant we wouldn't be moving to another base in the U.S. during that time). So it seemed smarter to buy a house and make an investment rather than renting an apartment again.

"We're here," Kelsey said. "Welcome home."

We parked in front of the house. I leaned over and gave Kelsey a kiss. We jumped out of the car. She took me by the hand and led me indoors. She showed me the new furniture she'd bought, a leather couch and a recliner. She'd hung up pictures already. The walls were painted cool colors. I loved all her choices. We were home, truly home.

"We need to have a party," I said. "A big housewarming party."

Kelsey just grinned.

Sure enough, we held that party a few days later. My parents flew down from Michigan. Josh and Deanna were there, and some of the guys from my unit came over. I manned the barbecue. The smell of charcoal-fired hamburgers drifted over the neighborhood, and I felt like the luckiest man alive. Kelsey and I had a dog, two cars, and now a house. We were a young family living the American dream.

Still, I couldn't help but notice the way Josh Buck picked up his young daughter and carried her around, showing her the backyard. I held that picture in my mind for a long time, and I wondered why, even though Kelsey and I had so much, something still felt like it was missing.

FOR A SOLDIER, garrison life stateside is just like any other nine-to-five job, except the hours are longer. At the start of a day at the base, I woke up at five, threw on my PT uniform (shorts and a T-shirt), and drove to the base to get there by six. They played reveille, and we'd do PT for an hour and a half. Most days that meant we took a run, anywhere from two to ten miles. Other days we did wind sprints that lasted forever. We did push-ups, sit-ups, calisthenics—whatever the PT leader wanted us to do.

I was too big of a guy to be much of a long-distance runner, so although I could hold my own, I was often back of the pack. Weights were my big thing. I had a home gym and could bench 250 to 265 for multiple sets and squat 315. In the army, your job is to be in shape. I lifted on my own time, usually after work.

After PT, we showered, dressed in uniforms, had breakfast, and were ready for the rest of the day's work by nine. Each day's work was different. We kept our skills sharp—marksmanship, combat lifesaving training, weapons detail, whatever it took. We might do more training. We might take inventory somewhere.

We finished our day anywhere from 4:30 to 6 p.m., depending on what was going on.

After I drove home, Kelsey would have dinner ready for me. I'd play fetch with our Lab Buddy, and Kelsey and I would talk about our days. We were homebodies mostly, and for the first six months or so after my deployment was over, we mostly just hung out and had fun. On weekends we went to movies and out to eat. We had friends over to play cards or board games, and we had lots of laughs over our favorites: Cranium, Apples to Apples, and Catch Phrase. We barbecued steaks, hamburgers, bratwurst, or chicken. Sometimes, I'd have a rum and Coke after the day was done.

Fortunately, after I got home, I didn't struggle with any past memories of combat, although I know any number of soldiers who do. I told a few stories to Kelsey about our unit's time in Robat and BMG, about going without a shower for so long, and about some of the firefights we got into around Impala and Corvette, but she didn't like to talk about those things much—and I understood that. I found I could shut off the memories pretty easily. My logic was straightforward: I was a combat soldier. That's what I did. I told my mind to go to certain places, and I refused to allow it to go to other places. I found that I could reconnect with my family best that way, although I knew other guys handled things differently with equal success.

In December, we traveled up to Michigan for two weeks to visit my folks. Kelsey wasn't feeling well. Like a dope, I didn't clue in at first to what might be making her feel that way. After we went home, Kelsey went into the bathroom, took the test, and came out, her brow furrowed, and asked me to drive to the nearest Walgreens to get another test.

Sure enough, the Walgreens test confirmed her hunch. We didn't know what to do first. A bunch of emotions swirled together. We called my parents. We called Kelsey's parents. They were all excited for us. All I could think was, *Oh my gosh, this is real—*

I was gonna be a daddy.


ONCE THE SHOCK wore off, my main concern was trying to save money. I started looking at car seats, cribs, a stroller, a bassinet, a bigger car. Braces. Summer camp. College. Kids sure can be expensive. Officially, we decided not to tell anyone else we were pregnant until after twelve weeks, just until we were sure everything would be okay. But I was so excited I kept telling people left and right at work. It was so awesome. I'd be like, "Okay, I just told you that, but you can't tell Kelsey I told you. Okay?!"

I went to all the doctor's appointments along with Kelsey. I was there when we first heard the heartbeat. I was there at twenty weeks when we had the ultrasound and first found out our baby was a girl.

*A baby girl.*

I couldn't imagine anything more incredible.

Kelsey began to "nest" at home, like pregnant women often do. We bought a crib and a changing table and a dresser and a bunch of baby stuff, and I got busy with wrenches and instructions, assembling it all. Kelsey brought home color swatches of paint and asked me what I thought. "Whatever you want is fine by me," I said. (That's a phrase wise husbands know is best to say.) I laughed when I took a look at myself one day—me, the tough combat warrior, painting one of our bedrooms the girliest shade of pink you've ever seen.

Kelsey drove a sporty 2010 Mazda3 at the time, and she loved the car, but the car seat wouldn't fit. I hemmed and hawed and cursed and shoved and finally managed to install it, just to show

Kelsey that the front seats would hardly go back, and she was like, "Okay, just sell it." I nodded.

Kelsey hates going to car dealerships, so without her along, I traded in her Mazda for a Ford Freestyle, a station-wagon crossover type thing, and brought it home, but Kelsey opened the driver's door and shook her head.

"It smells like a cat," she said.

She was right. So I took the Freestyle back, played hardball with the car dealer and got my money back, then went and bought a Ford Sport Trac, basically an Explorer pickup truck. It was bigger than the Mazda, my payments were good, and when I brought it home, Kelsey jumped in and took off for a drive right away. So that was her car.

One day I looked at a calendar and squinted. It seemed like our kid was never actually going to arrive. But before I knew it the due date was three months away, then two months, then four weeks. Then two weeks. Then it was only a matter of days. Kelsey's mom flew into town to help out. With two days to go, Kelsey went in for a checkup. The doctor said, "Okay, she's ready. That baby needs to come out now!"

We went into the hospital on September 26. They induced labor. Kelsey was a real trouper. She got an epidural, but it only worked on half of her body, so it was really rough. Her mom and I sat with her. My job was to keep calm and keep a cool washcloth on Kelsey's forehead. I didn't joke around at all then. I just wanted labor to be over for Kelsey as quickly as possible. Fourteen hours of pain later, at four in the morning on September 27, 2011, our daughter was born.

Wow. I made some weird noises in the back of my throat. There our kid was, with goo all over her, and she was wrinkly and scrunched up, and all I could think was that she was the most beautiful thing in the world.

"It's okay to cry," the nurse said.

I didn't know how to cry. So I just kept making my weird noises.

I cut the cord and helped with her first bath. We had planned that her name was going to be Madison Avery. But when she arrived, she didn't look like a Madison Avery. She looked more like a Chloe Lynn. So that's what we named her.

I thought back to that housewarming party where everything seemed perfect, but still one thing had been missing. Chloe Lynn was that one thing. With her in our lives, nothing felt missing anymore. A feeling of totality came over me. Of completeness. We were no longer alone. We had a child. Our family was now three.

As I cuddled Chloe beside Kelsey's hospital bed, I couldn't wait for us to take our daughter home. I promised Chloe that I would show her around to everybody we knew. I would build her a swing set in our backyard soon. A good sidewalk ran outside our house, and she would love to go for stroller rides with me whenever I took Buddy for a walk. Already I loved this child with a love that went beyond words. I would provide for her and play with her and teach her how to do things and show her the way forward. I would defend her and fight for her, and in that long moment of wonder and joy in the hospital room, I held her and looked at her and marveled at the mystery of life, of things too great and powerful for words.

SOMEWHERE DURING THAT first full day of being in the hospital with our newborn—I think it was only an hour or so after Chloe was born—a nurse came and got the baby and took her to the nursery for a while so Kelsey could get some sleep. We'd both been up for a long time—something like twenty-seven hours by then, and our emotions had ridden a roller coaster. Kelsey hadn't

Me goofing off with my big sister, Sarah. I was the jokester of the family, although Dad says I never knew when to quit.

I hoped I'd have a career in the NFL one day, but I settled for playing in community college instead. This is me in eighth grade, a proud Vassar Vulcan.

Mom and Dad made the fourteen-hour trip from Michigan to Fort Bragg in January 2007 to see me off on my first deployment to Afghanistan. I teared up and got on the bus quickly so nobody could see me cry.

Kelsey and me having lunch on our first date— a week-long whirlwind trip to Cozumel, Mexico, while I was on a short break during my first deployment. We had a fast, exciting romance from the start, and we haven't slowed down since.

Right before we were married, Kelsey and I went to Maine to meet her side of the family at her grandma's farm. That part of the state has a lot of ticks, and Kelsey didn't want to get any, so I told her to climb on while we walked out into a field. My role has always been the "strong man" in the relationship.

I couldn't believe how beautiful our newborn daughter was. Chloe was so tiny, so wonderful. I was more scared to be a new parent than I was to be in combat.

Maintaining a sense of humor while on deployment is essential. When we took breaks, we often played baseball or Frisbee, fighting the tension by staying loose.

Seeing my brother-in-law, Josh Buck, on our second deployment to Afghanistan was always welcomed. It felt great to have a piece of home so close by. Other soldiers didn't get to see any family for a full year.

This was the last picture taken of me, April 8, 2012, at our strong point while on my third deployment to Afghanistan. I'm sporting my Vassar Vulcan hat out of hometown pride. Two days later, on April 10, I'd be critically wounded.

The evening after I was hit, my hometown of Vassar held a candlelight vigil at the high school football field to pray for me and my family. I felt deeply honored to have so much support from my community. *[John Cook Photography]*

Four days after being wounded, I turned twenty-five while in the hospital. My guys sent me this picture of themselves as a way to let me know I was still in their thoughts. This is 1st Platoon, Bravo Troop, 4/73rd Cavalry Squadron, 4th Brigade Combat Team, 82nd Airborne Division—the guys I lived with, ate with, fought alongside of. Brothers.

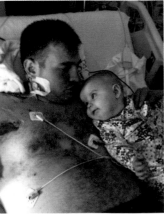

This picture means so much to me. I was in ICU at Walter Reed, and this was the moment I saw Chloe for the first time after being wounded. I was scared to see her again, fearing how she would react. Internally, I was wondering if I could ever be a good father and husband again. Chloe just looked at me, smiled, and nestled right in. I was still the same to her.

This was the first day I walked. After one lap around the room, the staff said I could stop, but I kept going. I was covered in sweat and exhausted. My limbs were trembling. But I was elated and I walked three laps. I'm tearing up in this photo, telling the therapists and prosthetists how thankful I was for all their hard work.

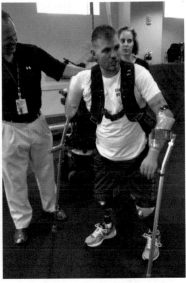

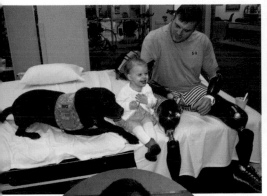

Kelsey and Chloe came to therapy with me and cheered me on. I wanted to get better for them. The service dog's name is Deuce.

This was a monumental day, the first day of me walking using taller prosthetic legs that have knees. I was almost my full height again. Kelsey and I are pictured with my physical therapist, Kerry, and my number one leg guy, Dave.

With every day, week, month, I got stronger. It was a milestone for our family to be able to travel back home to North Carolina for a few days to celebrate Chloe's first birthday at our own house. I practiced making my mom's famous stuffing for a Thanksgiving celebration.

About five months after being hit, while still in rehab, I had set a goal to walk the Tunnel to Towers 5K along with Corporal Todd Nicely. I rubbed my leg raw and it was bleeding into my liner, but I finished it. Later I fell down on stage in front of 25,000 people. It was a pretty awesome day.

I enjoyed finding new ways to be an adrenaline junkie. Here, I'm downhill mountain biking in Crested Butte, Colorado, with Adaptive Sports Outdoors.

Learning how to drive again while at Walter Reed was huge for me. It was my last bit of healing to regain full independence. Big thanks go to driving rehab specialist Major Tammy Phipps for all her guidance and training.

I started the Travis Mills Foundation as a way to help other wounded servicemen and their families. This photo was taken at one of our first retreats in summer 2014, two years after I was wounded. Left to right: Drew Mullee and his son Easton; Andrew and Tory Smith; Jennifer Mullee; Kelsey, Chloe, and me; and Taylor and Danielle Morris.

A ceremony was held for us on October 15, 2014, when Kelsey, Chloe, and I moved into our new smart home in Maine, built by the Gary Sinise Foundation, which builds adaptive homes for critically wounded service members. Kelsey and I were completely overwhelmed by the support of the foundation and our community, thankful and blessed that so many people came together to allow us to have a place to call home.

Three years after being wounded, this is me running strong on Memorial Day 2015 at the fourth annual Miles for Mills 5K in Maine. This event has developed into a fundraiser, now held by my foundation to help other wounded veterans. *[Mark & Deanna Photography]*

During Maine's winters, I love taking Chloe for a ride out back of our property with my action track chair. Buddy, our yellow lab, enjoys coming along. I'm never going to sit back and let the world pass me by. If Chloe wants to go out and play in the snow, I'm her dad and I'm going to take her.

eaten fast food in nine months, and right before she dozed off she murmured that she was totally craving some Chick-fil-A. So I headed out to get her a chicken sandwich and some French fries. But before I left the hospital, I swung past the nursery to check on Chloe.

They call it the father bear instinct.

Two morons in scrubs were standing in front of the nursery jabbering away about Belgian beer. Chloe was inside the nursery. I could see her through the glass. She was screaming her head off. And she was unattended!

I found a nurse and said, "I'm Travis Mills. What's going on with my baby's doctor?"

She motioned toward the two Belgian beer dudes and said, "Oh, the doctor for the Mills baby is right over there."

One of the dudes heard her, shrugged nonchalantly, and said, "I don't have a baby in there."

And the nurse said, "Yeah, you do. The Mills baby."

"Oh," he said. "That baby."

So—ahem. Let's just say Father Bear growled. This was a military hospital, I might add, and this was my first experience standing up for my kid. I got in the guy's face and politely explained—as only an infantryman can—that he needed to quit talking about Belgian beer and tend to my crying baby daughter, and if he didn't do so immediately, then I'd rip off his head and spit down his throat.

After that, he hustled.

I went and got the Chick-fil-A for Kelsey, and when I got back I asked if the doctor had been in to see her.

"Yeah," Kelsey said drowsily. "And he was super nice too. Kinda overly nice. Like he really wanted to reassure us that everything was going to be okay."

I just smiled.

■ ■ ■

Having a new baby is a bit like going to boot camp. You do things you aren't used to doing. You don't eat on the same schedule. You don't sleep. You're exhausted. You're confused. And in that crazy state of confused exhaustion, you can find yourself on edge, the same slippery slope where you don't know whether to laugh or cry.

I received ten days of leave, so I stayed home those first days after Chloe came home. Having a new baby in the house was awesome and exhilarating and exhausting all at once. Being a new dad was also scary. It was scarier than anything I'd ever done, scarier than combat. Scarier than the fish in Higgins Lake. When I held Chloe, it felt like I was holding the most delicate thing in the world. Like a fresh egg you take out of the fridge. You're scared you'll drop and crack it.

Kelsey was sore from the delivery and was nursing for the first time, which I learned isn't the easiest thing to do. The lovely Miss Chloe liked to be held pretty much nonstop—and insisted we do things her way. It's tough for new mothers to find time to sleep. I took Chloe as much as I could. Once, I fell asleep on the couch while holding Chloe and I rolled over. Kelsey saw it and was afraid I'd crush Chloe, so after that I was banished to sleeping with her in the recliner, where I couldn't roll. When she wasn't sleeping in my arms, Chloe slept in a little bassinet in our bedroom. Kelsey and I both slept so lightly that we heard her and woke up anytime she turned over. I'd get up and change her, and pass her to Kelsey to nurse. Before long, I found that I could get up and change the baby without ever really waking up.

A week or two passed in a sleepless fog, but soon we became a well-oiled pit crew. I needed to go back to work on the base, and I found that life at home was just like being overseas. When you're in an FOB or a security post, you never sleep more than four hours a night. So I was used to it. I wanted Kelsey to get more sleep, and I wanted to make sure she was taken care of. So I slept the first shift from 8 p.m. to midnight. Then Kelsey would sleep uninterrupted, and I'd take over from midnight to 5 a.m. If Chloe slept during my shift too, then we'd have no problem. But if Chloe was up, then I was up too, and it was a rougher night. But I'd rather be the one with the rough night than Kelsey.

In the early mornings, we enjoyed watching *Mickey Mouse Clubhouse* together. I'd set Chloe down in her bouncy chair and I'd sit in my recliner and move her chair up and down for her with one hand.

Days turned into weeks, and weeks turned into months. The older Chloe got, the more she could do.

One day while lying on her stomach, she held her head up. We all cheered.

Not long after that she rolled over by herself. We all cheered again.

In no time, she was scooting around. It was an exciting and mega-proud time as a family, and Kelsey and I were both amazed at the things our absolutely brilliant and beautiful daughter could do.

MY MILITARY CAREER was going forward too. I went to college for six months, then took another course in advanced leadership, then attended jumpmaster school. Jumpmasters are expert parachutists who train other soldiers how to become paratroopers. When a group of paratroopers jumps out of a plane, the jumpmaster leads all aspects of their jump. So I was in charge of checking people's equipment and throwing them out of an airplane. If there are any rigging problems, it's the jumpmaster's fault.

At first, I felt thrown to the wolves at jumpmaster school. The highly rigorous training takes about a month, and involves passing six intense exams. Almost everyone fails at his first jumpmaster school and I proved no exception. I retook the school, anxious that I needed to get everything down perfectly. My dog Buddy turned into a first-rate study partner. His faithful sitting beside me encouraged me that I could do this.

On my final test, I had fifteen jumpers, and I was responsible for making sure they all came down alive. I came in confident and was determined not to show any nerves. I checked all their riggings, we all went up in the air, we did more checks, and everybody went out the door. Everybody landed safely. On the ground I asked, "Hey, how many people think this was my first jumpmaster duty?"

No one raised his hand.

Fine by me. They couldn't believe it was my first time. That's what coming in confident can do. To become a jumpmaster in the 82nd Airborne was no small accomplishment. I was really proud of that designation, and I loved the actual work.

After I became a jumpmaster, I regularly taught soldiers how to become parachutists. On one jump, I had a kid who froze and wouldn't go out the door of the plane. The army gives you three chances to jump on your own, but his three chances came and went and he still didn't go. He was a good soldier, and I knew he'd make a good paratrooper if given the right incentive. So I picked the kid up by his shirt and pants and threw him out of the plane. He thanked me later.

On another jump, another kid didn't want to go. He was also a good soldier, and I knew he could do the job, but his nerves were getting in the way. I gave him a little kick in his back, and out he went. He also thanked me later. Once a soldier makes their first jump, they almost never have trouble again.

I ended up staying stateside longer than originally planned. I had a job offer to become a squad leader in a different unit, but then a new spot opened up in my same unit, and I took that instead. In early 2012 I was promoted to the rank of E6, staff sergeant. I was the youngest E6 in my unit, and I was put in the senior E6 spot as a weapons squad leader. This meant I'd be in charge of two teams of soldiers, each of which worked with a big 240 machine gun. From a weapons perspective, the heavy guns are the most crucial part of any dismounted patrol (a patrol that's on foot, not in vehicles). Without the two 240s rocking, the rest of your platoon doesn't have much protection at all. So my job was to lead my two machine gun teams to either kill the enemies first, or to keep the enemies' heads down while our other guys maneuvered up to kill them. This new position is exactly what I wanted—a frontline leadership role. I thrived under pressure, and I wanted the stress of it, the challenge of it.

A third deployment was coming up, beginning in February 2012, and I didn't need to go on that deployment if I wanted to opt out. You can't actually "decline" a position in the army, but since I'd been on two deployments already, this one was optional for me. Kelsey didn't want me to go overseas again. Chloe was going to be just under five months old at the start of my third deployment, and Kelsey loved having me at home. I loved being at home too. But I also knew I was needed elsewhere.

That's a hard feeling to describe unless you've been there yourself. By then, I wasn't working with the guys from my second deployment, even though many of them were still in the 82nd. But even my new guys already seemed like brothers. As an E6, I'd handpicked all the privates for my squad, and I'd helped train them and worked with them for nearly a year already, basically ever since my second deployment ended. A bond forms quickly under these conditions. As an NCO, your job is to lead, protect, and inspire your guys. If they were going overseas, then there was no way I'd let them go alone.

The guys in my squad were Sergeant Cobia Farr, my assistant gunner from Tennessee. PFC Eric Hunter, a great soldier who was always joking around, always in trouble. PFC Jon Harmon, who carried the most rounds of anybody and never said no to a fight. PFC Armando Plascencia, the squad designated marksman who could spot targets and take out threats like nobody's business. PFC Ryan "The Riot" Theriot, my assistant gunner—I always had a lot of confidence in him. PFC James Neff, who was like a little brother to me. And PFC Brandon Fessey, a big strong kid and our quiet ammo bearer.

Nobody was going to mess with my squad. These young men were headed for war, because that's what their country asked of them. And they were all going to come home alive, because it was my job to make sure that happened.

Sometimes on a training exercise, I might sing and tell jokes and be goofy and have a good time, but when it came down to a mission, I was all business. I drew out plans. I made sure everybody knew what to do and where to go. I made sure things got done right. I would never leave my guys stranded. It was a pride issue. I had a duty to them, and as a leader I was their best option for success.

That way of thinking takes some getting used to. When it comes to fighting a war, the officers and the politicians have the big plans in mind. They can tell you why you're fighting and what needs to get done on a large-scale level. But as an infantryman in charge of a squad, my main concern is my guys.

Honestly, I don't know if I ever went overseas because I was concerned about the Afghan people themselves. It's undoubtedly that way for some soldiers, but on any deployment I went on, I wouldn't say the care of the Afghan people was foremost in my mind. Don't get me wrong, there's no hatred or dislike for them on my part. But whenever I deployed, I wasn't primarily thinking about helping them build their country or build schools or help the people win the right to vote. Even though all those things are worthy causes.

The reason I went overseas was because of the soldier next to me. The guys in my squad. Our job was to protect America and keep the Taliban at bay. I'd trained my men. I'd taught them all I knew. It was my job to take care of them. I couldn't imagine them deploying without me.

BY FEBRUARY 2012, when my third deployment was scheduled to start, coalition forces had been fighting the Taliban in Afghanistan for more than eleven years, and there was talk in the media that the war in Afghanistan was dying down. But I was wary of the talk.

Earlier, in 2010, President Obama had sent a surge of some 30,000 new additional troops into Afghanistan (who joined some 70,000 troops already there), and a lot of headway had been made in terms of capturing or killing Taliban leaders and destroying caches of their weapons. On May 2, 2011, al-Qaeda founder and leader Osama bin Laden (who'd enjoyed safe haven in Afghanistan with the Taliban for years—and from his base in Afghanistan had declared war against the United States) was killed by a team of Navy SEALs in Pakistan, where he'd eventually fled to after 9/11. Then, in June 2011, President Obama slowly began to pull troops out of Afghanistan—a plan that would take several years. Other coalition countries followed suit.

Yet even though troops were leaving, a lot of work was still needed. (History has shown that from 2011 to 2012, the number of Taliban attacks continued at roughly the same rate—about

28,000 attacks per year.) My unit's job on my third deployment was basically the same as it had been before—to partner with the Afghan government and help them establish security on their own. Specifically, we were headed to the Maiwand district in the south of Kandahar province, a rural and highly violent area. The new Afghan government might have been growing stronger as a whole, but its influence was not reaching outlying districts, which were still hotbeds of Taliban activity.

Josh Buck was wary too. A week before we deployed, Josh and I sat in his garage, and we both had a strange, ominous feeling about this upcoming deployment, a feeling I'd never felt before. I looked around the garage at the shelving, the bicycles, the boxes, the lawn tools, and said starkly, "Josh, I don't know if I'm coming back from this one."

"Dude, you're going to be fine," Josh assured me. But concern clouded his eyes, and I could see it.

For this deployment, Josh was going to be at Camp Stone, near Kandahar, and I'd be in a strongpoint about fifteen miles west of him. He had another decision about whether to reenlist coming up soon, and Josh was talking about getting orders to go to Hawaii next and me going with him. My third deployment was considered a "filler"—only nine months long at most, and our colonel had volunteered us for this. We all knew it was going to be nine months in a viper pit.

If you asked me, Hawaii sounded like a much better bet.


ON THE EVENING of February 23, 2012, I hugged Kelsey for the last time and gave her a long kiss. She was going to move back to Texas to stay with her folks while I was gone so they could help with the baby. Our house near the base was going to stand empty until I returned.

"I love you, Kelsey," I told her. "I'll see you soon. I already miss you."

She was in tears. A beautiful mess. Josh was leaving on that same deployment too, but a day later than I was. So he came to see me off and support his sister. I hugged him and he hugged me back.

Chloe was five months old and sleeping soundly in her car seat. She never even woke up when I kissed her cheek. I unstrapped my daughter, picked her up, and cradled her tightly, one last time, in my arms. She inhaled deeply, smiled, and carried on sleeping.

Then I waved goodbye.

Walking away from my loved ones, I had to ask myself if this third deployment felt different from the first two. I had a child to think about now. A family. I knew there would be tense days and firefights ahead, but honestly I wasn't afraid of dying. I wouldn't be reckless and make myself an easy target, and I didn't want to die. But I knew that if I got hit, then I got hit. If it happened, then it was meant to be.

As a soldier, it's not like I talk about my emotions every day. I don't write poetry. I don't watch romantic comedies as a rule (just Mickey Mouse Clubhouse with Chloe). I'm trained to kill people. That's what I do. You've got to be tough in the 82nd. You've got to be as hard as life. You don't want to show weakness ever, particularly with any of your guys around. When you're overseas and out in the middle of nowhere and you have twelve to twenty guys with you, you can't take a seat and say you're done. As a leader, I couldn't throw my helmet down and complain that things weren't fair. You have to make the best of it. You have to keep going. You've got to be as tough as they come.

But even so, as I walked away from my wife and child and brother-in-law, the wind struck my eye, and I wiped away the wetness with the back of my sleeve.

# MY LAST DEPLOYMENT

**I**T FELT FAMILIAR. WE TOOK ROUGHLY THE SAME SERIES OF flights to get over overseas as I'd taken on my last deployment. From the States we flew to Ireland, and then to Kyrgyzstan, then Kandahar. In Kandahar, there was a lot of sitting and waiting. Finally, we jumped on a Chinook helicopter with our gear and took off, headed toward our new place of residency at a triangular-shaped strongpoint in the outback of Afghanistan.

Our strongpoint was so small it didn't even have a name. It wasn't big enough to have a FOB designation. The biggest FOB near us was Sarkari Karez, a couple miles away, and the biggest town near us was called Maiwand (sometimes called De Maiwand), with a population of a couple hundred people. It's a bit confusing; the town and the district both shared the same name—Maiwand. Maybe 50,000 people total were sparsely spread throughout the district. The region was considered a hotbed of Taliban activity.

In addition to the village of Maiwand, we had six or seven clusters of villages in the area around the strongpoint that we were responsible for. The village names all blur together in my mind now: Mahmudabad, Danday, De Maymand Chinah—I don't remember all of them. Our platoon's mission was to travel around to these clusters, sift out the Taliban from the civilians, and try and clear out the bad guys while protecting the good. Most of the time we'd be partnered with an Afghan platoon, trying to help them take the lead and facilitate patrols of their own.

Everywhere I looked around the strongpoint I saw barren dirt. Looking north, I could see a big mountain pass. To our south lay a huge dried-up wadi about half a mile wide. Another five miles south of that was another mountain pass. Barren landscape isn't safe. We knew the Taliban lurked everywhere throughout this district. We just didn't know specifically where "everywhere" was. I thought back to my first deployment—how it was a picnic compared to what this was going to be. I wasn't positive what the days ahead would hold, but I suspected we'd soon see blood. I never thought it would be my own.

ON OUR FIRST day there, we went out on patrol with the guys from the 10th Mountain, who we were replacing. Nothing happened. The rest of my guys arrived the next day. We took over from the 10th Mountain and they left.

On the second day, we went out on patrol and talked to some of the key leaders from the villages in the area and gave the kids kites. Only one boy played with his kite, and the rest of the children all beat him up. This was another indication of the Taliban's influence in the region, although the meetings with the elders went okay and all was quiet.

For our patrol on the third day, our CO figured it would look good if we could flush out some Taliban. Officially, a mission such as this is called "learning our battle space," and the idea is we'd deliberately go out and try to pick a fight. The village to the farthest south in our area of patrol was called Maiwand Karez, by far the worst village of all the ones we were responsible for. A lot of Taliban-controlled drugs ran through this region, and the intel on this particular village was that they hated Americans the most. Our lieutenant, Zac Lewis, talked with me and the other squad leaders to get our input about what we wanted to do.

I liked Lieutenant Lewis a lot. He was a couple years older than I was, and this was his first deployment. In personality, he was a reserved guy, a college man who'd majored in finance and had worked in an investment firm for a few years before joining the military. He spoke quietly and cautiously and kept himself together almost to the point of being tightly wound. But I could tell his tight personality only sprung from the desire to lead our platoon the best way possible—and I respected him for that. It's not easy for a brand-new officer to walk into a unit and try to lead a platoon, particularly when the NCOs under him already have combat experience. While we were back at Fort Bragg, I took it upon myself to publicly joke around with him as much as possible. I knew it would be good for him and would help loosen him up and ultimately become a better leader. He didn't like being touched, so I'd purposely pick him up and give him a huge bear hug, or I'd swing him up and over my shoulders for fun. He'd squirm and roll his eyes and call me names and laugh it off, and the platoon could all see he was going to be an okay guy because he could take it. I knew he'd be a great leader to follow.

We squad leaders all agreed to go to Maiwand Karez and set the tone for this deployment. Lieutenant Lewis took the message back to our CO. We wanted to come in strong, so the Taliban would know we were there and meant business. If we could get inside the village, then good, we'd do that. But if the fire was too heavy and all we could do was go down there and set eyes on the village, then that's what we'd do to start.

Our platoon left our strongpoint in the early morning. Maiwand Karez was only about three kilometers away, but we were hiking extremely slowly. Because of the severe IED threat, it would take us several hours to cover that distance.

We moved over the ground in four columns. One soldier walked in front—he's called the mine hound. He had a metal detector with him and he swept the ground for IEDs—back and forth, back and forth. The metal detector would also pick up changes in the density of the dirt, so theoretically it could find IEDs made out of glass and plastic. The mine hound was always extremely vulnerable to potential gunfire because he was so focused on the ground, so directly behind him walked a SAW gunner, who covered the mine hound with his machine gun. Behind the gunner walked a team leader who looked for visual indicators of IEDs—wires, some dispersed dirt maybe, anything that didn't look like it should be there. He also marked lanes to the right and left with a can of shaving cream to indicate a clear pathway for the guys behind to walk in. Everybody else walked in a single-file line, each man five meters away from the next.

I think most people who picture combat think that direct fire is the biggest threat to soldiers on a foot patrol. But one crazy thing about this area of Afghanistan was that we were at a far greater risk from buried IEDs than we were from direct fire. It was all connected to the Taliban's vicious strategy for IED placement. In the movies, if guys take fire, you see them running and diving for cover. But we couldn't do that in this area, particularly this far along into the war. The Taliban must have watched the same movies, because we'd learned that they had deliberately placed IEDs in areas that a man would run to and dive for if he was trying to take cover. So whenever we took fire, we were trained to stay exactly where we were. It sounds counterintuitive, but we'd actually have a greater chance of survival if we didn't dive for cover. Instead, we'd take a knee or go prone and fire back from there. Under fire, if our guys broke off to flank the enemy, then we'd still move at a slow walk, because everywhere we moved was potentially a minefield.

It took us more than four hours to walk to the village. We set up on the north side while half our guys came in slightly east of the village. The plan was that one element would establish a base of fire while we flanked from the north. One of my machine gun teams was with me, and my other team was with the other element.

As soon as we set up, a bullet zipped in. Right behind it came another. A firefight broke out and for the first little while, it was just small arms fire from the Taliban's AK-47s, nothing major. By the smoke plumes, the enemy fire looked to be coming from the wadi on the other side of the village. We shot back and started maneuvering to see if we could push the enemy back. An hour passed and then another. Then another. Gradually we moved forward and through the village. It was dirt poor. Everything was closed in the village. No one was running around. All I saw were mud huts and mud walls and narrow alleyways. No civilians anywhere. We saw some yellow jugs at one house that looked like they contained materials for making explosives, but that was it. Eventually the firing died down completely and for about thirty minutes on the other side of the village there was absolute silence.

In front of us lay the dry riverbed. It was wide, about 800 meters, maybe half a mile. Our CO was with us on this mission and told us to cross the wadi to see what was on the other side. There was no cover whatsoever in the riverbed, which meant we were completely open to attack. The area was wide, low, rocky ground—and I could tell by the concerned looks on the faces of the other squad leaders that none of us thought this was a good idea.

I set up my gun line on the edge of the riverbed with my Alpha team on the right and my Bravo team on the left. Sergeant Farr was team leader of Bravo and I knew he'd do a good job. The idea was that the rest of the troops would cross the riverbed in between my two gun teams. I gave both teams the sectors of fire, the limits where they could and couldn't shoot, so they wouldn't hit the guys walking between us. With our two gun teams in place, the guys from the first and second squads slowly started to walk across the riverbed. Everything was quiet. That eerie sort of quiet that you fear isn't going to last long. Our men followed the mine hound, walking at a snail's pace.

When our men were halfway across the wadi—completely vulnerable—one enemy bullet zipped in. Our men all took a knee. When a bullet zips in it makes a whistling sound, almost like a really quick *whip*. Another bullet soon followed, and suddenly the area around the wadi completely erupted with heavy fire. Our men flattened out. This was like no fire I'd ever seen before. Bullets kicked up all around us. Artillery shells boomed. Mortars. Rockets. Everything was pouring toward us with fire and fury.

Bullets zipped in and hit all around our fingers, our helmets, our arms, our legs, *whip, whip, whip*. You could feel the extreme velocity of the fire. This was our lieutenant's first firefight ever, and he didn't panic, but I knew he needed to make a decision soon—keep our men walking forward or bring them back. He kept the radio to his ear. He was shouting and someone was frantically yelling back at him from the radio. Everywhere I could hear the dire sound of constant lead. *Boom! Boom! Boom!* The Taliban knew exactly what they were doing, and they were walking the mortars closer to us, zeroing in their coordinates to land a direct hit. Shells landed twenty meters away from our men. Then fifteen meters. Our guys were pinned down. They'd stopped moving.

From the far side of the wadi, my gun teams fired back with everything we had. Our guns were all set to cyclic, the maximum rate of fire. My men were shooting prone to make themselves smaller targets. But I noticed that two of my guys were shooting in the wrong spot. They were shooting too close to where our other guys were positioned and were liable to shoot them. Plus, we needed to keep our heads, particularly in a heavy firefight such as this, and conserve ammo. No one knew how long this would last. Someone needed to set them straight. It was time to move. I sprinted over to my other gun team and slapped their heads to make sure they were firing in the correct position, then yelled at them not to burn through their ammo all at once. They calmed down, their training took over, and our machine guns spewed out bullets in deadly measured increments.

Our lieutenant's decision still hung in the air when I noticed out in the middle of the wadi that one of our guys was down— Sergeant Butler. He yelled, "I'm hit! I'm hit!" One of his team leaders, Sergeant Marty Miller, ran over to him and swept his hands along Butler's body to check for blood. Miller ran back to our lieutenant to report and yelled that he couldn't find any. Out in the wadi, Butler tried to stand but fell.

Lieutenant Lewis decided right then to bring everybody back. I hate to lose a scrap, but it was the right choice. Pushing forward with mine hounds was going to take too much time, particularly now that we had a casualty out in the middle of the wadi. Plus, it was going to be nearly impossible to land a helicopter to evac Butler anywhere in a hailstorm like this. Our guys started to fall back to where we had been.

Bullets still raged all around us. Butler had his arms around two guys. They were trying to pick him up. But every time he took a step he fell to the ground in pain. Bullets smacked all around them. Mortars continued to fall. *Boom! Boom! Boom!* Everywhere was dust and confusion and smoke. The two guys could have dragged him to safety, but something was happening that impeded that process—I couldn't tell exactly what.

My mind flashed to a moment back in the States when I'd had a disagreement with Sergeant Butler. He was older than I was, maybe late thirties, an E6, same rank as me, and in charge of the first squad (I was in charge of the fourth). Butler wasn't a bad guy, but he ran his mouth, and we had our differences. He'd said something, and I'd said something, and we'd disagreed. That was okay. It brought a fun level to work.

Here in the middle of a firefight, I didn't care about any disagreement. I tossed my M4 to First Sergeant Michael Parrish and sprinted out into the riverbed. I was still wearing my body armor, but essentially I was weaponless. If I'd kept my rifle, it would have only slowed me down. I ran down to where Sergeant Butler lay. He was probably fifty meters total away.

"It's my leg," he shouted. "I can't put any weight on it."

"Shut up!" I yelled. "Get on my back now. Let's go!" Without waiting for him to answer, I grabbed his right hand with my left, squatted down, and threw him over my shoulders in a fireman's carry. He was probably 185 pounds. I hefted him up, and ran him back to safety.

We got behind a berm and I kept going another fifty meters, then I set Butler down so a medic could tend to him. I was sweating something fierce and just about to gulp a drink of water when my first sergeant yelled, "Mills, I need you over here right now!" So I ran over to him on the edge of the wadi, got my M4 back, and took charge over the two gun teams again. He needed to get everybody off the line, and there were still a few more men to go.

We called in Kiowa helicopters to help provide covering fire. When they showed up, the enemy quit firing for a short time so as not to show their position. That gave us enough time to run Sergeant Butler back to the casualty control point, an area set up by the platoon sergeant to collect the wounded while out on patrol. But the Kiowas didn't stick around long—and they didn't dare land to evacuate Butler. In a hot point like this, it's any Taliban's dream to blast a coalition helicopter with an RPG.

Eventually we all got out of there safely. We hiked out the same way we went back in, slowly and cautiously through shaving cream lines with a minesweeper leading the way. Butler was carried on a stretcher, and we took turns carrying him. When we neared the strongpoint, I ran ahead of my guys and high-fived them back into the strongpoint while singing the 82nd Airborne song. This was the first time a lot of our guys had ever seen combat, so they were shaky and a number of them were smoking. I said whatever I could to encourage them. They did the right thing. That's how they were supposed to handle a crazy situation like that. You just want to keep their spirits up so they don't freeze the next time they're in battle.

Two guys caught me outside my tent. They'd deployed before but had been with a different unit then. Earlier, both of them had wondered out loud why I'd ever been promoted. They'd fought under other NCOs, and the other NCOs were always serious, never joking around about anything. But these two guys had changed their tune now. They said that after seeing me in today's firefight they'd follow me to hell and back. It felt like a pivotal point in my leadership.

No one was hurt except Butler. We had an aid station at the

strongpoint, but it was limited to bandages and Neosporin—the stuff your mom would have at home. What we needed was an X-ray machine. It turned out that Butler wasn't shot after all, but he'd torn up his ACL something bad and couldn't set any weight on the leg. Since his condition wasn't critical and resources were limited, they decided to evacuate him the next morning when an aircraft would normally depart from the strongpoint. Driving him to Kandahar wasn't an option due to the high risk of the area around us.

Later that night we relaxed a bit and were all joking around, just letting the stress of the day wash out of us. I said something to Butler about how he'd need to get a desk job now. It sounded condescending, I confess, and he didn't like that and called me cocky and said a couple of other words my direction. We exchanged a few more jabs and things escalated. I ended up saying that if he didn't have a bad leg I'd come over to where he was and punch him to pieces. Despite our attempts to unwind, the tension of the day was still running high. But this is how a brotherhood is: tempers can flare in the military, but guys get over stuff fast.

An hour and a half later, Butler said, "Hey, Mills, I gotta use the bathroom."

And I was like, "Okay, I'm coming." I picked him up and carried him to the john.

Our disagreement was over. Just like that.

Later that night, we could see heavy lights on in the villages around us. They were holding Taliban funerals. We listened in on our Icom (basically a walkie-talkie with a police scanner built in), and they were saying prayers and naming off the guys who'd been killed.

I can't say we felt remorseful. It could have been our guys' funerals. It was only our third day here and already we were taking heavy fire. We knew we were in for a real battle on this deployment, and we were ready to go back out to the fight and do our jobs the following day.

The next morning I carried Butler to the helicopter. His knee was all swollen up.

"Take it easy," I said, and set him down.

"You too," he answered.

Those are the things you do for your fellow brother-in-arms.

Later, a couple of my higher-ups said I should get the Bronze Star for my actions in running into the wadi under fire to save Butler. My commander wanted to put in for a higher medal for me, but I told him not to bother with the paperwork. It was what it was. I was just doing my job. Later on I received a Bronze Star for all my actions during the deployment.

FROM THEN ON, we took fire almost every day. Day after day after day after day.

It might have been a week in, we headed out to a village called Khik, about three or four kilometers away from the strongpoint. It would take at least a five-hour hike to get there. The 10th Mountain had come into heavy contact with the Taliban there, so we were pretty sure it would happen again. We knew that when it came to Khik, we weren't just going to stroll in and talk to the leaders. So our orders were to take bigger rucksacks, talk to the elders, stay the night in or near Khik, then come back the next day.

It was early morning, almost daylight, when we left the strongpoint. Conventional wisdom would reason that any platoon out on a mission would be safer to travel under the cloak of darkness. But because of the threat of IEDs, it was actually safer for us to travel during daylight. Again, we were moving through barren land with no cover. The same dry riverbed (wadi) generally runs east to west, but it changed course and paralleled where we were on this hike.

About an hour in, the sun's rays streaked across the land. In the distance near the wadi, three vehicles careened along the landscape, traveling fast in a dusty convoy, heading straight toward the village of Khik. Two of the vehicles were pickup trucks and one was a car. There was no road where these vehicles were driving, only the edge of the wadi, and all three vehicles were traveling at an unnaturally high rate of speed. Maybe fifty to sixty miles per hour. Normally, civilians will travel at about twenty when there are no roads around. I could see military-age men packed in the back of the pickup trucks and inside the car. I had a strong hunch who they were.

Sure enough, about thirty minutes later, another cluster of vehicles traveled the same stretch of ground. Same high rate of speed. Same age of men packed into the vehicles. They were glaring our direction, obviously not happy to see us.

It was the Taliban on their way to work. Their work was to set up around the village of Khik and blast us once we got there. They wanted to keep us from talking to the village elders inside, from making any allegiances with them, from helping them in any way. Seeing this deadly commute prompted an unnerving feeling. Frustration. Anger. Because of the rules of engagement, we couldn't do anything about these vehicles. The men weren't shooting at us. They were only driving by us *on their way* to shoot us. It felt like being in high school again on the football team. You're the home team and you see the other team arrive and take the field. We knew we'd be battling these exact guys later in the day. But for the moment we couldn't do anything except give them the stink eye. Equally unnerving was that it still would take us a while to arrive at Khik. By then, they'd have had more time to set up and build up their defenses.

An hour passed. We continued our slow pace behind the minesweeper. Finally we arrived at the outskirts of the village.

We set up behind a karez hole for cover. Used for irrigation, a karez hole is sort of like a giant molehill with water in the bottom. The opening of the hole is maybe 10 feet by 10 feet, and the drop down inside is maybe 50 to 60 feet. If you fall in, it's going to be a bad day. We took off our rucksacks, and Lieutenant Lewis set up a sniper team overlooking the village, a weapons squad on another karez hole closer to the village, and two rifle elements. I set up my guns and called in our grids. All was completely dead silent. We knew it was the calm before the storm.

The village was maybe the length of two football fields away. With security now set up, the lieutenant led our second squad, about eight men, toward the village to make contact. They moved at a snail's pace, always sweeping the ground for mines. I had to hand it to the lieutenant—he was right in the middle of this action, doing his job fearlessly.

Sure enough, when our men were not quite halfway from us to the village, the air erupted in bullets. Shooting at our men were the same Taliban members who'd been driving by us all morning. The fire wasn't coming from the village itself. It was coming from the neighboring areas. Once again, our guys were pinned down in the open. It was pretty heavy fire—lots of smoke, dust, noise, and lead—and there was an additional problem this time: my guys couldn't fire at the enemy!

From where the squad had stopped moving—directly out in the middle—we couldn't shoot our machine guns at the targets we needed to hit. Our own guys were right in our way. There was no means of getting a message to the squad by radio. That meant someone needed to run out into the middle of the fire and deliver the message in person. The squad was about thirty yards away. That would be my job.

I sprinted forward to our men, got in the face of the team leader, Sergeant Williams, and told him to move the squad. It was hard to hear and he hesitated. I started literally picking his guys up and shoving them forward. He got the picture in a hurry. "Follow Sergeant Williams!" I yelled at them. "Move!"

They started to move forward. Still under fire, I ran back to the karez hole and got my gun teams working. Our field of fire was now cleared, and we began ripping into the enemy. We fired and fired and lay down enough cover so the second squad was able to move into the village.

On some days, I attended these key meetings with the elders, but on days like this where the fire was flying, I needed to stay out by the guns. I'd be in on the debriefing later to hear what was said. Eventually the firing died down.

Our second squad spent the rest of the day in the village. Lieutenant Lewis talked to village elders through an interpreter and worked to gain an understanding of where their allegiances lay. We were all suspect of whatever the elders in Khik told us. Your job is more like trying to piece together the truth when you walk in there, rather than expecting you'll hear it being told openly.

Picture it this way. The villages in our area were neither totally "bad" nor "good," meaning neither aligned with the Taliban nor against them. Their allegiances were almost always fluid, and in a crazy sort of way this actually made sense for the civilians' survival. The village elders had seen a lot of combat in their area over the years, and they were used to sitting on the fence, switching sides depending on who dominated at any given time. In places such as Khik, they hadn't yet seen much influence of the new Afghan government, so it made sense for them to be allied with the Taliban sometimes. With no one to protect the village, the Taliban would inflict retribution on the villagers if the place wasn't allied with them.

I talked extensively with Lieutenant Lewis about this afterward, and the longer we were in Afghanistan, the less we believed the conflict had much to do with actual religion, although Islamic extremism acted as an umbrella to influence every action. More and more we could see that the war had a lot to do with money.

The Taliban is basically a drug cartel. Some 87 percent of the world's heroin originates in Afghanistan and the Taliban controls the bulk of this destructive business. Back in 2000 when they were still officially ruling the country, the Taliban had publicly collaborated with the United Nations and banned poppy farming in Afghanistan for about a year, which sounded good if you believed the surface reports. But we had our doubts. See, the ban initially proved effective, and some 75 percent of the world's heroin suddenly disappeared. But opium can be dried and stockpiled, which later reports showed the Taliban had done. Their eradication of heroin only drove the price up for them to sell their stockpiles at big profits. After that, the Taliban changed their mind about poppy growing, and drug production in Afghanistan once again boomed. The Taliban raked in the dough.

Religious extremism and wars were key components that drove their drug business. Poppy fields lay all around the village of Khik. Already, tiny green buds dotted the soil, watered by the very karezes we took cover behind. The Taliban wants to keep the Afghan population uneducated, impoverished, and desperate. That way, they could walk up to any old Afghan farmer in Khik and say, "Hey, you're broke. You've got a wife and five children to feed. We'll give you a thousand dollars to plant your field with poppies. In six months' time, we'll come back and the crop will be ours. If your field isn't ready for harvest, then we'll kill you. How's that sound?"

That was Lieutenant Lewis's theory anyway, developed from his studies and firsthand interaction with village elders, and it made sense to me.

NEAR THE DAY'S end, our second squad emerged from the village and joined the rest of us behind the holes. We figured we'd get hit again soon enough, and supplies were low, so we made a decision to head back to the strongpoint that night rather than risk a night out in the open near Khik. Our men ate a few rations, then we headed out. Sure enough, another firefight erupted as we started to walk away.

During this firefight, a sniper's round cracked six inches from my head. I'd never flinched in a battle before, but this felt too close. Quickly I ducked and turned my head away. Then I was angry at myself for flinching. In disgust, I jumped on top of a berm with my rifle and ripped off a magazine in the direction of the sniper. My magazine was spent. I yanked it out of my rifle. Before it hit the ground, I had another magazine inserted and was firing again.

Finally, Lieutenant Lewis yelled at me to get down and into the prone position. He was right. I was frustrated, but it wasn't a whining frustration. It was an angry frustration. I was sick and tired of this stupid war. Sick and tired of all the evil around us. Sick and tired of a system that harmed people and removed all their opportunities to make better lives for themselves. Sick and tired of anybody shooting at my guys!

Standing on top of a berm might have seemed rash. But I wanted my men to see my example. And I also wanted the Taliban to see. We were fearless and tough. If they wanted to fight us, then we'd get out there and beat their asses every time. I wanted to show dominance. I wanted to show I wasn't afraid.

When that firefight was finished, we picked up and slowly moved out again back to the strongpoint. We cleaned our weapons, went to sleep, got up the next morning, and went out on another patrol again.

That became our pattern in my third deployment. Every day we went out. Every day we got in a firefight. Every day we came home, only to do it all over again the next day.

How much did we shoot? I was the ammo NCO at our strongpoint, and it was my job to inventory the ammo. On an average day we went through 1,200 rounds (bullets) for each of the big machine guns. Then each rifleman would run through an additional 100 to 180 rounds on his own. The count varied a little from day to day, and we didn't ever want to waste ammo. We just did whatever it took to keep the enemy at bay.

Day after day after day after day.

# 11

# APRIL 10, 2012

S**PRING ARRIVED IN AFGHANISTAN AND WITH IT THE RISE OF** poppy season. The temperature rose, and as we patrolled from village to village, I noticed that crops were coming up. Although much of the district was still rocky, brown, and barren, in other sections an unusual smell of freshness filled the air and a faint color-wash of green layered the hills.

Daily firefights continued, along with a mounting sense of frustration. Thanks to new rules of engagement put in place by the Obama administration in conjunction with Afghan president Karzai, our hands had become more and more tied in terms of what we could and couldn't do.

On my first deployment, if we believed our lives were endangered, then we could respond with appropriate force. But by the time my third deployment rolled around, if we were out on patrol and approached a group of known Taliban fighters, we would need to convince our commander (who was often not present with us as a ground unit) that the fighters were armed and a genuine threat before engaging.

I respect the office of the presidency, and I'm sure these rules were put in place with good intentions. In fact, the new rules of engagement sound relatively benign on paper unless you're actually in a combat situation and can see them lived out firsthand. It's then that you see cracks in the armor.

In the strongpoint, we had a security camera up on a pole about thirty feet high that fed us real-time video coverage in a 360-degree view. One night that spring, with this camera, we saw Taliban fighters placing IEDs in the ground near the villages directly around our strongpoint. But because these fighters weren't shooting at us, we couldn't do anything to stop them. We inquired up the chain of command if we could shoot mortars at them. The answer was no. We asked if we could go out and engage them in a firefight. The answer was no. All we could do was go out the next day and try to find and remove the IEDs, or find the Taliban who placed the IEDs, get them to shoot at us, and then shoot back. From the perspective of the soldiers on the ground, it was no way to fight a war.

FOR WHAT WOULD turn out to be my last big mission, we loaded into a Chinook about 3:30 a.m. and flew ten kilometers (about six miles) to a compound that had known Taliban fighters and weapons inside. Our mission was to take all three houses inside the compound, detain the fighters, and turn them over to the ANA.

This mission was a follow-up to our earlier mission in Khik. Throughout that mission, we'd had various helicopters checking in on us. The Taliban don't fire on these, because the aircraft can then see their positions on the ground and destroy them. Observers in the helicopters were repeatedly able to see two motorcycles follow the same path to and from a certain area. Any pattern like that is legitimately suspect. So over the next week, surveillance aircraft monitored these three compounds (where the motor-cycles had gone) and confirmed that known Taliban fighters frequented the compounds and were bringing in and carting out caches of bomb-making equipment and small arms. I never heard if the surveillance aircraft were drones or what. These actions were done at a battalion or maybe even a division level.

With us on this follow-up mission were two women, Sergeant Whitney Longwell and Specialist Jen Russell. The army calls them FETs (Female Engagement Team), and they're armed soldiers, but their specialty isn't fighting. Throughout Afghanistan, it's considered disrespectful (and in practice is virtually impossible) for American soldiers to talk to female Afghan civilians. So our FETs had learned a smattering of the language in about three months of language school, and then while on deployment they would go out on select patrols to build relationships and see what they could learn from female civilians. They'd also search Afghan women for weapons if that was suspected, which is why the FETs were included in this mission. The main language used in our area was Pashtun, an extremely difficult language to learn, so most FETs needed to use interpreters too. Our interpreters were all male, so although the system was a great idea, it wasn't perfect in practice.

The compound was L-shaped, with one building positioned at each corner of the L. Our helicopter touched down some distance outside the compound. We were at least four hundred meters away, far enough away so the helicopters wouldn't announce our presence, and we hopped off quietly. No yelling. No voices. Using hand signals on the ground to spread out and do the mission. Even if the people inside the compound heard helicopters, they probably heard them regularly overhead in that region, so we weren't afraid our cover would be blown. The sun was barely coming up. We ran to the compound, set up the heavy guns to cover the compound, then headed inside the first building without any resistance. I stayed on the guns outside to provide security. This is what was recounted to me later:

Inside were two men along with their wives and some children. Everybody was still asleep. Our men woke them up. We weren't yelling or anything, and the women covered themselves with burkas, and the children looked at us wide-eyed. I didn't like the idea of storming a compound when there were children involved, but seeing the children didn't change our actions. If the men involved hadn't been making bombs, trying to kill us, then we would not have had this problem to begin with.

In the second compound, our men found four military-age males along with six hundred pounds of homemade explosives, plus RPGs, launchers, ammo, and a number of rifles and other weapons. We also found a huge amount of opium along with Taliban recruiting videos and bagged fertilizer, the main component in making homemade explosives. One of the Taliban's hands was burned from the kind of acid it takes to make IEDs. Another man turned out to be the owner of the compound.

In the third compound, we didn't find anything, but that was okay. Overall, we considered this mission a success. The secure-and-search of the three compounds happened quickly, maybe twenty minutes total. We took no casualties, seized a huge amount of weapons and drugs, and were set to turn over several detainees to the ANA. We were supposed to blow up the weapons we found, but the ANA wanted to keep those, so we planned to turn those over to them too.

That's when things took a turn for the worse. The Taliban doesn't use encrypted radios, so all this time our interpreter was scanning the radio. He could hear that the enemy knew we were there. They were bringing in reinforcements. They were surrounding us.

At first we weren't overly concerned, because we knew we were getting picked up and flown out. So as soon as the search of the compound concluded, we used our code word to get picked up. But as luck would have it, there'd been a mistake at brigade and they'd promised the same aircraft to another unit. That meant we needed to carry all these assets, plus lead the detainees, and walk the ten kilometers back to the strongpoint. Ten kilometers doesn't sound like far to walk, but we needed to mine-sweep the whole way—and do it while potentially under fire. So it was going to be a long, long day.

That's not a fun message for a platoon leader to give to his squad leaders, and it's certainly not a fun message for a squad leader like me to relay to his teams. It's like saying someone's almost for sure going to get shot. Initially I was angry at the poor planning, but on the outside I played it off with a shrug and said, "All right, guys, we know what we need to do, so we might as well get walking." The reaction from my men to the situation was a mix of anger, concern, and frustration. But we decided to make the best of it. We were 82nd Airborne, after all. We trained for desperate moments such as this, and we were used to being surrounded by the enemy.

So we started to walk.

The first and second squads went first along with one of my guns. The third squad came after that, and then after that came the other half of my squad, the fourth. For much of the time, I walked dead last, because I wanted to make sure everybody was covered and I didn't want to leave anybody behind. Overall, we walked in two large groups in a sort of leapfrog movement, where one group bounded ahead while the other group covered the first. Then the second group bounded to the first while they took a turn and covered us.

We weren't far out of the compound when suddenly we took fire. Bullets zipped in from behind a tree line in the distance and we all took a knee and fired back. The two FET members were near me, and it was the women's first firefight. One of them yelled, "What do we do?!"

"Just keep shooting!" I yelled.

They stepped up to the challenge and shot back. They weren't scared. Or at least they didn't show it.

After a while the shooting died down, and we moved forward. Dangerous terrain lurked everywhere. Bullets could come from other compounds, from behind huts or foliage. A couple trucks whizzed by on a road in the distance. We could hear the Taliban on our Icom radio. They were planning movements and calling in reinforcements, more weapons and ammunition. Essentially, their plan seemed to be to shoot at us for a while, then pack up and move to a new location down the road where they'd shoot at us again, and so on and so on until we got back to our base. It didn't take much brains to figure out that was a smart move for them. They were driving. We were walking. For us, our only plan was to keep moving, always on the lookout for our next point of cover and concealment. If you're standing still, then you're a sitting duck. You always want to keep moving, even under fire.

Sure enough, not long after that, we got into our second firefight of the day. Bullets whizzed in all around us and we fired back. We fought for a while, then the fighting eventually died down, and we moved on.

Not long after that, our third firefight of the day began. Bullets zipped everywhere. There was a lot of smoke and dust and noise. The firefight died down, and we kept moving.

Then we got in a fourth firefight. Then a fifth. Then a sixth. My backpack was full of ammo when the day began. Gradually it grew lighter and lighter. Each fight grew more intense. The day stretched longer and longer. We became more and more tired. One of my guys' backpack was still full and he looked like he was going to topple over. I made him take my lighter bag and I took his full one in exchange. He didn't want to do it, but I made him. My guys would go until they fell over rather than admit they needed help.

When a seventh firefight started, I was with another sergeant and he yelled "Fall back," so we fell back behind a building. Mortar rounds were falling everywhere and when we fell back we were pinned down behind this building, so we opened up with our weapons to fight our way out of it. I had Neff, our gunner, with me, and I fed Neff rounds. I told another guy to shoot grenades toward the enemy until I told him to stop. The whole situation sucked, and we just shot at whoever was shooting at us until the firing died down enough for us to pick up and move out again.

We fought the whole way back to the strongpoint. It was a grueling day. But I'd made it a point on other missions to run ahead and sing to my guys the 82nd cadence when they returned into our gates. I was exhausted, but I wasn't going to let them down, today of all days. I ran ahead, started singing, and high-fived them all in.

A firefight is sometimes called a TIC (pronounced *tick*), which stands for "Troops In Contact." *Klick* is another term for a kilometer. Afterward, we named that day the "Ten-Klick-TIC." We'd had seven firefights in six miles. Our speed was one mile per hour for six hours. None of us had been injured. All in all, it was a pretty monumental day for our platoon.

Unfortunately, not every mission would prove so successful.

★ ★ ★

THE MORNING OF April 10, 2012, dawned bright. It was four
days before my twenty-fifth birthday, and we were now six weeks
into this deployment.

The day was scheduled to be a day off for us, so I got up and
had breakfast. I called Kelsey to tell her I loved her, then I lifted
weights in the prison gym in the strongpoint. Then I just hung
out until late afternoon when that tip from the informant came
in. Another regular day. Another regular patrol.

We suited up, locked and loaded, and headed out to hike the
four hundred yards to the village.

"Check this area" was the only order I gave.

I called Riot up and asked him where he thought we should
put up the gun. He motioned to exactly where I thought we
should put it and I said, "All right, go get Neff and bring him up
here."

That was it.

Riot left to go get Neff, and as he did, I set my backpack
down. The backpack touching the dirt was all it took.

Such a simple act of war.

JOSH BUCK WAS my first family member to hear that I'd been
wounded by an IED. He was at Camp Stone when Sergeant Carmen, a close friend of Josh's, called him on the phone, but Josh
initially missed the call. Carmen had been Josh's platoon sergeant
for five years, then had moved up to become the brigade senior
medic. All the message said was that Josh needed to call him back
and that it was important.

It was a bright sunny day at Camp Stone, and Josh had reen-
listment on his mind. He was thinking about going to Hawaii

soon. Josh called Sergeant Carmen back. He figured the phone call was nothing and they'd just catch up, like they often did.

"Hey—got your message. What's up?" Josh asked.

There was a moment of silence. Josh wondered if the call had been dropped. Then Sergeant Carmen said, "Hey, brother, I wanted this to come from me and nobody else. One of your friends got hurt today."

"Who?" Josh asked, his voice intense.

Again came a moment of silence. Sergeant Carmen cleared his throat, then said, "It was Travis."

A barrage of strong emotions shot through Josh. He stifled the urge to throw something and asked, "How bad is he?"

"He's still alive," Sergeant Carmen said. "Right now he's a triple amputee. I'm sorry to have to tell you this, but I figured you'd want to hear it from me first."

Josh bit his lip and said, "You're right. Where's he at?"

"Kandahar."

Josh said thanks and slammed down the phone. His heart pounded. His whole body filled with fury. He knew the potential to get wounded comes with the job. It happens. But it's still a shock when you hear of it. This was his brother-in-law. His sister's husband. His niece's father. His close friend.

A ferocity and concern rose in Josh like he'd never felt before. He kicked a chair. He punched a wall. He walked into the first room he came to and flipped everybody off, then walked outside, now feeling light-headed. His legs felt weak and he tumbled down a ramp he normally walked down every day. At the bottom, he picked up rocks and started throwing them. He never broke down like this. He was usually a composed person who thrived in chaos and under stress, but that day while throwing rocks, he started crying. Screaming. Cursing at the sky. It was the only time in his life he'd been out of control with emotion. Only then did he look at his hand and realize he'd broken it when he punched a wall. He couldn't feel the pain of it. He just felt numb.

Josh knew he wasn't allowed to phone any family members yet. The army needs to report the initial act of wounding officially to next of kin. But Josh knew he was going to be in an extremely vital position over the next few days. After official reports are made, the army typically calls with updates every twelve hours. Josh would be allowed to call with updates, and he could provide these sooner—and in more detail—than the army could. He knew our family would want those updates as soon as possible.

He ran to his commander, explained the situation, and jumped on the next helicopter heading to Kandahar.

KELSEY RECEIVED A call at 11:53 a.m. her time, while standing in her parents' kitchen in Dallas, Texas. She was making lunch, a tuna fish sandwich.

Chloe, then six months old, was happily playing in her walker nearby. Kelsey had taken Chloe to her first Easter egg hunt a few days earlier and had shown the video to me the evening before. It was nearly the time in the day when I usually called, and Kelsey was looking forward to saying hello.

The caller ID indicated the phone number was from North Carolina. Kelsey didn't recognize the specific number, but she reasoned it might be someone from the base. She answered the phone. It was my commander back at Fort Bragg.

The caller said straightforwardly that he had bad news: I'd stepped on an IED in Afghanistan. Kelsey reeled, then thought to ask, "How bad is he?" The commander told her that I was a triple amputee.

Kelsey never hung up the phone. Her knees gave out. She

fell to the floor, screamed one long continuous wail, and shouted, "Oh my God, oh my God, oh my God."

Here's how she described the moment later in a journal:

*I could not wrap my head around the pain my husband must be feeling. I was all alone in the house, and my actions upset my daughter to the point where she was screaming.*

*I could do nothing to soothe her. I couldn't pick her up. I couldn't look at her.*

*My body felt like it was being torn in two. I wanted so badly to be able to talk to Travis and to let him know I love him and that I thanked God he was still alive.*

Kelsey called my dad in Michigan, but when she tried to tell him what had happened, little would come out. My dad knew something was wrong and he kept repeating, "Is he alive? Is he alive? Is he alive?"

Kelsey couldn't answer. The call dropped. She phoned her mom, and Tammy rushed home from work to comfort her daughter and take care of Chloe.

All the rest of that day Kelsey stayed glued to the phone. Calls came and went. For the time being, army officials told her to stay where she was. They might bring her over to Germany. They might not. I'd be brought stateside soon, and probably then Kelsey could travel to where I was.

Kelsey later wrote,

*I don't know how to explain this feeling. I didn't sleep for a week. I didn't eat. I lost ten pounds the first week, because I was just sitting, waiting for phone calls.*

★ ★ ★

My dad had spoken to me the day prior to my injury. I knew my parents were really concerned about this deployment because it was in such a hostile area. For that reason, I'd phoned them more often than I had on any other deployment, although I never said anything specifically about what was going on.

During my first deployment, my dad had a job driving a truck. His shift started at midnight, and he'd turn on the news and drive into the early morning. He'd hear reports, like three troops had been killed in Afghanistan, and it would be a long night for him. When no one knocked on their door the next morning, it was a good thing. He told me later that he just learned to live with this tension. He just prayed it wouldn't be his son.

On my third deployment, when the call came, my dad was with two of his friends loading up some scrap machinery into his trailer. Kelsey's voice came on the phone, but my dad had bad cell service in the area, so it was hard to hear. Kelsey was hysterical, saying she was so sorry, so sorry. But he couldn't get any more information out of her. He knew something very bad had happened, but he didn't know initially if something had happened to me or maybe to Chloe. When the call dropped, he yelled to his two friends, "Unhook that trailer and winch. I need to go now!" And he took off like a flash.

He raced over to the supermarket where my mom works. On the way, he was able to reach Kelsey again by cell. She got out the word *Travis* and that I'd been gravely injured, but she couldn't say much more than that.

My mom was at work when my dad burst in, pulled her aside, and told her I'd been hit. She remembers standing on the floor of the supermarket with him, as they hugged each other in a tight embrace. My dad's reaction was that he was badly shaken up, while my mom was nearly in shock. He rushed home to wait by the phone, while my mom went into the store's business office, filled her supervisor in, and asked the supervisor to put me on their church's prayer chain.

When my dad reached home, he saw that the army had called and he'd missed it. Soon another call came in. It was the army again, and a military official reported that I'd been hit by an IED and that I was gravely injured. The caller asked if my mom and dad had passports so they could fly to Germany if needed. My dad said they did. The caller told them to pack light and to be ready to go at a moment's notice.

My mom went home and called my sister and her husband, and my brother and his wife, so they could hear before the story hit the news. Then Mom called her neighbor and asked her to put me on another church's prayer chain. I think before long I was on the prayer chains of all the churches in Vassar and Millington and all the surrounding communities.

From that point on, everybody at home lived by the phone. My dad described it this way:

*Until you go through something like that yourself, it's hard to describe the feeling. There's no eating anymore. You don't leave the house. There's a lot of pacing around. You just wait.*

*Whenever the phone rang, we jumped. You look at the phone and don't know if you want to answer it or not.*

I WASN'T THE only man in my squad who'd been hurt that day.

PFC Ryan Theriot, my soft-spoken gunner with a shock of dark hair, had also been hit. He loved the 82nd and was a tremendous soldier. When the blast went off, he initially thought he'd stepped on the IED himself. The blast knocked out his hearing momentarily, blew the lenses out of his sunglasses, and knocked him down. He also had some big chunks taken out of his legs.

When he came to and his hearing returned, he heard me yelling for him, looked around, and saw me on the ground nearby. By that time medics were already working on me. Riot was bleeding from the face and body and legs and he started to yell because it hurt so much. Another medic tended to him.

PFC Brandon Fessey was also hit. He's young-looking, with sort of an all-American boyish face with a quick smile and a low voice, another tremendous soldier. Right after the blast, he didn't realize he'd been hit at first. He was also bleeding from the face and he noticed blood on the front of him, but he wasn't sure if the blood was his or not. He ended up with a concussion and some other injuries, although fortunately he wasn't hurt as badly as Theriot.

Fessey was the mine hound for the mission, but I don't blame him for anything that resulted. Mines can be as unpredictable as a shark, and we were swimming in an ocean full of them. It's not hard for a mine to fool a minesweeper. Ultimately, the safety of my men was my responsibility. If I blame anyone, I blame myself.

Sergeant Daniel Bateson was one of the first medics to work on me while I was still on the ground. Normally, he has a low voice and a quick laugh. That day he was all business. While he was still on the run over to me, he opened his bleed kit and an airway kit and got out a tourniquet. His first thought was that what he was seeing was not real. I looked like a mannequin amputee that the army might use in a training exercise. "Nobody lives from this," he whispered to himself. But his training kicked in and he went right to work. Sergeant Hambright also rushed over and started working on me, as did Sergeant Bruner and Sergeant Voyce. My torn limbs were as raw as hamburger, and I was covered in dust and blood and grime. They slowed down my bleeding and packed me up good and tight.

Then the Blackhawk came. They loaded Fessey and Riot on the helicopter first. Then they loaded me on. Riot and I were on the floor. Fessey was sitting up. At that point, one of my legs was still attached to my body by a few strands of skin and ligaments. The medics had flopped it over and wrapped it underneath me so I wouldn't stare at it anymore.

After the helicopter took off, Riot was in a lot of pain, and I was ordering the medics in the Blackhawk around, trying to make sure my guys were cared for. Fessey was saying something like "Dude, I'll be fine."

Later, Kelsey received the following private message via Facebook, describing the events of my evacuation from the perspective of one of the flight medics who worked on me in the air:

To Kelsey Mills,

My name is 1SG Waite. The other flight medic was SSG Hockersmith. You belong to a family of warriors. Other wounded soldiers in the aircraft were injured and screaming. But your husband was more worried about them than himself.

It's very noisy in the aircraft, and you can't hear without a flight helmet. SSG Mills made SSG Hockersmith take off his flight helmet so he could hear his questions about his men and get an answer. He then apologized to him for making him take his helmet off. I couldn't believe it. Here he was severely wounded and apologizing to us for the inconvenience.

His face was dirty and there was dust in his eyes but he never shed a tear. I replay in my mind a moment when he looked at another wounded soldier and winked to reassure him that all would be okay.

My crew is still on duty in his unit's area now. We go back to Kandahar on Monday, but we won't go back the same way. I am an E8, but this E6 is the example for myself and others to emulate.

Respectfully
1SG Shane A. Waite,
C 3/2-5 Lightning Dustoff

THE INJURIES TO myself, Fessey, and Riot hit everyone in our platoon hard. About a week after the blast, our lieutenant, Zac Lewis, wrote a bulk letter to his family and friends. Here is part of his email:

*As [my wife] Tori mentioned, this past week has been one of the most challenging of my life. I want to say thanks to my friends and family for your support. You really have no idea how much a few words of encouragement can mean when you are at a time and place like this. Thanks again.*

*My platoon is in a very active area of operations in southern Afghanistan. Our mission is to close with and destroy the enemy. There is no "outside the wire" here, because there is no wire. My boys are simply always on alert. We haven't had a shower since we've been in Afghanistan. We've run nonstop missions and have been very successful at accomplishing these without experiencing any injuries to our own.*

*I'm just trying to paint a picture of life here, and not trying to make you feel sorry for us. Trust me, I belong here with these guys, and we are a family. Rather, I want to paint a picture because I'd like to tell you about Travis Mills. I know you don't know him, but it would mean a lot to me to be able to spread his story.*

*My platoon's string of missions without injury came to an abrupt and violent end last week when we hit a dismounted IED during combat operations. I had three paratroopers injured from the blast. One injury was minor, one was severe, and one was simply beyond words.*

*The most severe injury was sustained by my weapons squad leader, Travis "Big" Mills. I'd like to take the opportunity to tell you about him. Even under the conditions that I've described, he is the best of us. He was the biggest guy in the platoon and has the biggest heart to go with it. He was eager to please and always cheered us up. He led from the front and was injured because of it. He preferred that he take the injury over any man in his squad. He was the most fearless person I have ever seen in combat.*

*When we weren't in combat, he was great to have around. He woke up every morning and sang a bunch of different songs to us . . . usually Kesha or Britney Spears or the songs of some other girl band. We had this ritual. Anytime we finished a patrol where we'd had a firefight, once we returned to the strongpoint, he would run to the front of the formation and sing songs about the 82nd Airborne. He would do dance gestures and all. He even did it for the brigade commander when he came to visit. It was a big hit.*

*He laughed at how serious I am and how I don't like to be touched. So he made it his personal mission to make me laugh. Usually this involved an overly aggressive and a little-too-*

*intimate man-hug followed by a middle school style dance where he'd grind on me. He kept me sane. I laughed at his antics constantly. In combat, there is no one we would have rather been with. He risked his life to save others constantly, and I can recall two times specifically that he literally saved me.*

*Needless to say, I took his injury hard including the personal guilt that a leader feels when he is responsible for his men. So, I wanted to tell you these things.*

*Everyone is asking how I'm doing. Yes, I am hurting, but you know I am going to be ok. More importantly, Travis is going to be ok. The truth is, I've seen things here so terrible that I'll never be able to put them into words, Travis's injury being at the top of the list.*

*But I've also seen things here so wonderful that I'll never be able to put them into words either. I know that it sounds crazy, but it's true. How do you put into words the spirit like the one I've just described in Big Mills?*

*The reality of it is that I have the honor of leading people like Travis. There are many more in my platoon just like him. So, while I've seen some things I'd like to never talk about again, I've seen just as many things that I'll spend the rest of my life trying to explain to anyone who will listen. I've seen a tremendous love and care between brothers that have only each other to rely on, and have only one care . . . to bring each other home.*

*It's a selfless, deep, everlasting bond that I consider myself lucky and absolutely privileged to be a part of.*

*Thank you so much again for your support, but know that I am fine. I am exactly where I need to be right now. My family here is taking care of each other, and we will persevere as one.*

# 12

# PAIN

JOSH BUCK ARRIVED IN KANDAHAR BEFORE I CAME OUT OF MY first surgery. My blood type is A positive, and I'd required so much blood during this first surgery that they'd needed to rush back to the nearest FOB and solicit donors.

Josh was still bombarded by strong emotions. To hear him tell it, he basically walked into the hospital, grabbed the first guy he saw, and blurted out, "My brother-in-law is here. You need to take me to him right now!"

The dude told him to cool down and pointed him in the right direction. Eventually Josh found where I was, and a nurse told him to wait in the hallway. That same nurse had treated me before I'd gone under, and she told Josh that I'd been strong and had kept asking about my guys. The last thing I'd said before I went under was that I just wanted to hold my baby girl again. The nurse was in tears as she recounted this to Josh—the severity of my injuries had shaken up even the medical staff—and Josh said it was good to have somebody to cry with. He was taken to a holding area, and he was able to connect with Riot and Fessey to see how they were doing. They were going to be okay.

Josh saw me right after I came out of that first surgery. He described how the sight of a big guy like me not filling up a hospital bed was a picture that just about killed him. Immediately, the medic in him went to work. He checked out my bandages and examined the tubes running in and out of me. He saw the remains of my right arm bandaged high, nearly at my shoulder, and thought, "My God, are they even going to be able to attach a prosthetic to that?" The remains of my legs were bandaged where my knees used to be. My left hand was still attached at the time, and Josh thought, "Well, at least that's better than nothing." In Kandahar, I wasn't put in a private room, and across from me was a wounded Afghan. Josh needed to consciously catch himself because he didn't want to direct any of his anger toward this person, but he remembers thinking, "Dude—was this worth it?!"

I was still unconscious and would be for some time. Josh contacted hospital administrators to get them to check with the army's casualty affairs notification program to ask if Kelsey or my parents had been notified. Josh learned that no family notifications had been made yet, and that it might take two to three days. He furrowed his brow at the length of the timeline and said, "Then you need to change your process, because his family needs to know." The people he talked to were helpful, not policy pushers, and said they would speed things up. A few hours later they tracked Josh down and indicated that Kelsey had been notified. They let Josh use an office and a private phone. Josh first phoned Deanna, his wife, to relay the news. She'd already talked to Kelsey and had heard. Then Josh phoned Kelsey. She was sobbing, wailing. Josh swallowed his own surging angst and tried to stay calm for his sister. Kelsey was just inconsolable.

"I need you to settle down and listen to me, because I need to tell you what's going on," Josh said. "What do you know so far?"

"I know he's a triple amputee," Kelsey said, and lost it again.

"You're right," Josh said matter-of-factly. "He's also missing fingers on his left hand, and the doctors aren't sure yet if they can save that hand. They think they can, but they don't know for sure." He relayed that my kidneys had initially been failing but I was on dialysis now and my kidneys were improving. Trying to be reassuring, he said, "You know, Kelsey, if a wounded soldier makes it to the hospital in Kandahar, then the hospital has a ridiculously high survivability rate. Something like 99 percent of the wounded soldiers who make it to Kandahar end up leaving the hospital still alive."

Kelsey took notes on all the information; Josh promised to call again as soon as he had any updates. After he hung up with Kelsey, he called my parents with the same news, and then contacted the commander of the hospital. Josh knew I'd be transferred to another hospital soon, and he asked to be transferred along with me. The commander was very helpful and said yes.

Our division commander was in Kandahar when I was there in the hospital, and he and army personnel held a brief Purple Heart ceremony right after I was brought out of surgery. This is the award given to soldiers when they've been wounded in battle. In a situation as grave as mine, they want to do this as soon as possible in case a soldier doesn't live. I was still unconscious. Josh accepted the medal on my behalf. The division commander pinned it on my blanket. A picture was taken, which I've never seen. They were very supportive and said to relay to Kelsey their concerns and prayers.

The nurse brought Josh some of my personal effects that I'd had on me when I was wounded. Among them was my wedding ring. My ring finger had been destroyed, but one of the medics at the scene had thought to find the ring. It was caked with blood and dirt. Josh asked hospital staff for a couple of alcohol wipes. He sat in the hallway and painstakingly scrubbed until every bit of blood and grime was gone. I was still sedated, and this gave him something productive to do to take his mind off things, he said. He vowed that the ring would not be out of his possession until he could give it to Kelsey.

When the job was finished, he put my wedding ring in his pocket next to my Purple Heart.

GETTING HIT WITH an IED is like having a heap of broken bottles hurled at you by a pitching machine—an extremely powerful and completely vicious pitching machine. Any uncovered body part gets shredded.

Doctors said the stumps of my arms and legs looked as shredded as raw hamburger. Imagine your arm jammed into a meat grinder. Someone had turned the handle on me until huge amounts of my flesh and bone were simply gone.

Fortunately, Kevlar body armor had covered my torso and shielded me from the bulk of shrapnel, so my internal organs were intact. My heart was good. My liver, lungs, colon, and intestines were fine. My kidneys were shaken up but otherwise okay, and that was about it internally. In one place, shrapnel had ripped through my body armor and left a jagged golf ball–size hole. If I hadn't had my armor on, I would have been ripped in half.

Unfortunately, body armor only goes over your trunk. Maybe someday they'll design body armor for limbs, but right now a soldier couldn't move if he had body armor on his arms and legs. I suppose limb armor could be hinged, but even then it would be too heavy. You couldn't fight in it.

My helmet had protected most of my head. My brain was fine.

I had glass shards and bits of rock embedded in my face and all through my cheeks. What the doctors couldn't pick out was left to emerge on its own. For months a zit would pop and a piece of glass would come out.

My hearing and sight were okay.

My man parts were okay, if anyone's wondering.

It was just the rest of me that was messed up.

I REMEMBER LITTLE about being in Kandahar. Altogether, I was there for a day and a half. From Kandahar, they transferred me to the U.S. hospital at Bagram Airfield. It's officially titled the Heathe N. Craig Joint Theater Hospital, and its facilities are as good as any hospital in the United States. The transfer was a regular part of the process of evacuation. All casualties departing the theater go through Bagram, but I couldn't tell you exactly what the reason is for this.

We flew to Bagram on a C-130. It's a large four-propeller plane, and ours had been modified so the inside was a large functioning hospital room. Josh stayed with me throughout the transfer, and he said the plane was full, the casualties were stacked two high in cots, and the critical transport team was extremely professional.

But Josh couldn't be next to me for every procedure. He wasn't officially my next of kin either, so he wasn't consulted on decisions that doctors needed to make quickly. Shortly after arriving in Bagram, on April 12, two days after being wounded, I was taken in for another surgery. Later, when Josh came into my room to check on me, my left hand had been removed. My forearm had been amputated just below my elbow.

Josh found a nurse, his eyebrows lowered, and he asked, "What the hell?!"

"It was necrotic" was all the nurse said. This happens when not enough blood flows to tissue and the tissue dies. She was matter-of-fact, cold.

Josh called Kelsey and relayed the information that I was now a quadruple amputee. He wanted his sister to hear this piece of bad news directly from him. He kept it together for Kelsey. Then he called his wife, relayed the same news to her, and broke down into tears.

WITHIN A DAY or so I was transferred again from Bagram to the Landstuhl Regional Medical Center in Germany, again as part of the normal evacuation process. We flew on a C-17 to Germany along with a critical care transport team. This time the casualties were stacked four high. Josh went with me and was able to stay in the holding barracks at Landstuhl.

Kelsey heard the news from Josh and wrote the following in her journal:

> I haven't been able to breathe since Tuesday at 11:53. I want so badly to talk to Travis, to touch him, to be by his side. It is killing me to sit here helplessly.
>
> Today is April 13, 2010, and I have been in contact with his doctors and nurses in Germany. He had his third surgery today where they washed out his wounds. He is now in recovery with a slight fever of 101. His kidneys are working well and he is able to maintain a somewhat stable blood pressure on his own. He has opened his eyes a few times, and they are bringing him up to a light sedation. He opens his eyes on hearing his name or my name.
>
> He is still on a ventilator to help him breathe, because he is so heavily sedated, but when they bring him to lighter sedations

*they turn it off and he is able to breathe on his own. Later, they said they'll bring him out of his sedation and take the ventilator out completely, and he should, God willing, be able to talk. The nurse assured me that I could talk to him if at all possible.*

*He's so far away from me now. I feel so completely useless and helpless. I know the man he is, and how he brightens any room with his presence. He is handsome, funny, athletic, caring, giving, worrisome in the best possible way, loving. He is the essence of all things good, and he is such an amazing father and husband.*

*I know Travis will overcome. He's hanging on, hanging on for Chloe, for me, for his parents. He loves life, and I know that he will be strong and persevere through this. I'm not saying there won't be times of doubt, depression, anger, hurt, disappointment, but I will be at his side, and I'll assure him he'll get better.*

*I will be there every agonizing step of the way.*

*I love him so much.*

FOUR FULL DAYS after the wounding, they let me come out of sedation gradually, and I woke up for the first time. Josh said I looked confused and scared. Josh's face was the first I saw, and it must have registered to me at some level of consciousness that I wasn't alone.

"Travis," said one of the doctors. "Can you hear us?"

I took a few deep breaths and croaked out a faint "Yeah."

I had a tube down my throat, and the doctors told me I needed to cough once or twice to help get the tube out. I coughed, and somewhere above me Josh said, "That dude is really tough." The tube slid out.

"Okay, Travis," a doctor asked. "What's your last name?"

A few seconds went by. I just stared at the face above me. Then I said, "Mills."

My voice was raspy, and the word came out lower than a whisper. No one above me said anything, so I said it again, this time a little louder. "Mills."

Somehow I thought that wasn't loud enough, or maybe they hadn't heard me, so I said it as loud as I could. "MILLS!"

The doctors looked happy. All my exertion barely yielded the volume of a strong whisper, but seeing my resolve to keep repeating my name louder and louder, that's the point where Josh knew I was going to be okay. I wasn't going to die. They told me to get some rest.

I fell asleep, and Josh went to go get a sandwich. He hadn't felt like eating since before he'd met me in Kandahar. When I came to again, Josh was there at the hospital bed. This time I had more presence of mind and decided to ask a few questions of my own. Only he and I were in the room then.

"My soldiers?" My voice was still raspy, barely a whisper, and I was groggy from all the meds. "How are my soldiers?"

"They're both alive," Josh said. "And they're doing awesome because you took the brunt of the explosion for them. If Riot or Fessey had stepped on that IED, they might be dead because they're smaller than you. Riot's here in Germany with us. I can go get him later if you'd like."

"Yeah," I said. "I'd like that."

Josh nodded at me. "We'll do that, then."

A few moments of silence went by. I knew I'd been wounded, but I didn't know how badly. I knew I couldn't move my arms and legs, but that's all I knew. I looked at Josh and stone cold asked him outright, "Am I paralyzed?"

"No, man," Josh said. "You're not paralyzed."

"You don't need to lie to me," I whispered. "I can take it."

"I'm going to tell it to you straight." Josh knew I'd want to know the truth. "You're not paralyzed, but both your arms and legs are gone."

A little sound erupted from me, somewhere between disbelief and horror, half gasp, half laugh, almost a snort: "Hmph."

Then I shook my head as if saying no and closed my eyes. I wasn't sleeping after that. I was awake. But I wasn't saying anything to anyone anymore. The reality of how badly I'd been wounded hit me with as much force as the initial blast. I couldn't take the magnitude of what I'd been told.

I lay there for some time without saying anything. Josh stayed by me. He was silent as well. Eventually I drifted into an uneasy sleep, and when I awoke a few hours later, Josh was still there, and I still refused to talk to anyone. I glanced at a calendar on the wall. The date was April 14, 2012, still the same day as when I'd heard the news I was a quadruple amputee.

It was my twenty-fifth birthday.

I COULD CALL Kelsey if I wanted to. But I didn't want to talk to her. I choked at the thought.

Josh was still sitting on the chair next to my bed, and I was still silent, still not wanting to talk to anyone. Why was I so damn embarrassed to call Kelsey? I wasn't a sissy. I wasn't afraid. I loved her so much. I just couldn't take the thought of her being married to a man without any arms or legs.

Thoughts swirled around the insides of my mind. *They'd gotten me. Those damn Taliban got me. I always thought I was pretty tough. Nobody ever messed with Travis Mills. The Taliban wasn't ever supposed to win. I was always the sort of husband who took care of things for his wife. I lifted the heavy weights. I opened the jars. How was I supposed to do that now?*

Two harsh words gradually formed in my mind and stayed there, words worse than any swearwords I could think of. Those two words contained all my dismay and anger and hatred and fear and anguish and heartbreak. Those words directly related to my new reality, to my will to move forward, and I wanted to scream those words with every ounce of my being, but for now I held my tongue because I ached all over and all within me. The pain was so bad.

Part of the pain was the thought of what I'd become. I could hardly picture the new me.

Yet the pain was more than emotional. It was physical pain—it coursed through my body. I felt like I was on fire.

I tried to focus on my breathing and take stock of why my pain was so bad. Even with all the medications flowing through me, I still felt like I was in a red-hot vise. I could hardly take it. I knew Josh would never lie to me, but my arms and legs still felt like they were attached. My hands felt like they were burning, like someone was clamping them inside an industrial furnace— but my hands weren't there. The flames were eating away my ligaments, my nerves, my skin. My legs—my phantom legs—were clamped in that same fire. Bolts of agony surged from limbs that weren't there and registered to a brain that still was. The pain came and went. Came and went. Came and went.

Josh started in his seat and leaned closer. "Travis! You need me to get the nurse?"

I didn't say anything. I was itchy and sweating bad.

He pressed a buzzer, then went and got a cool cloth and laid it on my forehead. The nurse came in and upped my morphine.

Just before I went under again, everything that I'd always drilled into myself rushed through my mind. *Never show fear. Don't ever let your guys see you in pain. Don't cry out.*

Even when I'd been lying on the ground right after the blast,

I'd felt pain then, but I hadn't showed it. When that IV was shoved through my chest, that was painful, but I wasn't going to complain then. You don't let people down. You just don't.

But this time the pain was so bad. It was still so bad, even with more painkillers in me now. So bad. So bad. So bad. This time, I wanted to do the unthinkable. Those two words began to vocalize within my throat. "Josh," I said.

"Yeah—what do you need, buddy?"

I swallowed and whispered the two words.

"I quit."

# THE COMA

HE PHANTOM PAIN CAME AND WENT. MOSTLY IT CAME AND stayed. Sometimes I had moments where I was thinking clearer, and I wasn't quitting then. In my soul, I know I never did. In a moment of unbearableness, I'd whispered to Josh that I wanted to end it all. Maybe I even whispered it more than once. My memories of that time swirl; they aren't linear. Sure, I thought about suicide. I never formulated a plan, but the thought of not being around anymore had its appeal. Those were my most depressed moments. Right at the beginning when I knew this was my new reality. Before I could work up the stomach to call Kelsey. Before I started thinking that there was still hope of going forward.

In Germany, they wheeled Theriot into my room. The Riot had some holes in his legs in addition to the cuts in his face, but he was healing fine. He's a big guy with broad shoulders and huge arms, and he tried to smile at me, and I tried to smile at him. It was good to see him, although it looked like he didn't know what to say to me.

I found out later that Riot knew I hadn't called Kelsey yet. He knew I needed to. But how would a private ever say that to a staff sergeant? How do you say that to someone you look up to?

"I'm sorry," I whispered to Riot. "I'm so, so sorry."

"It's not your fault," Riot said.

"I shouldn't have let you get wounded. I'm sorry."

"Don't be sorry, Sergeant Mills," he said. "It wasn't your fault."

But I was sorry.

Sorry for everything.

INSTEAD OF CALLING Kelsey, I called Lieutenant Lewis.

He was still in the outback of Afghanistan. Still in daily firefights. I tried to put a smile in my voice and I said, "Sir, I got something for you."

Without missing a beat, I sang a phrase or two of the 82nd Airborne song, just the same way I had always sung to the guys whenever we returned from a combat mission and I high-fived them back into the base. My voice was raspy and not too loud, but I croaked out,

*All the way Airborne, Airborne all the way.*
*Drive it on, drive it on.*

Externally, I was so messed up, but inside I was still a weapons squad leader. I wanted to be fierce when I spoke with my commanding officer. I wanted to reassure my guys that I was okay.

I could hear the smile in the lieutenant's voice, and he thanked me. Then he explained that they'd run an air assault mission the night after I'd been wounded. They were certain they'd taken care of the same savages who'd planted the same IEDs that had got me. On that mission, in my honor, each soldier in our platoon carried something that had belonged to me. A magazine of ammunition. A grenade that had once been mine. I thanked my lieutenant for this. My unit was still out there in the thick of the battle. Still doing their job.

Our conversation didn't last long. I was exhausted. I asked that he take care of my remaining squad, and he promised he would.

I apologized that I couldn't be there to help out for the rest of this deployment, and he reassured me I'd get better soon.

I told him in a couple of months I'd meet him and the rest of the guys at Green Ramp in America (the name given to the location where the unit would redeploy to at Fort Bragg). I'd be there with bionic arms and legs on, and I'd give Lieutenant Lewis a big ole bear hug, same as I always did. He said he was looking forward to it.

"I'm sorry I let you down, Lieutenant" was the last thing I remember saying to him.

"You didn't let us down," he said.

I HAD THE presence of mind to call John Becker, my Presbyterian minister from my childhood days. He was living in Ohio and retired now, but I knew he was still strong of spirit and faith. I didn't want to talk to him necessarily. I wasn't liking the idea of God much at the moment and my anger and dismay were still clouding everything else.

I wondered if God was punishing me. Maybe I was a bad person. I was filled with frustration. Self-loathing. Doubt.

I didn't come to any conclusions then. But I called Reverend Becker for a specific reason: I wanted him to do something for me. Something that meant much.

"Can I ask a favor?" I whispered, my voice raspy.

"Anything," Reverend Becker said.

"Call my mother. Help my parents through this."


THAT SAME DAY, still my birthday, I called my parents. I didn't really want to speak to them. I think they could tell that, even though I tried to hide my true feelings. They told me happy birthday, and I broke down and they did too.

We composed ourselves and talked some more, just about this and that.

Then I said to my dad, "How could they get me like that? What did I do wrong?"

"You didn't do anything wrong," he said.

"I stepped on it and went flying through the air. I did a 180. It was crazy."

"Well, Travis," my dad said, "the important question is 'Did you look good doing it?'"

I chuckled. I love my parents so much. It hurt to laugh. My dad was trying to cheer me up. I loved him for that. "Yeah," I said. "I looked pretty awesome."

Here's how my dad later described the feeling of that first phone call with me:

*When you first hear your own son is hit, you can hardly take in the news. This was my Travis. My son.*

*You don't hear the word amputee. You hear "gravely ill," the better chance that he's going to die. Then we heard triple amputee. Then quadruple amputee. But we still weren't thinking that word. In my mind, all I could think was that I wanted my boy back. I didn't care how. No arms and legs—that didn't matter. I just wanted my boy back—that's all that mattered.*

*When we first talked with him, I could picture his face. I
knew I'd see him alive again. That's what was so important.
That's what saved us from going over the deep end.*

I FELT LIKE eating something solid. For some strange reason,
Oreos came to mind. And pineapple juice. In regular life, I ate
the occasional Oreo, but I never drank pineapple juice. Yet those
were the only things that sounded good. I asked a nurse if she
could get me some. She did.

Somehow that request found its way to Facebook—that I'd
wanted Oreos and pineapple juice. That's not an easy request to
fulfill when you're overseas. Some army guys saw the post and
sent me a case of pineapple juice.

ON APRIL 15, the day after my birthday, I summoned the nerve
and called Kelsey for the first time.

"Hey, babe," I said. "I love you. I'll see you soon."

That was pretty much all I said. I was hurting, sore. I just
tried to keep the conversation short and light.

Inside my head, I was a mess, a runaway freight train. All
these thoughts kept rushing around uncontrolled. *How could I
ever be the husband and father I needed to be? I couldn't even give my
wife a hug anymore. I couldn't hold her hand. And that was only the
beginning. How would I ever drive again? How could I work and earn
a paycheck? None of that was ever going to be possible. Kelsey didn't do
anything wrong. She didn't deserve this. Why would she ever want to be
with someone like me?*

I wanted her to leave me.

I wouldn't blame her if she did.

But Kelsey was thinking the exact opposite. She wrote in her journal,

*I was able to talk with him late last night and the result left me feeling saddened. He seemed like talking to me was upsetting him, and he told me he had to go only after a few short words. I understand that he is feeling embarrassed and scared and feeling like a failure . . . I mean, I cannot even begin to imagine the roller coaster of emotions he is feeling right now.*

*My brother told me that Travis is nervous to see me because he doesn't know how I will react or if I will continue to love him as my husband. These worries seem so trivial to me, because I will love him through sickness and health until death do us part—I did not use those words lightly when we got married. I will be by his side every day for the rest of our lives, whether he likes it or not. I know his natural reaction will be to push me away because of embarrassment or feelings of letting me down, but I just wish I could constantly reassure him that my love for him is unwavering.*

*Josh said that Travis is having phantom pains, saying his feet and hands hurt when he knows they aren't there. That just shows how powerful the human brain is, and I know he will be able to use his arms again. The thing that keeps choking me up is the times he would squeeze my hand three times to mean "I love you" or rub my back or feet while I was pregnant. Or how he'd just make me breakfast. He'd do all the hard things for me. Now it's my turn to do all those things for him.*

*The fact is that this isn't going to get better for a long time, but I do have hope and I do have faith. I love him so much. He really and truly is Superman in every sense of the word.*

★ ★ ★

THEY TOLD ME I was going home.

Back to the States anyway. Plans and flights got rearranged once, and my meds were making my mind loopy. At first I was medically ready to fly, they said, but then my condition wasn't good enough, so flight plans were delayed a day. Then another day. I freaked out and became angry, combative. For some time all I did was yell profanities.

Then I was in tears.

Not bubbling tears. Just rolling tears. Frustrated tears. Sad tears.

"I just want to go home," I said to Josh. "Just send me home."

Then a shiver of fear went through me and it dawned on me anew where I was again and what had happened to me. Sometimes I forgot for a split second. It's one thing to talk to someone you love on the phone. It's another thing to see that person again. To not feel like you're you anymore. And then I wasn't sure if I ever wanted to go home again.

"Josh," I said. "I can't do this. I don't want anybody to see me like this. Here I am lying in bed, shitting on myself. What am I ever going to do?"

"It's going to be okay," Josh said. "Nobody is going to judge you for being hurt. The whole purpose of the Taliban is to get us. Sometimes they win one. But that doesn't mean we're destroyed."

My mind felt all dark inside. We were quiet for a long time then.

"Kelsey will probably leave me," I said to Josh.

"Dude—" His voice was steel. "My sister will *not* leave you."


BEFORE I LEFT for the States, I had another phone call with Kelsey, this one longer.

Kelsey described it in her journal:

*Travis was finally able to call and talk to me. Really talk. He asked for privacy, and when the nurse left the room he broke down on the phone in tears saying, "I can't take care of you with no arms and legs," over and over and over, and "I have always taken care of you, that's my job. It is not your job to take care of me."*

*I reassured him everything would be taken care of and he had nothing to worry about. My love for him does nothing but grow, along with my pride and respect.*

And in a later entry,

*I was informed yesterday by Travis's surgeon that he will not be able to fly today because he has a slow bleed in one of his extremities. They are not sure which one, but once they get him into surgery to do a washout they will be able to see it and stop the bleed. They say it is a very slow drop in his hemoglobin levels, and nothing to be worried about. However, they would rather have him completely stable before they fly him over the vast Atlantic Ocean.*

*I heard he has been awake today a lot and my brother has been by his side, although Travis has not asked to talk to me or anyone else family-related today. The nurse, Flo, said he is on a roller coaster of emotions right now, and that he will be for a long time to come, understandably.*

*A chaplain was able to see him today, and Travis was open to talk, which is a very good sign. The chaplain was able to help him better understand what has happened and what this means. I mean, all this tragedy is hard for any one human to process, and Travis has done it with superhuman abilities. Later, when I talked to Flo, she said Travis and Josh were both sound asleep in Travis's room.*

Kelsey wrote another entry, this one addressed just to me:

*Travis—one of your nurses, Major Kate, told me that they brought some music in for you to listen to and that you were dancing around and singing to Kesha. And then "Amazing Grace" came on and you started crying. I know how much this song means to you and what it means to you. Soon you will be able to snuggle with Chloe and hum her this song. I thank God that you will have that opportunity to hold Chloe again, and that Chloe gets her daddy back and is able to be raised and protected by you.*

*You are a hero in every sense of the word. A superman. I love you so much. Words cannot express my gratitude for you surviving this. I would not have been able to live without you.*

ON APRIL 17, five days after the blast, I was cleared for travel and flew from Germany to Andrews Air Force Base in Maryland. Josh stuck by my side. We had another great critical care transport team. Those people were really something else. On our way, we heard that my parents and Kelsey were flying over to Maryland to meet me.

Once we landed, hospital staff loaded me and a bunch of other wounded guys up in a huge semi-truck of an ambulance and we navigated the Beltway over to Walter Reed Army Medical Center in Bethesda. A number of the other wounded guys were marines, and marines don't respect anybody who isn't a marine. But Josh said these guys were respecting me. One of them said, "This is a tough, tough dude."

I was pretty out of it, but my mind was with it enough to make some crack to one of the medical staff that we were all rolling along in a "meat truck." He grinned.

Right away when we arrived at Walter Reed, they needed to do another surgery on me. I'd had some stitches open up on the flight over. This surgery occurred maybe twenty minutes after being wheeled through the front door.

I heard that Kelsey and my folks had arrived. At first I said to Josh that I didn't want to see her. I was still feeling like less of a man. But Josh said, "Look, she just wants to tell you that she loves you." Josh went to go prepare them, to sort of explain what it was going to be like to see me for the first time. His leading line was "Remember—he's still alive. But it's going to be a bit traumatic to see him. Just be prepared."

When we saw one another, everything was sort of a bustle of activity all at once. I couldn't look my parents in the eye. I was standoffish with Kelsey. I didn't want to look at anybody or have them looking at me. Medical staff were all around doing their thing. It was noisy and confusing. Since Kelsey was physically present in the hospital, she needed to sign a bunch of paperwork right away to allow them to cut some more off my leg so they could sew it up again. Everything happened really quickly. She felt queasy and overwhelmed and was trying to read through the forms, and I snapped at her and said, "Just sign the damn papers!" I don't know what was wrong with me. I never talk to her like that. She signed the paperwork while I was getting prepped. Then they took me in for surgery. That was our romantic first meeting.

When I came out of sedation, it was the following day. There was some family trouble. I tried to piece together the story. My dad had become really sick on the flight over and needed emergency surgery for diverticulitis. He didn't want to have the surgery because he wanted to stay with me, but I saw him and told him to go take care of himself. I insisted. So they took him in for surgery, and he ended up in a hospital room seven doors down from me. As he recovered, he could take his IV pole and walk down and see me. Josh flew back to Fort Bragg and got Deanna, who was six months pregnant, and they both flew back to Walter Reed.

Beside my hospital bed was a small stand-up plaque with a Bible verse on it. I don't know where the plaque came from. Somebody gave it to me. I read the words slowly in my mind.

> *Be strong and courageous. Do not be afraid; do not be*
> *discouraged, for the LORD your God will be with you*
> *wherever you go.*
>
> JOSHUA 1:9

*Hmph*, I thought. I wasn't too happy with God just now. *Where was God when I stepped on an IED?*

The thought was barely out of my head when I heard Kelsey say it was time for me to meet Chloe again.

*Chloe!*

In all the bustle, it hadn't dawned on me that my daughter was here too. Tammy, Kelsey's mom, had flown over with them, and she'd been taking care of Chloe when Kelsey and my parents had first met me. I took a deep breath, letting the announcement sink in.

I wondered if Chloe would start crying at the sight of me. I wondered if she'd be afraid of me. I had white monitors affixed to my chest, and the stumps of my arms were all taped and bandaged and a bit bloody. I had tape on the side of my face from my ear to the base of my neck, and it was holding some sort of tube in place. Chloe was not yet seven months old. At the very least she'd have forgotten who I was.

Kelsey brought her over to me, laid her on my bare chest, and held her there so she wouldn't slip or fall. Chloe's hair was downy and soft. She was dressed in a wonderfully crazy-colored polka-dot jumper.

I lifted my head to look into my daughter's face. She smiled, perfectly calm. I looked her in the eye, and she looked up at me. She was the first person I'd looked in the eye—and it felt fine. For several moments, we held each other's gaze.

"I love you, Chloe," I said.

She cooed.

I was the same dad to her.


CHLOE WAS GONE from my room, and I was trying to be polite to the doctors, but I kept having these terrible phantom pains. They came and went, but mostly seemed to stay and grow. The fire burned hotter and hotter. The morphine wasn't doing much. After a while the pain grew unbearable.

I gritted my teeth and tried to keep it together. A nurse was in the room. "I'm sorry," I said, "but if you could just please give me a little more pain medicine. My fingers are on fire, but I know they're not there." Then I screamed. And I don't ever scream.

What I didn't understand yet was that the severe pain I experienced came from the injured nerve fibers in my limbs. An injury such as mine can trigger a progressive, falling-domino type of sensation where the neurons fire more than normal. The phenomenon is like a car engine revving past the point of redline and staying there. All pain is magnified. It's a horrific, searing feeling you wouldn't wish on your worst enemy.

I don't know how long this extreme pain went on. Minutes. Hours. Days. I yelled and yelled again and again. I could hear murmurs of the doctors above me talking to my family members. No, they didn't know if the pain would ever subside.

Images swirled in my head. Time meant nothing to me at this

point. I remember telling a nurse that I wished I would die. Time passed and the intense pain remained. One night my dad was with me and I begged him to turn my leg around. "Dad! I know I don't have a leg, but it's backward. You've got to turn it around." I cried out all that night, my dad told me later. I screamed. I shouted. I thrashed about in agony.

A doctor showed me a chart and said, "Travis, on a scale of one to ten, describe your level of pain."

"Ten," I said.

They administered some sort of painkiller as part of a medicinal study on me. I don't remember what it was.

Again the doctors asked me to describe my pain.

"Ten," I said.

They tried a second study. Afterward, the same question.

"Ten," I said.

They tried a third study. I don't know how long these studies took to implement. When this study was over, they asked the same question.

"Ten," I said.

I couldn't stand the torment.

"I want to die," I said again. I didn't know who was listening. I didn't care. It was the truth. I was as tough as they come, but I couldn't take these phantom pains. It felt like I was being filleted alive. The skin was ripped off me. Spikes were driven through my heels. My toenails were yanked out. Gasoline was rubbed all over my skinless flesh. I was screaming again. Screaming. A match was tossed on the gasoline and my body exploded in fire, burning, burning, burning.

"There's a relatively new and controversial experimental study," a doctor's voice said from above me. "It's only ever used on extreme cases. Basically, we pump him full of Ketamine and put him into a coma. We leave him there for a while, then bring him back out. It's like turning a computer off and then rebooting it again. The hope is that we can reset his pain tolerance. It's not a guarantee. And there are risks."

"What sort of risks?" came a voice off to one side. My eyes were closed. They were having a meeting about me, and I didn't hear the answer just then. I'd heard that on the street, Ketamine is known as Special K or Cat Valium. It's similar to PCP. I'd never tried either, but I'd heard that if you take enough Ketamine, it feels like you're not in your body anymore. You have wild hallucinations. Sometimes people describe the feeling as "near death." On the street, they call this being plunged into the "K-hole."

Okay, then. If I had one chance in a hundred of feeling better again by going into a Ketamine coma, then that's where I would go. I was awake enough at one point to agree to the procedure. I knew I might never wake up again. I knew it might fry my mind completely. I might become a basket case for the rest of my life. I didn't care. Anything was better than this unbearable level of pain.

FOR FIVE DAYS straight, they fed me 600 milligrams of Ketamine per hour around the clock. I heard later this procedure has only been done thirty times in the world.

In the coma, I saw nothing. I felt nothing. I heard nothing. I thought nothing. I remember nothing.

After five days in a coma, I started coming back to reality, feeling slightly awake. You'd think that the first thing I'd do would be to say my wife's name really softly—*Kelsey*—all romantic, like you see in the movies. But I just yelled a bunch of words. I felt hazy, frightened, confused, and I yelled that whole first day I was off the Ketamine. I let loose with one long string of loud gibberish. They needed to reassure patients in other rooms that I wasn't being tortured. "Oh, he's coming out of a Ketamine coma," they said. "Just let him yell."

For the next four days, I was in and out of hallucinations. I didn't sleep at all during that time, and within the hallucinations, I saw everything perfectly. I mean—*perfectly*. At first, I was chasing two kids from my hometown. They stole something from Walmart. The kids and I were in a car accident. They crashed through my window. I thought I killed them. Then they were alive, and I said, "Hey, why didn't you tell me I got hit by an IED, you jerks."

Then I was with Genghis Khan. Ole Genghis and I were fighting a real barbarian horde. Genghis had a big hairy beard and he smelled something awful. Arrows flew by me. I fired back.

Then I looked outside my window. A SWAT team was coming into the hospital. Two teams. And the two teams were shooting at each other. Real bullets. Zipping in and landing an inch from my head just like we were back in Afghanistan.

Two of my cousins and I were riding skateboards along with Rob Dyrdek on the TV reality show *Fantasy Factory*. The show might have been on TV while I was in the room, but I thought I was actually on the show.

I was playing hockey in the NHL. I played for the Washington Capitals. We were on the ice, and the ice was cold. I skated around with pads on and a hockey stick in my hands. Fans were screaming. The puck came toward me. I slapped it hard against the boards, and into the net it flew.

A fifty-year-old go-go dancer crawled on a leash down the hallway of Walter Reed. She had a red bikini on, and she was old and wrinkly. I could see her clearly in the hallway. But I was still in my bed too. I was in two places at once. I wanted to go talk to her, but something held me fast in the bed.

Kramer from *Seinfeld* stopped by. He sat in my room with a head full of high wild hair, and I saw him as clearly as I'd ever seen anyone. We carried on a conversation for at least two hours.

"Giddyup," Kramer said. "I'm useless, Jerry. Yo diggity dog. It's like a sauna in here."

"But it's not a legitimate business," I said. "Those pretzels are making me thirsty."

"Stick a fork in me, Jerry, I'm done," he said. "What day is it, anyway?"

"It's just the first day," a voice said. Only it wasn't Kramer anymore. It was my father. I think.

A tube was stuck down my throat and I tried to spit the tube out. I shouted, "Hey—take this tube out of my neck!"

"It's okay, buddy," said a voice. "We'll get it out for you, buddy. Just hang on, buddy." This was a nurse. A male nurse with a bald head.

"Is the tube out yet?" I shouted.

"Not yet, buddy. Don't worry, buddy. We'll get it out in a minute, buddy."

I hated this man. I hated him desperately. I shouted, "Stop calling me buddy!"

Kelsey later told me those words actually came out of my mouth. But I was talking really slowly in this hollow Cookie Monster type of voice, dragging out words so they were almost unintelligible. "STT-OO-PP-PPP . . . CALL-INNNNG . . . ME-EE-EE . . . BUDDY-YYYY!"

Everyone thought at the rate I was handling coming out of the Ketamine coma (or wasn't), I was going to have permanent brain damage. It was quite frightening for everybody who saw me, I was told later, but I had no idea I was putting them through this terror.

Once, somebody was stealing Chloe. That hallucination was the worst. She was out in a field, and somebody was running after her, wanting to hurt her. "Don't touch my daughter!" I yelled. "I'll kill you!"

The times when I was semi-lucid, I was still frightened. Angry. Confused. Insistent. I could talk sometimes. Sometimes I couldn't. It was my mother's birthday, and I gave her a necklace. I think that actually happened. No, it was Mother's Day. Maybe that was it. I accused my dad of stealing from people. My dad never stole from people. But I was certain he did. My brother, Zach, came for a week, but I accused him of never showing up. My dad showed me pictures. Zach was here. So was my sister, Sarah. Everybody was here. The pictures were real. I made my dad phone Zach at three in the morning because I was convinced Zach was choking to death on a chicken bone. Dad placed the call. Zach was fine. Sleepy, but fine.

One night my mom was in the room with me. My eyes were as big as marbles and I was hallucinating. My heart pounded out of my chest. Fortunately, I never wigged out on my mom during that whole time. I think I wigged out on just about everybody else. Later, she told me she'd asked a nurse that night when I was coming back. The nurse didn't have a good answer. "He might not ever come back" was all the nurse could say.

JOSH WAS IN my room.

I could see him clearly.

"Josh," I said.

"Yeah?"

"I see dead people. Don't you?"

"There are no dead people in the room," Josh said flatly. "Go back to sleep, Travis."

Five minutes went by. "Josh?"

"Yeah?"

"Those dead people are still there."

"Are you serious?"

I cracked a grin. "I'm just messing with you, dude."

"You jerk," Josh said. But Josh was smiling. If I was cracking jokes, then he knew I was back from the effects of the Ketamine, truly back. He leaned over me and pressed his forehead against my forehead. He'd been doing this every so often ever since I'd been wounded. A manly sort of bonding. Just to let me know family was there.

"I don't want to die anymore," I said. "I don't ever want to quit."

Josh was crying then.

So was I.

My pain was gone. My hallucinations were over. The Ketamine coma had worked. My mind was clear. Nothing was destroyed. Josh straightened up and sat back down again. I looked over to the side. The same plaque with the Bible verse was there. I couldn't help but read the verse again.

> *Be strong and courageous. Do not be afraid; do not be*
> *discouraged, for the LORD your God will be with you*
> *wherever you go.*
>
> Joshua 1:9

Earlier that verse had made me so mad. But when I read it this time, that anger wasn't there, at least not to the same degree it once was. My anger wasn't gone completely. But in my mind and soul I felt for the first time a flicker of hope. My situation sucked, yes. But I was beginning to see some perspective. There was much work still to be done. Huge work. An enormous challenge lay ahead of me, yet the thought of that challenge didn't repulse or dismay me anymore. Back in normal days, I'd loved a challenge. The quest to succeed in the army had always been a challenge for me. My situation now as a quadruple amputee held out the same sort of dare to succeed.

Sure, if I could have changed things, I wouldn't have been in this situation. But I *couldn't* change things. Being a quadruple amputee was my new reality. I could quit for good. I could shut myself off from the world. I could will myself to die.

Or I could fight forward and keep on living.

For higher reasons I would never know, I was being called to walk a new and unknown pathway. I would need to be strong and courageous, just like I'd always been. I wouldn't be terrified. I had a wife and daughter I needed to live for, and God said He was with me.

I stared at that plaque by my bedside.

I stared at it for a long time.

14

# THE FLOOR IN FRONT
# OF ME

LTOGETHER, I WENT THROUGH THIRTEEN SURGERIES, THOUGH
I couldn't tell you exactly what each one did or the exact
dates when they occurred. I don't remember much about
the actual procedures, and some of the surgeries happened right
after the blast while others happened as late as eight and nine
months later.

But I remember seeing myself in a mirror for the first time.
This was maybe three weeks in, right after coming out of the
coma. My eyes were swollen, my face was puffy from the drugs,
and underneath my eyes were deep dark circles. Between losing
my limbs and my lack of eating solid foods for three-odd weeks,
I'd dropped a total of 110 pounds. When I was in Afghanistan I'd
weighed 250. I was now down to 140. I hadn't weighed 140 since
sixth grade. I felt the wrong kind of skinny, a concentration camp
kind of skinny, where nutrients are deficient and muscle mass has
been lost. Not to mention limbs.

I wasn't happy about any of this. I felt self-conscious about how I looked, embarrassed, even ashamed. All the things I couldn't do anymore loomed large, frustrating me. Small stuff even. If I had an itch, I couldn't scratch it. If I wanted a drink of water, I had to ask someone to get it for me. I couldn't blow my nose without someone holding a Kleenex. When I went to the bathroom, somebody needed to wipe my butt—that was the worst. Indignities and inconveniences were now a regular part of each day. I felt out of control. Dependent. Grieved over what I had lost. Altogether, even though I began to progress forward, the mirror proved a stark reminder of my new life. I don't think I could look in a mirror for about four months without breaking down.

The medical staff at Walter Reed proved great as a whole, but some were definitely better than others. Using a bedpan irritated me because I had two big cuts on my butt that would bleed. Those cuts hurt. One nurse was particularly great. Lieutenant Bussells. He figured out a way to pad my bedpan with foam. Plus he always used heated wipes. Nice.

For a long while, I wasn't able to put into words how I felt, but I know now that if you've been wounded it takes time to work through your anger. You're angry about little things, about big things, about things you've never been angry about before. You need to work through the new harsh reality that your world has changed. You can't do the same things you once did. For me, I didn't even look the same as I used to look. And I didn't look like other people, ordinary people.

I soon learned that whenever somebody new saw me, he was bound to give me a long look before turning away. Either that, or the person would glance away quickly, stare at the ceiling, and deliberately not look at me again. Some looks contained pity. Some contained shock and horror. Some contained gratitude and respect. I couldn't control the looks I received from others. I could only control how I reacted to the looks. If a person wondered what happened to me, then my preference was that he should just ask me. It didn't bother me to talk about it. I'd just tell him I was bitten by a shark and we'd have a laugh. That would set us both at ease, and then I'd explain how the injury really happened if he wanted to know more.

The truth is this took a while to work through, and some days I was growlier than others. One morning I needed a test and was wheeled down the hall to another room. A kid was hanging out in that part of the hospital visiting someone. I needed to wait out in the hallway before going into the test room and the kid stared wide-eyed at me, her mouth agape.

Normally I like kids, and I tried to shrug it off. But the kid kept staring—and staring and staring—and the kid's parent saw her do this but didn't do anything about it. Finally, fed up, I hissed to the kid, "You know who did this to me? The bogeyman in your closet and the monster under your bed."

Just then I was wheeled into the test room. I chuckled darkly to myself. Hey—chalk one up for Uncle Travis.

On another occasion, a representative for the army's mental health unit came by my room. I know that some guys go to counseling after they've been wounded, and it works well for them. But I'm pretty straightforward as a rule, and I didn't think counseling was for me. She started asking me all these questions, but I just gave her my name, rank, and serial number, then pretended to be asleep. She sighed, exasperated, then came back a while later. I was eating cereal, but as soon as I saw her I closed my eyes again and feigned snoring. I didn't think my problems were anybody else's business. I knew what my problems were. I could see them plainly. My stumps were all too obvious.

■ ✦ ■

THE ONE SILVER lining to the particular type of wounds I'd received was this: despite the severe extent of my injuries, my cuts were surprisingly clean. What was gone was gone. What was still left was still there. Basically, surgeons just cleaned my cuts, folded skin over my stumps, then stapled and stitched up the loose skin. All I needed to do after that was heal. I had no skin grafts. No burns. No internal organ damage. No brain damage. No intense recurring pain after the coma had done its work.

My right arm had been blown off near the top of my biceps. The main artery in that arm had been severed when I was wounded, so the arm bled really badly at first, and then the wound scarred up on the front of my right armpit where shrapnel tore through it. That's my shortest limb, and I had a shoulder and a tiny bit of an arm left there.

My left arm was the one they'd amputated at the hospital. I had the biceps, elbow, and about half the forearm left.

My right leg was ripped off in the middle of the knee. I didn't have a kneecap or a joint anymore. The leg was amputated again surgically about two inches above the knee, so it's shorter than my left leg. I had scars around there from big holes they needed to sew up.

With my left leg, I still had the limb down to the kneecap, but that's it. That was the leg that had still been minimally attached after the blast. Medics had lashed it underneath me for the flight to Kandahar. When doctors removed my clothing on the operating table, my leg came off with my pants.

I had a scar that ran down my back about four inches. And I had a big dent in my butt cheek where a big piece of meat was gone. The dent didn't hurt, but it made my twerking look funny. I'm just joking. My twerking looks phenomenal.

It took a while for me to realize how lucky I was—in a manner of speaking. Despite the severity of what I'd been through, I could still go forward. I didn't need to wait long for my body to recover before I went to work. My new mission was to get better. My immediate task was to learn how to function in my new world. And I could do that. I genuinely could.

One visit helped enormously. A guy about my age walked into my hospital room about five days after my hallucinations stopped, and I did a double take. He was wearing shorts and a short-sleeved shirt and I could see that he was a quadruple amputee just like me, except that he had prosthetic arms and legs already in place. He was walking on his own, unaided by a wheelchair or canes or crutches or anyone holding him up. I wondered at first if I was seeing another hallucination.

"Hi," he said. "My name's Todd Nicely." He was friendly and forthright, and he asked me if I wanted anything. I said a ginger ale, and he walked over to the fridge, bent down, grasped a can of pop, opened it up, and handed to me.

I was like, "Wow. How'd you do all that?"

"It gets easier," he said.

Todd was a marine corporal who'd served a tour in Iraq before doing a second tour in Afghanistan. In March 2010 he was leading his men single file across a canal on a crude bamboo bridge in Afghanistan when he triggered an IED hidden at the far end of the bridge. Todd was only the second American quadruple amputee in the history of modern warfare to survive his injuries. I was the fourth. (Army Sergeant Brendan Marrocco was the first, Todd was the second, Marine Sergeant John Peck was the third, and then one more soldier, Navy Petty Officer 2nd Class Taylor Morris, was injured like this about two months after me, making five surviving quadruple amputees to date.)

Todd and I didn't talk long, but just seeing him function so well encouraged me immensely. He was already out of the hospital and rehab. More important, he'd moved back into his own house with his wife.

"Things will get better," he insisted. "You'll walk. You'll drive. You'll feed yourself. It'll take some time and hard work. You'll need to learn how to do everything all over again. But you will overcome this. You will."

Long after he left, his words rang in my ears. Todd's words and example proved part of the turning point for me. I came to see that what had happened, happened. I needed to quit blaming God. I needed to drop loathing myself. I needed to stop being embarrassed about the way I looked. I needed to quit thinking my injury was caused by something wrong I did. I couldn't dwell on the past. I had to set new goals so I could go forward. I knew there would be huge hard times ahead. Rigorous rehabilitation and a steep learning curve. But I needed to keep pushing forward. I had nothing else to do at Walter Reed except get better.

The weekend passed, and early Monday morning I buzzed for the doctor. When he came around about 6 a.m. I told him I was going to the gym for rehabilitation.

"No, not yet," he said.

"No yourself, Doctor," I said. "This is going to happen. I'm just lying around here in this bed. I gotta start moving."

"Call me at one p.m. when I come around again. Let's talk more then. I still don't think you're ready."

I shook my head. "Look, Doctor, I'm going to do this, and I'm going to do this today. Either you let me go to the gym or I'll sit in my bed and do stomach crunches until I hurt myself. What's it going to be?"

He smiled. "Why the big rush?"

I had pictures of Kelsey and Chloe on the wall so I could see them from my bed, and I told him to look at those pictures. "I've got a family," I said. "I've got to be there for them."

He told me to slow down and take things easy. It would probably take me three full years to get better. (At this point, I couldn't even sit up on my own.)

I told him I didn't have that kind of time. My family needed me. They were my motivation. I had to become again the husband and father I'd always been, and I had to do it double time.

He smiled again and said, "Okay, let me think about it. I'll be back at one."

I called him at 6:30. At 7:00. At 7:30. At 8:00. For four hours straight I called him every half hour.

Finally he'd had enough. He let me go.

My FIRST DAY at rehab was nothing impressive. I was only there for an hour—that was all I could take. And everybody knew this—including the doctor, who called them ahead of time and basically said, "Look, this guy won't take no for an answer. Just humor him, okay?"

Todd Nicely met me at rehab. I introduced myself to the staff in the occupational therapy wing and they had me lie on my stomach and stretch out my core and remaining limbs to the extent I could. They put a heating pad on my back. Then I fell asleep. I was finished.

But I went back the next day.

And the next. And the next. And the next. I went to rehab every day from then on. It took me about a week to learn how to sit up again. I needed to build up my muscles and figure out new ways of moving. At first, any movements I did were small. Like bobbing a balloon up in the air time and time again. Then I figured out how to roll over. Soon I did a sit-up. Then another. I went through range-of-motion drills where I moved the remains of my appendages in any direction I could. I did stretches. Soon I gained some speed. I started to feel limber again. Once I got going, I did sit-ups until I thought I'd pass out. I did leg raises without any weights, then leg raises with weights attached to the remaining parts of my limbs. I did arm pulls that were just brutal. Kelsey came with me and would often bring Chloe. My daughter loved sitting on a little mini-trampoline they had there. Sometimes I did ab crunches with Chloe sitting on my stomach for added resistance. Those were the best. Kelsey was a rock—always there for me. Chloe became my life force—her presence spurred me to drive harder. At first I was only able to work at rehabilitation for two hours a day. Then it became four hours a day. Before long it was eight hours a day, five days a week. My job of getting better turned into a regular forty-hour workweek. The only bad thing about recovery turned out to be the weekends, because the occupational and physical therapy staff weren't there and I couldn't work toward getting better.

My two favorites were occupational therapist Josef Butkus and physical therapist Kerry Quinn. Joe hooked my longer arm to sensors, and as I flexed my muscles back and forth I learned to drive a car on a video screen. If I messed up, the car crashed into a wall and exploded. "Hey, Joe," I said with a grin, after a crash. "Do I really need to blow up all over again?" We shared a laugh and he said, "Sorry, Travis, that's just how the game works." The idea was to learn how to use my remaining muscles to make new and different movements.

After four weeks in the hospital, I was fitted for a prosthetic arm for the first time. They put plaster on my arm and pulled it off to make a mold. When everything fit right, they made me a socket out of carbon fiber. Each remaining limb would shrink for about a full year after the injury, so they would need to make different sockets as the limbs grew smaller.

I learned that the advances made in prosthetic technology were breathtaking. At the end of the American Civil War, if you lost a limb you'd get a broomstick with a hook on the end. By the end of World War II, it was a plastic stick with a hook on it. Today, we have robotic arms with microprocessors in them and even the possibilities of hand transplants. The technology is only going to get more advanced from here on out, they told me. Scientists are working on being able to regrow limbs in a lab. They're already able to regrow ears, some muscles, and some bones. New technology allows for spray-on skin cells.

Putting on my arm for the first time felt pretty cool. The arm was robotic and had a hand that could open and close when I used the same muscles I'd used to drive the car in the video game. At first I could only wear the arm for about an hour before it started to hurt. But I increased the duration an hour at a time and soon was wearing the arm all the time.

I started off learning basic tasks. How to stack blocks with the hand. How to stick a clothespin onto a plastic holder. How to mash one Lego block into the next. I graduated to learning tasks such as holding a toothbrush and picking up a bottle of Gatorade. I got better and better at using the hand, at making finer and more precise movements with it. The funniest thing to me was that I could rotate the hand at the wrist in a complete 360-degree circle. The motion wasn't a wave, like a normal hand would do, but a roll. I could rotate the hand completely upside down and keep going like a car tire turning in circles at the end of an axle. I developed a favorite joke, shaking hands with an unsuspecting person while rotating my hand around at the same time. It always threw the person for a loop.

My parents and Kelsey stayed near the hospital at a place

called the Fisher House. I got my first overnight pass, and my parents and Kelsey wheeled me over to the house. We had dinner together. It was lasagna, and I was able to feed myself for the first time with my new arm. That felt really good. I stayed with Kelsey at the Fisher House that night. That was even better.

I got another prosthetic arm made up, so now I had both a right and a left. The therapists worked with me to relearn any number of daily tasks. Grabbing a fork. Making a peanut butter sandwich. Putting a Hot Pocket in a microwave and heating it up. I got to where I could pick up a plastic baby spoon and feed Chloe her lunch. Every baby is a bit messy when eating, and I could even gently brush the sides of her face with the spoon to clean off dribbles. I bought a slushie machine so we could all make slushies in occupational therapy. All the other rehabilitation patients and I were pretty excited about that. I made two or three slushies, handed them out, then said, "Okay, if all the rest of you want one, you can make them yourselves."

The prosthetics team was simply amazing—Dave, Pete, and Jaime. These guys work with amputees every day, helping to make our lives better. I went back to them again and got fitted for two legs. As a rule, I don't like having my legs touched, particularly by dudes. Dave and Pete worked on my legs while Jaime worked on my arm, and they all worked on me so much that I grew to accept it before long.

Getting a prosthetic made up is a bizarre experience. There's no parallel to it if you're not an amputee. You go to a private room and strip down to your boxers and they put Saran wrap all over you. They take cast material and slather that on and hold it on your arms and legs while it hardens. They talk to you this whole time, and with legs they've got to get into intimate areas, and they're always saying, "Oh, just relax. You're doing great." They pull off the cast material and make check sockets first out of plastic. (The socket is the piece of the prosthetic that your limb fits into.) Eventually they'll make your sockets out of carbon fiber, but carbon fiber is so expensive, they don't want to mess those up or have to make them twice. So they work with the plastic check sockets first, fitting them and seeing where they need to shape those so they fit perfectly with your body. Then they build the carbon fiber pieces and fit you to those, and after you learn to use them you're off and running.

Rehabilitation is a real team effort. The guys who make the prosthetics do their part. The physical therapists get you strong enough again to use them. The occupational therapists help you use the prosthetics and understand how they work. There's not enough credit given to all the team members who help make it possible for guys like me to live a normal life again.

And they were all cool about it too—at least the ones who worked with me were. Their attitude was that they weren't around to babysit me or take it easy on me or even to motivate me. They were here to help me get better when I wanted it. They treated me like a grown-up from moment one. The responsibility was up to me. If I rose to the challenge, then I'd go forward. If I didn't, then I'd sit around for the rest of my life watching TV. It was my choice.

Occupational therapy is pretty much designed to make a person upset. Each daily task was a challenge to relearn, and that took time and effort. Things I could do normally would take ten times as long. The staff helped break down every task into steps. Before I brushed my teeth in the morning, I needed to put on my arm, then consciously maneuver the arm to the toothbrush to pick it up, then consciously get the hand at an angle where I could grasp the toothbrush, then work to grasp the toothbrush, then grasp it firmly enough, then maneuver it to my face, then hold it still while I shook my head around to brush my teeth. Nothing felt fluid or straightforward at first, and I needed to develop patience, something I'd never had much of before.

All this time I continued working on physical rehabilitation too. I continued with the arm stretches and leg stretches and worked with weights attached to my nubs, all the while trying to get ready to take my first steps. One big question still remained: would I ever walk again?

EVEN THE ACT of positioning my body fully upright took some doing. I was sitting up by then, but overall I'd been on my back for so long, I wasn't used to being fully vertical anymore. Staff checked out my stumps first to make sure they could hold weight. They hooked me up with short, unbendable legs at first, strapped me to a specially designed table, and slowly tilted me upright.

At first the tilt was only 45 degrees. The blood rushed all around my body. It was a burning, uncomfortable feeling, I could hear my heart beating in my ears, and I broke out in a bad sweat. After I got used to that, they tilted me all the way vertical so I could stand. Before my injury, I'd been six foot three inches tall. With my short legs on, I was only five foot five. The first thing I did after standing was hug Kelsey. It felt different to look up at her instead of down, but I didn't care. This was another turning point for us. I was on my way.

On June 7, three days shy of it being two months after the blast, Riot and Fessey came to therapy to visit me. It was going to be a big day. I was planning on taking my first steps. Riot and Fessey were both healing nicely, and they'd come to watch and cheer me on.

Hospital staff tilted me up, fitted me with arm crutches, and with a harness tethered the back of me to a hook on the ceiling.

The hook moved on a track so I wouldn't fall flat on my face if I tripped—the system was called a Solo-Step. Two therapists positioned themselves on either side of me to help if needed. My dad was taking the night shift with me at the time, so he was in his room sleeping. But my mom and Kelsey were there to watch. If all went well, the therapists' goal was for me to walk one lap around the room.

I took one step and then another. My legs felt like they were in cement. I kept going. Three steps. Four. Five. My steps were shaky and jerky—it hurt so bad. I wobbled, then righted myself. My arms and legs burned, but I kept going. I told everybody how thankful I was that they were letting me do this. Kelsey was in tears. My mom too. Riot and Fessey were cheering me on. Kerry Quinn, my physical therapist, kept shouting at me, "Opposite crutch, opposite foot!" But I lifted my crutches right up off the ground and took a few more steps without any support from my arms. "Get those crutches on the ground!" she yelled. But she wasn't mad. She was as ecstatic as I was.

"Hey—I told you I was going to walk today!" I yelled back to her with a grin.

After the first lap around the room, the staff said I could stop, that was enough work for one day—but I wasn't stopping. I wobbled again and lost my balance and set my crutches down but didn't fall over. Then I put myself together again and kept going. I was covered in sweat. My limbs were trembling. I was exhausted. I broke down and cried. It wasn't sadness. It was elation. I was coming back for good.

That day, I walked three laps.

For my second day of walking, my dad got to come see me. I told him I was going to walk five laps that day. But I walked half a lap and fell over, my legs in spasms. I felt so weak and tired, that was as far as I could go. The therapist said the second day a person is often weaker because of all the work done the day before. I was tearing up. "I'm so sorry, Dad," I said. He hugged me and told me it was okay.

The following day, I was riding in my electric wheelchair heading out to eat with my family. I still wasn't very strong at the time. As I went over a doorjamb, I went too quickly, hit the bump, and tumbled out of my chair. Instead of landing on my butt (which I should have had the presence of mind to try and do), I instinctively stuck my right leg down and landed full force on my stump. That's like landing on the end of a broken bone. I yelled and writhed in pain. That was the end of my walking for a while. I was bruised and sore for days, but fortunately nothing got broken.

It took ten more days before I was permitted to walk again. I walked that day and the next. I walked and walked. Every day after that I came in to rehab to walk more and more. I kept plugging away at my next goal and my next. To learn how to walk without crutches completely. To walk up steps. To pick myself up from the ground if I fell down.

I graduated to a set of taller legs with manual locking knees. I was now six feet tall. My taller legs felt like the real thing. "Watch me go!" I yelled to everyone in the room on the first day I tried them, and gave a little shoulder shake of a dance. "I'm 82nd Airborne. I'm as tough as they come. Never give up. Never quit!"

SOME DAYS WERE harder than others. Much harder. And it wasn't because of rehabilitation.

On June 7, 2012, the very same day I walked for the first time, my platoon had gone out on patrol like usual in Afghanistan, half a world away from me. Two of our men were clearing an area outside of Maiwand when they struck an IED. Both were gravely wounded. It took several days for the news to reach me.

The area they were in was narrow—an alleyway about seven feet wide—and dangerous to stay in for long. Our medics and evacuation team needed to move quickly to get them out. When the helicopter landed, medics were still working on the two wounded men.

The mine hound searched the pathway from the wounded to the helicopter. Everything looked okay to proceed. An eight-member team placed one of our wounded, PFC Brandon Goodine, on a litter, picked him up, and started carrying him to the helicopter. Unknown to anyone, an IED was hidden near the corner of a building. The mine hound had picked up a false reading due to the proximity of the bomb to the wall. The IED exploded. The entire eight-man team carrying the litter took the brunt of the blast. The shrapnel scattered, and thirteen men total were wounded that day.

Among the seriously wounded was PFC Stefan Leroy, our radio telephone operator (RTO). He lugged around the big backpack radio with him and was Lieutenant Lewis's right-hand man. PFC Leroy was a special kid. He'd signed up to be a scout, but the lieutenant had handpicked him to be his radio operator instead because Leroy was mature for his age and intelligent. The RTO is the only private who directly reports to the lieutenant, and he went out on every mission. PFC Leroy lost both his legs.

Also among the seriously wounded was PFC Jon Harmon, one of the guys from my squad. He was our ammo bearer, who carried rounds and took rear security. He was one of my toughest soldiers and never said no to a fight. The news hit me hard. Harmon had lost both his legs too.

PFC Goodine, age twenty, was wounded in the first blast and was the soldier carried on the litter when the second IED was struck. Another special kid. As a teenager, he'd been a bit aimless and had kicked around doing this and that. Then he'd fathered a daughter when he was only seventeen. He knew he needed to do the responsible thing, so he married the girl he got pregnant and joined the military so he could provide for his wife and daughter. But Brandon's motivation was even greater than that. He saw a higher call to the military. He wanted to make a difference in the world.

The second explosion killed Brandon Goodine.

Everybody in our platoon loved Brandon. He was a quiet kid who manned his rifle and followed orders explicitly without ever complaining. He was from Georgia and loved NASCAR. He loved his wife and daughter more than anything. I couldn't believe he was gone.

When we'd started my third deployment, we had 32 men total in our platoon. Including the injuries to Fessey, Riot, and me, it meant 16 men total were now taken out. Half my platoon was gone.

With this news, my getting better took on an even deeper meaning. As a platoon, we were hurt but not destroyed. My guys were still out there going on patrols every day, still getting in firefights, still getting the job done.

I wanted them to know I was never going to quit now. I wouldn't quit for me. I wouldn't quit for them.

# 15

# TO WALK, TO RACE

RETTY QUICKLY I MOVED OUT OF MY HOSPITAL ROOM AT WAL-
ter Reed to their outpatient building number 62. They call
it the "Warrior Building." It offers kind of an apartment-
like setting, and Kelsey and Chloe were with me here. It felt good
to be out of the hospital. They started calling me "the mayor of
62" because I walked around like I owned the place. As I became
more independent, I could come and go more as I pleased.

Most of my time each day was still spent in rehabilitation.
But I started to tackle a few other activities too. One day not long
after I got my legs, a doctor whispered to me, "A patient needs to
talk to you on the fourth floor. I can't tell you who it is because of
confidentiality issues. But if you just go up there, I'm sure you'll
find him." He gave me a knowing look, like he'd already talked to
someone on that floor about what he was asking me to do.

Instinctively, I got what he was saying. Enthusiasm is conta-
gious. Not everybody has the will to go forward, and sometimes

a soldier will need a bit of a push. Like back when it came to my jumpmaster duties. A soldier might be accomplished in every area, but if it's his first jump out of a plane, he might need a bit of a kick to help him get out the door. I went to the fourth floor, smiled at a nurse who recognized me, and asked, "You know anybody here I might want to talk to?"

She nodded and motioned to a room two doors down on the left. I walked straight in, took one look at the soldier in the bed, introduced myself as Staff Sergeant Travis Mills of the 82nd Airborne Division, and said, "You can do this." We talked for a bit, and it was amazing to see a soldier respond to a firm, encouraging stance, same as if he was back in basic training. He just needed to be told he could go forward. He needed a kick out of the door of the plane.

After that, doctors called on me regularly to do the same thing. Or I'd just take it upon myself. I'd go walk up and down the hallways of the hospital and into people's rooms, introduce myself, and see if I could encourage any of the other wounded veterans. All branches of the military were represented at Walter Reed, and we became a real brotherhood.

Kelsey and Chloe would often come with me as I made my rounds from room to room, and it's amazing what good things can happen when somebody knows you're cheering for him. Some of these guys didn't have any family and friends who'd come and visit. Man, I'm not sure how a guy can make it without a support system like that. When I was at my worst, Kelsey would stay with me eighteen to twenty hours a day. She was amazing. Another family member would take the night shift with me, so I'd never be alone. We had a strong network of family and friends we leaned on. That was so important.

Sometimes when I made my rounds, I took my wheelchair because it was easier to roll longer distances than it was to walk. I'd wheel myself into a room and just tell the guy there that things were going to get better. Sometimes if a guy was new to the hospital, I'd bring other wounded veterans with me too. We formed a sort of welcoming committee. At one point we had nine guys all going around on visiting duties, trying to offer any encouragement we could.

When Kelsey and I were staying at 62, I convinced Kelsey to go back to Texas for a few days to see her parents. This foray into independence was important for me. Her mom had been really great and had stayed with us for several months before going home. My parents too. My dad was retired, so he was able to stay a bit longer. My mom was still working, so she took a leave of absence for about three months and stayed at the hospital until I could walk again, then she went home. Kelsey's dad, Craig Buck, had quit his job so he could help out with me, and we'd become great friends in the process. But they were gone now and it was just Kelsey and me. Kelsey didn't want to leave me all alone at first. I pointed out to her that I'd still have all the hospital staff nearby, so it wasn't like I was actually going to be all alone. But this was an important step of my rehabilitation. We talked about it for several days, and Kelsey was still hesitant, but I insisted.

Right before she left, I went outside the apartment to go get some Subway sandwiches for dinner. I was in a motorized wheelchair rolling along on the sidewalk near Walter Reed, and a text came in from a buddy. I glanced down at my phone, which was on the seat between my legs. Just then the path curved a bit, and I was going too fast. One of the wheels slipped off the sidewalk, and, boom, I flipped over. (Note to self: Don't text and drive.)

Lying on my back in the bark dust with my heavy motorized chair flipped over on one side, I thought, *This isn't good. This definitely isn't good.* But I wasn't going to call for help after making such a big deal to Kelsey about how independent I was. Figuring out how to fix this was something I needed to do by myself.

Fortunately just then a man walked by, stopped, and asked if I needed help. He righted the chair for me and helped me back up into the chair. I'd landed in a bunch of woodchips and had a bunch of those stuck to the back of my shirt, but I told him to not bother about brushing those off. I thanked him then proceeded the rest of the way to Subway, ordered the sandwiches, paid for them, and headed back to the apartment with the Subway bag.

When I rolled through the doorway of our quarters at 62, Kelsey took one look at all the woodchips stuck to me and her eyes sprang open wide. She asked what happened. I came clean and told her the story. She really didn't want to let me stay alone then. But I said, "Kelsey, look, I'm okay. I got back up." She eventually conceded and went to Texas. While she was away, I kept going to physical therapy each day. I even went to an Orioles ballgame with some friends. Developing the confidence to be left alone and knowing I could still function okay was a big deal to me. I didn't just want to sit around. I wanted to go out and handle things by myself.

It's amazing what you can accomplish once you make that all-important decision to go forward. I don't mean to say that determination is everything when it comes to healing from an injury. But I'd say that determination is vastly underrated. Here's how it factored in for me: I knew I could choose to go the other direction if I wanted to. I could choose to quit. If I'd wanted, people would have spoon-fed me for the rest of my life. I could have stared at the ceiling for the next sixty years and spent the rest of my life angry, frustrated, grieving, and dismayed. I was very aware I had that free choice.

party I was in my wheelchair with my short legs on so I could stand for short bursts if I needed to, and I looked a bit out of place in pictures I've seen since then—this big guy on short legs. But what was important was that I was there for my daughter's birthday. I was happy to be alive and to be in the pictures and to celebrate this important milestone with my family. I didn't take that simple truth for granted.

I was there.

I WANTED TO do something big. I wanted to do something beyond myself, something to tell myself that the worst was behind me, something that might even inspire others. Right after Chloe's first birthday celebration, I signed up to run a 5K race in New York City. They call it the Tunnel to Towers 5K, and it's held in honor of Stephen Siller, a heroic firefighter commemorated after 9/11.

On September 11, 2001, Stephen Siller was in Brooklyn when the first plane hit the first of the Twin Towers. He'd just finished the night shift at the Brooklyn firehouse and was heading home to Staten Island when he heard the news and called his wife to tell her he'd be home late. He tried to drive over to the city to help, but he couldn't get through the Brooklyn–Battery Tunnel because the traffic was already gridlocked. So he strapped his sixty pounds of firefighter gear to his back and ran from the tunnel to the Towers. It was the last run of his life. He was believed to be somewhere on the 80th floor of the South Tower when it fell. He was thirty-four.

About 20,000 people were set to run the commemorative race in 2012. I was going to walk, not run, but I knew that even walking would pose a challenge. I hadn't been on my legs very long. Kelsey came with me, always my amazing support person.

Or I could deliberately choose to go forward. I could choose to heal.

Somewhere along the process, I decided not to be known as a "wounded warrior." I don't mean disrespect to anybody who goes by this title, and I still use it from time to time because it's convenient shorthand for describing veterans who've been through combat-related injuries. But if you still think of yourself as "wounded," then you're still focusing on your injury. I wasn't going to do that. I was healed. I had my scars, but I was the same "me" as I'd always been. I'd be a man with scars who chose to live life to the fullest and best.

WHAT WAS LEFT of my unit came home from deployment in August, and like I'd promised, I traveled to Fort Bragg to be there when they returned. It was a quick trip all in all, a thirty-six-hour turnaround before heading back to the hospital. But it was important for me to be able to do this. On the way to the base in the van, Kelsey and I were running late. When we got to the base, I showed the guard my ID, but I'd grown a beard by then and looked different from my picture. The guard said he was going to search us, and I adopted my best sergeant voice and said sternly: "Look—my guys are coming home in half an hour and I told them I'd be at Green Ramp to meet them. I was wounded in Afghanistan, and you're going to get out of my way."

The guard took a closer look at me, saluted, and without another word let us through.

We drove around the base, parked, and found the right hangar. This all took some doing and we were nearly late, but when the plane touched down, I was waiting on Green Ramp where I'd promised I'd be. I had a fresh uniform on and was standing on my tall legs. It had been a long walk from the parking area to the ramp, and my legs were hurting something fierce, but I didn't care. When my guys started walking off that plane I stood straight and proud and saluted them the best I could. Saluting was hard, because my right arm is so short. But I brought my head down to my hook and made the gesture of honor.

My first sergeant, Michael Parrish, had returned earlier on a different plane, and I spotted him in the hangar along with a couple of my buddies. As soon as I saw him, I started tearing up. He walked straight over to me, and I said, "I'm so sorry. I let you down."

He gave me a hug and said, "Sergeant Mills, you're one of the best combat squad leaders I've ever seen. You never let me down."

Lieutenant Lewis was there. It was so good to see him again. He gave me a big hug, and I said, "Welcome home." The remaining guys in my squad deplaned and we all said hello and gave each other hugs. Cobia Farr, the assistant gunner. Armando Plascencia, our marksman. Eric Hunter, the gunner. James Neff, my other team's gunner. We didn't have a lot of time, because some four hundred people were being ushered off the plane quickly and into the holding area. When I saw Daniel Bateson, our medic, I said, "Hey, there's the guy who saved my life." We gave each other a quick hug, looked each other in the eye, and he moved on with a grin.

A kid from a different battalion got off the plane and he tried to hug me. I didn't know him, but I guess he thought everybody else was hugging me, so he should too. It was an awkward moment and I said, "Hey, man, if you don't know me, then you don't need to hug me." He looked startled for a minute then grinned. It made a funny story to tell afterward.

■ ■ ■

I HEADED BACK to the hospital at Walter Reed. Even though I'd come so far in my rehabilitation, I still had a long way to go. Doctors and therapists were saying I'd need to spend about another year in and out of rehabilitation. But one day while at the outpatient building at the hospital, I took my first bite of a Johnsonville jalapeño-and-cheddar bratwurst and suddenly had the strongest desire to be back home again—and this time for longer than thirty-six hours. I remembered barbecuing bratwursts in my backyard, and the feeling of wanting to be at home—my own home—nearly overwhelmed me. That's what I'd done so many evenings before my third deployment. After work I'd come home, we'd have a good barbecue dinner, and I'd play fetch with my dog in my backyard until he tired out. That's all I wanted again: I wanted to be with my family and my dog and have a barbecue.

We decided to do it. We flew back to Fayetteville, North Carolina, and spent about four days in our own house again. We hadn't rented it out while I was on deployment and the house was just sitting all that time. Even the cable TV was still turned on. It felt so good to be back in a place that was familiar to both of us. Our house wasn't equipped the same way as the apartments at Walter Reed were, and it was harder for me to get around and use our own bathroom and shower and stuff, but we managed.

While in Fayetteville, we celebrated Chloe's first birthday, a little bit early. A bunch of families from the neighborhood came over to our house, and sure enough we had that cookout with hamburgers and hot dogs and bratwursts and lemonade and soda. I called a company and had a bounce house set up in our backyard. A bunch of little kids all ran around and jumped like mad in the house. We had a smaller birthday cake made up just for Chloe, and when her cake was placed in front of her she hesitated, took one cautious lick, then plunged her face right in. During the

When the race began, I felt swept along by a surge of adrenaline. People jostled all around me. I limped along about a quarter mile or so at a good clip and pretty soon began to hurt. My stumps chafed inside my prosthetics, but there was no way I was going to quit. The course went underneath the water and uphill out of the tunnel. When I walked out of the tunnel, I had to squint into the bright sunlight that hit my face. Along the route, the streets were lined with banners that commemorated lost firefighters and lost soldiers. People held signs up encouraging us along. Firefighters were there wearing their full gear in honor of the event. On I pushed. My right leg began to bleed. The inner thigh chafed so raw that it dripped blood into my liners. But I kept going. I passed the one-mile marker, then the two-mile marker. Only one more mile to go. Both my legs were burning. My back hurt. I told myself I was going to do it. I pushed through and reached the final marker. Everybody cheered. The race wasn't comfortable or fun, but I was proud to have crossed that finish line.

After the race, we headed over to the Freedom Tower to attend a memorial event being held there. The former mayor of New York, Rudy Giuliani, spoke, and Gary Sinise, the actor who'd played a disabled veteran in the movie *Forrest Gump*, said some good words. I'd met him once very quickly at an earlier event where he'd asked me to say the Pledge of Allegiance. He'd asked me to come up on stage at this event too. I did fine getting up onto the stage, but on my way over to where I was supposed to sit I stubbed my foot on an extension cord and toppled over. They were introducing me at the time, and I fell in front of 20,000 people. The mayor's bodyguard picked me up and tried to right me, but he didn't understand that my knees don't lock in place, so I kept falling down and for a few tense moments it sort of looked like he was giving me the Heimlich. Kelsey ran up, locked my knees for me, and got things squared away. I'd gone beyond being embarrassed when things like that happened. I'd found that if I laughed it off, then other people relaxed. The program finished, and attention quickly turned to the Lt. Dan Band with Mr. Sinise on electric bass, which took the stage and cranked up the volume. It was a good day, and I was glad I did both the race and the event, but, boy, was I exhausted at the end.

Kelsey and I went back to our apartment at the hospital and I did some more rehabilitation. Not long after, I traveled back to Vassar, Michigan, to attend the homecoming game of my high school. I outfitted Kelsey and Chloe with *Vassar Vulcan* T-shirts so they'd fit in for the festivities. The school and town held a parade and asked me to be in it. Thousands of people showed up—they'd been following my story in the newspaper for some time now. I rode in the back of a Jeep with two good friends from town. The parade route was lined with well-wishers, and many of them held signs that said, "Welcome home, Travis." They were smiling and waving and yelling out encouragement to me. Seven or eight news affiliates interviewed me afterward and it was good to feel part of the community again. I knew they'd always been supporting me.

After the parade, the school held a pep rally and bonfire. At the request of Coach Leveille, I spoke to the crowd and the football players before the game and got them pumped up. Both teams played hard, and Vassar won the game, I'm happy to report. I felt truly blessed to be back in my hometown in a role like that. I was thankful for their cheers and signs and good wishes. Thankful they always had my back and respected my service. Grateful that they'd prayed for me and rooted for me and hadn't given up on me. Honored to be chosen again to speak to the football team.

We spent some time with my parents, then headed back to the apartment at the hospital. At the end of October, I was able to take Chloe trick-or-treating. Kelsey dressed her up really cute as

Minnie Mouse, and we went to about three houses and that was it. Chloe had a blast, even for that short of a time, and it felt good to me to be able to do some of these basic things with my daughter. Since I'd been back, she'd learned how to crawl and walk, and I'd learned how to walk again right along with her. It's hard to fully describe that feeling of walking through a neighborhood with my daughter on Halloween—how precious it felt—this was gold. With my prosthetic, I was able to hold her hand and even feel pressure on my prosthetic when she squeezed it. The evening was another marker of us simply being together as a family again, of me still being alive and of me going forward. Regardless of my injury, I was still going to be there for my wife and my daughter.

Later that evening, I renewed a silent vow to always be there for my family. I wanted to choose activities and hobbies that would bring us together and strengthen us all. Seeing Chloe grow up was a privilege that I'd just about lost, but now it was being handed back to me. Someday, I would teach my daughter how to ride a bike. I didn't know how I would do that, but it would happen. And if she wanted to take ballet lessons someday, I'd find a way of doing pirouettes with her. And if she wanted to play softball, I'd get a pitching machine set up in my backyard so I could teach her how to bat and bunt. One day far into the future, when Chloe gets married, I'll walk her down the aisle.

RIGHT AFTER HALLOWEEN, about seven months after the blast, I decided to stop taking all of my painkillers completely. I was sitting there in the apartment one morning and it was sort of an instant decision. I had still been taking a whole slew of medications up to that time—oxycodone, Lyrica, prescription-strength ibuprofen, a stool softener, and a bunch of other stuff. But I didn't like how it all made me feel, so I quit cold turkey. For the next four or five days, I experienced some bad pain, but after that the pain subsided. That was it. I never took any more painkillers after that.

Therapy continued. It was amazing all the things I needed to learn how to do again. My legs eventually adjusted to my sockets, the swelling went down, and I could wear the prosthetics for almost an entire day, although it still felt good to take them off every now and then and use my wheelchair.

Some of the hardest tasks involved using fine motor skills. You never think about how nimble and sensitive your fingertips are until you lose the use of them. My dad and I went out to get coffee once, and I picked up the coffee and closed too hard on the cup, spilled it, and burned myself. All part of the learning curve.

Picking up a credit card from the smooth surface of a table was one of the hardest things for me to learn. A credit card is so slim, and the tips of my prosthetic fingers are so wide, that it's nearly impossible to do. Staff helped me break the task down into steps. I learned to carefully slide the card to the edge of the table first and inch it over so the card overlapped air just a bit. Then I could clamp around the card from both the top and the bottom and pick it up, no problem.

Doing up the zipper on my pants was another basic yet hard task to learn. A zipper is so small that it is hard to grasp with the prosthetic. We solved the problem by tying a small length of cord to each and every one of my zippers. The cord made the zipper easier to grasp. Problem solved.

Eventually I learned how to do pretty much everything a man with two arms and legs could do. I practiced going to stores and getting a cup of coffee. I learned how to use a cell phone and to text using a stylus. I could swim using specially designed prosthetic arms with paddles where the hands would be. I figured out how to put on a shirt. How to plug my prosthetic arm into an electric socket when I was done with it for the night so it could get recharged. I could even shave my own face, although it's easier if someone did that for me. I even learned how to light a paper match—not even a wooden match, but a smaller, thinner paper one. I figured it's a function I'd want to learn so I could take my family camping someday. About the only thing I never figured out was how to put a ponytail in Chloe's hair. But, hey—I don't know a ton of dads who are good at this sort of thing anyway, even if they have two regular hands.

Standing up from a seated position proved one of the most physically difficult things to relearn how to do—and it continues to be physically difficult today. Think of all the intricate motions required to stand up from a chair. You've got to lean forward slightly, then push off with your arms while simultaneously pushing up with the muscles of both your quads and calves working in tandem. I didn't have any calf muscles anymore, and since my nub was so high on my right arm, there was almost nothing to work with there, which meant the bulk of pushing up my body's weight fell to my left arm. Therapists worked with me a long time on this. I learned to sort of throw my hips forward, then push up hard with my longer arm. I succeeded, but it continues to be one of the more difficult tasks I do.

On a mental plane, I didn't experience anything that might resemble post-traumatic stress disorder, but every once in a while I had dreams about the war and of being wounded. One night I dreamt I was on a mission with my platoon. The firefights were heavy and I was running around with my machine gun, taking care of business like I always did. When I woke up, I completely forgot I didn't have arms and legs. For a moment it felt like I could leap out of bed and go attack the day, same as I'd always done. Then I remembered my new reality. I lay there for one dark moment feeling sorry for myself, then mentally clapped my hands together as if to say "Enough!," got up, put my prosthetics on, and got on with my day.

We discovered that the bone on the end of my right arm had started to grow again. Bones that have been cut off can do that, we learned. It began to get pointy on the end and was causing a lot of nerve pain and bruising. I got frustrated. They offered to do another surgery to shave the bone down, but I didn't want to have another surgery. A buddy of mine, Tyler Southern, had been wounded and had experienced a similar problem. He told me he'd just beat his arm against a hard counter until the pain went away. It sounded horrific, but the principle was surprisingly sound. The process of repeated hammering against the end of the bone would chip the point away and pound out the end of the nerves. So I tried it. I beat the end of my stump against a counter until the bone chipped and the end went numb. Afterward it was sore and bruised, and the doctors were like, "You did what?!" But eventually the pain went away altogether, and I didn't need another surgery. That was a huge relief. All I wanted to do was continue moving forward.

Here's how Kelsey describes what it was like to go through the process of therapy with me:

*People call my husband a hero, and I know he's that, but he doesn't like to be called a hero. He's just doing what's needed.*

*I've always been independent, quiet, strong, an introvert. I've never been outgoing. When we were first married, Travis handled everything. But his being wounded has brought me out of my shell. There were many times, particularly right after the injury, where I had no choice. I needed to make phone calls.*

*I needed to make medical decisions. I became not only Travis's wife, but his nurse and caretaker too. That was hard, but I just thought, "Well, if he's doing all he's doing to get better, then I can certainly do this."*

*How did I help him? Often, I just listened and let him vent. Being wounded in that capacity is obviously a hard thing to deal with, and it's natural to feel so many things so strongly. He needed to work through a lot of emotions. I just listened.*

*Overall, I was proud of him. When he walked for the first time, I would show people videos of it later. I could feel so much joy from him. Since the day he started walking, he hasn't stopped. He's a beast. Even if he's feeling sore or tired, he'll put on his legs and walk around. He's the first at the gym, and the last to leave every day. His therapists loved him, because he was committed to putting in those long hours.*

*They say that something like 90 percent of marriages that go through a tragedy don't make it. But with us, it's brought us closer. It's made us stronger. We don't fight about stupid things that normal people get divorced over. Who takes the trash out? Who cares? We never fight about petty things anymore. We don't take life for granted anymore. We've started a new life now, and we're all together, and that's all that matters.*

*It's true, we lost a life that we thought we'd live. There's been heartache and sad days, but things could have been much worse. I could have lost Travis. Sometimes people will imply that losing him would have been easier for me. But that's a lie. There's no way I'd want to lose my husband.*

*When we got married, I said I'd marry him for better or worse, and I meant that. Sometimes, after the injury, Travis would say to me that I didn't need to stay with him, and I'd be like, "I'm not going to leave you, so shut up. I didn't marry you for your limbs. I married you for who you are, and you're still the same person."*

*That's the truth. When I look at him now, I don't see his arms and legs gone. I see the same man I married. And I love him for it. I'll love him always.*

# 16

# OUR NEW HOME

RIVING WAS IMPORTANT TO ME, AND WHEN I WAS STILL AT Walter Reed, they taught me how to drive again. A driving specialist, Major Tammy Phipps, helped me learn. The hospital had a handicapped-equipped van, and we figured out how I could grab the steering wheel okay with my new arms and how the gas and brakes worked when pushed by my prosthetics. Then it was off to the races. Tammy had a brake on her side of the vehicle too. When I first took the wheel, I felt as nervous as when I was sixteen and taking my first driver's test. We drove around the campus of Walter Reed at first. Then I graduated to slow speeds on city streets around the campus. Then faster roads. Then the expressway.

A foundation called Help Our Military Heroes bought me a wheelchair conversion van, and we took it over to Ride Away, another great company, which specializes in providing adaptive driving equipment. Their technicians sat down with me and figured out the best configuration to help me drive. A small lever was positioned near my short right arm: if I pulled the lever back, it throttled the car forward, and if I pushed the lever forward, it acted as the brake. On the steering wheel, they affixed a tri-pin clamp that gave me a really firm grip for my left prosthetic hand to steer with. On the door, a button was set up that my left thigh could hit. The button controlled the turn signals, horn, dimmer switch, windshield wipers, windows, and cruise control.

After I got the van, I took Kelsey out for a drive first. Kelsey was a bit nervous about me driving with Chloe aboard, so just the two of us went out and Kelsey was reassured. She had forgotten how great it was to be the passenger sometimes. I took Chloe out the next day and over to a friend's house. It felt so good for me to be able to drive my family around again. I mean—driving felt huge to me. I'd gone from basically just lying there in a hospital bed to being able to hop into my wheelchair to walking to being able to hop in my van and drive wherever I wanted. My dad jokes that I'm a better driver today than I was before my injury. He can even take a nap in the car with me driving now, but he never could do that before I was wounded.

In the winter, I went with hospital staff to Breckenridge, Colorado, and tried skiing. The first few times down the slopes I used a monoski, where you sit in a bucket and have support staff helping you along. It was fun, but if I fell over I couldn't pick myself back up. In the afternoon, I tried snowboarding while using my short legs. That was even more fun. I could clip in and out of the bindings by myself, and I got to the point where I didn't need to hold the hands of the instructors anymore. I got more and more proficient with snowboarding, and by the end of the day I was off the bunny hill and going down regular slopes. It felt pretty awesome to be able to do that. Kelsey had grown up skiing, so this was a sport we could all enjoy as a family again.

In the summer, we returned to Colorado and I went downhill bike riding. The particular bike I used was specially adapted with four wheels. To use the brakes you squeezed a lever between your thighs. I had both my right and left arms on and they were duct taped to the handlebars so I wouldn't lose my grip over the rough terrain, and I was strapped into the seat with a helmet on my head. We went up about 9,000 feet on this mountain, then flew down the side of the steep terrain. It was an incredible feeling to have so much freedom. Nobody needed to steer the bike for me. I roared down a narrow dirt trail and swerved around stumps and fallen trees. It was a full-on adrenaline blast. Before the day's end, I'd gone up and down that mountain five times.

On that same trip, I tried kayaking and canoeing. Kelsey loves kayaking. With my arms, I could hook on to a paddle and even bail out of the boat if needed.

Back at home I tried playing wheelchair rugby. It was fun, but my right arm wasn't long enough to help me move by myself, and there were no prosthetics allowed in the game. So unless the rules were changed, I decided that was a sport I wouldn't pursue.

I got to where I could actually run in my prosthetics. I was never much of a long-distance runner before being wounded, but going to a park and flying along a path on my new legs felt pretty awesome. Someday if Kelsey and Chloe want to run 5Ks, I'll be able to do that with them.

Due to all the medication I took, my hair started thinning, but eventually it grew back. That's about the only side effect I experienced from taking all those drugs. Another side effect of the injury (although not drug related) was that my body continually felt hot. Since I don't have any limbs anymore, my blood doesn't circulate the same distance in my body as before. Circulation helps a person lose body heat, so I find myself always warm, even on snowy winter days. Since the injury, pretty much all I ever wear are shorts and a T-shirt, even in winter. Plus, my legs are always capped due to the prosthetics, and they don't breathe very well through the liners. So my legs are always hot. At least that's what the ladies say.

ON PATRIOTS' DAY, April 15, 2013, we heard the horrific news that two bombs had gone off toward the end of the Boston Marathon. Three people were killed and some two hundred and fifty were wounded. More than two dozen people had limbs amputated, either by the blast or afterward in surgery.

Two weeks after the attack, I got a call from the general in charge of wounded troops. He was assembling a team of four wounded warriors to go to Boston to the Spaulding Rehabilitation Hospital and meet with some of the victims. So we did that. At first the staff and administrators seemed a bit reluctant to let us see the patients, like maybe they didn't agree it was a good idea. They took us on a tour of the hospital, but I was like, "So what? I already know what a hospital is like. I'm here to talk to people."

After they hemmed and hawed for a while, another guy on the team and I decided to take matters into our own hands. We slipped away from our handlers and took an elevator to the fourth floor. We found a nurses' station and said, "Hey, we're here from the army to talk to the bombing victims. We think it's going to be beneficial for them."

A nurse nodded and shrugged, and before you knew it, we were going from room to room and talking with everybody we met. Face after face went from discouraged to encouraged. We answered a lot of questions about how to do tasks without limbs. And person after person was like, "Wow, it can be done." It was a really good day. We came back the next day and met with one of the victims, who told us that after we'd left, he'd gone to rehab and worked out harder than he'd ever done before. That was our big message: *It does get better. You can overcome this challenge.*

We attended some therapy sessions with the patients. There were no photographers or publicity teams around. It was just us hanging out. A couple of patients were having a hard time that day in therapy, and I introduced them to an innovative tool that has helped me over many a rough patch. It's called the Ten Second Dance Break, and basically you just dance like a big goofball for ten seconds and then go back to work. Hey—it helps.

IN THE FALL of 2013, I was still at Walter Reed, and Kelsey and I decided to rent out our house in Fayetteville. The longer we were away from North Carolina, the less we figured we'd end up there permanently, particularly since I was just about out of the military for good. Kelsey and Chloe flew down by themselves first to pack the house up along with Kelsey's dad. A couple days later I drove my van down by myself. It's a six-and-a-half-hour drive from Walter Reed to Fayetteville, and this was the first road trip I'd taken by myself since the accident. That felt like a milestone right there. I drove by myself. I got gas by myself. I stopped at rest stops and fast-food restaurants by myself. The trip provided one of the last bits of emotional healing I needed.

I spent a few days in Fayetteville, then it was time to go back to Walter Reed. Kelsey and Chloe joined me for the trip home, and that was another milestone—them joining me in the van. I remember so distinctly pulling the van onto the freeway and looking in the rearview mirror. Chloe was having fun, watching a Disney movie on a DVD player in the back of the van. Kelsey was sitting in the passenger's seat next to me, calmly reading a book on her Kindle. I was driving my family on this road trip, just like

I'd been able to do before I was blown up. I didn't say anything out loud, but my pulse quickened and I felt a lightness in my chest at the thought of me being able to drive my family someplace like that again. Sheer excitement—that was the feeling. I could take my family on road trips again! You have to realize how huge that was.

At the end of November 2013, I officially retired from the military. We were back at the apartment at Walter Reed then, and first I went door to door in the hospital and invited all the friends I'd made to come to a celebration ceremony they were holding for me in the cafeteria. I was nervous at first that no one would come, but about two hundred people showed up. My mom and dad flew in to surprise me, and also my buddy Adam from high school days.

I'd been in the military for seven years and eight months total. And by then I'd been in the hospital for nineteen months total. I got up in front of everyone and said how I was going to miss the army and how thankful I was to be alive still. Then I blubbered like a baby, and everybody applauded and wished me well.

My retirement from the military meant I was done with therapy. I'd figured out how to do pretty much everything I needed to do. Walter Reed truly was an impactful place for me. The military has a brotherhood, but wounded veterans experience a brotherhood that's even deeper. You understand what other guys are going through. You can recover and go forward together. I don't think I'd be the same person I am today without Walter Reed and the staff there. I'd probably be sitting at home, miserable. Instead I'm leading my family, living life with every ounce of energy I can muster.

When we moved out of Walter Reed for good, we went to Texas for a while and lived with my in-laws. Our house in Fayetteville was rented by then, and it didn't make any sense for us

to move back if we weren't in the military anymore. Josh and
Deanna Buck were living in Oklahoma now, so none of our family were in Fayetteville, and it was important for us to live near
family. Even though I could do almost everything by myself, we'd
found it was still good to have help nearby. We lived with my
in-laws from November 2013 to April 2014, then when the Texas
heat got too much for me we went to Michigan for a while where
it was cooler, and lived with my parents. Residents of my hometown and the surrounding communities had held fundraisers
and helped my mom and dad modify their house with ramps and
decks and an ADA-compliant bathroom, so that was very helpful
anytime I came to visit.

We were contacted by Gary Sinise and staff members from
his foundation: they wanted to construct Kelsey and me a specially built adaptive home to use as our permanent residence.
This was incredible news. They were working in conjunction
with the Stephen Siller Tunnel to Towers Foundation, and the
representatives basically said to pick anywhere in the country that
we wanted to live, and they'd build us a house for free. The home
would be equipped with handicapped-accessible bathrooms and
all the newest technology available to help make life as smooth
as possible.

Kelsey and I felt overwhelmed and incredibly grateful. We
knew that having a home like this would help us enormously with
stability and with many challenges over the years to come. We
talked briefly about moving to Texas for the long term, but summers in Texas would be too hot for me to take. We talked long
and hard about moving back to Michigan for good, which got
my vote. But in the end we decided on Maine. Kelsey's parents
had moved in the meantime to Maine from Texas, and she had
many relatives in the area, so we were going to have a lot of support. That was fine by me. Michigan will always be in my heart,

but Maine was good too, and if Kelsey wanted to go to Maine, then Maine it was. My wife had been through the wringer for me, and I'd do anything for her. Right after I'd first come back to the States from Afghanistan, Josh had given Kelsey my wedding ring, and she'd given it back to me when I was conscious. I've worn it proudly on a cord around my neck ever since.

Foundation staff gave us a couple of guidelines for the house, and we sat down with an architect. I'd met Gary Sinise a couple of times, and I'd said the Pledge of Allegiance for him at that event once. Then a few months later at another event I got in line to meet him afterward, but he came up specifically to see me and say hello. He knew all these things about me; nobody was whispering in his ear. He struck me as a genuinely nice guy who wanted to use his fame and platform to help veterans.

The foundation built us an incredible two-story house. The shower and bathroom were set up perfectly for me to use, and an elevator would prove a big help. (Going up and down stairs is still one of the hardest things for me to do.) A ton of companies, both local and national, donated appliances, flooring, paint, you name it. The Carrington Charitable Foundation took care of the funding. If I had a thousand years to live, I couldn't express how grateful we are to all the people who helped. There are so many foundations set up these days in America to help support the troops. There are so many people who want to give back and help. I'm talking everything from multinational corporations who give big donations down to a retiree we met who makes decorative wooden canes for wounded warriors. There are a lot of good people in this world.

In October 2014, we were set to move in. They held a big ceremony for us. We drove up the long gravel driveway toward our new house for the first time, and covering the whole front of it was an enormous American flag so we couldn't see the house at first. Paul LePage, the governor of Maine, attended the ceremony along with his wife, Ann. When the time came for me to speak, I looked across the crowd and thanked all the tradesmen who'd helped build the house, plus everyone else who'd contributed. It was an emotional moment for me, and I spoke about the journey Kelsey and I had been on so far. This house was our own little piece of heaven. When all the speeches were over, Chloe led us all in chanting, "Move that flag!" The flag was moved, and behind it stood our new home.

It was beautiful, absolutely beautiful.

The house sits on twenty acres. A great organization called Truckin 4 Troops donated to me what's called an Action Track-chair, so I have two motorized wheelchairs, and the Action Track has special rubber tracks so I can navigate over rugged terrain outdoors. With the chair, Kelsey and Chloe and I can take walks around the trails on the property. There's space for everybody on the property, and Buddy the dog can run around to his heart's content. Each room is set up to be easily navigated by me no matter if I'm in my chair or on my prosthetics. The house was an incredible gift, a lifetime home for us, one more opportunity to receive and appreciate the incredible generosity of the people of America in support of the troops.

Not long after we moved in, we renovated an outbuilding on the property and made another living quarters with a garage underneath. When it comes to navigating day-to-day living with the prosthetics, I found I could do almost everything by myself, but it was still very helpful to have someone help me in the mornings and evenings getting up and getting ready for bed. So Kelsey's parents moved onto the property with us, and Kelsey's father became my right-hand man. I'd started doing a lot of public speaking by then too, and Craig started traveling with me to help navigate airports and hotels and rental cars and stuff.

I surprised myself when I found I really enjoyed public speaking. I'd begun to do some while I was back at Walter Reed, and the talks had turned out pretty well. After that, requests started pouring in from everywhere. Foundations. Universities. Corporations. Churches. Libraries. You name it. I had a PowerPoint presentation professionally worked up with pictures and all. In the presentation, I talked about my story and my family, about being in the military and the injury, and about what it takes to come back from that.

My main message is one that many people can relate to. Hard times come to everybody. When hard times happen, we have a choice to make. We can become discouraged and bitter, or we can choose to never quit. When life gets hard, the key is just to keep pushing forward. Instead of saying, "It could be worse," the key is to say, "It's going to get better." Then work with all your might toward that goal.

Once I was doing a radio promo spot, and the DJs and I were all riffing on each other in the studio while on air, and the main DJ asked me in fun, "I hear you're doing a lot of public speaking lately. What do you have to speak about anyway, dude?!"

"That's just the thing," I said. "Nothing really. All I do is walk into a room full of people and say, 'Hey, everybody, snap your fingers and wiggle your toes.' They snap and wiggle, and I say, 'Okay, your life's not so bad.' Then I drop the mic and walk away."

Everybody howled.

# 17

# NEVER GIVE UP.
# NEVER QUIT.

N ORGANIZER FOR A VETERANS MEMORIAL CALLED FREEDOM
Fest approached me and asked if I'd go skydiving to help
raise money for a veterans center and museum. Skydiving
was right up my alley. Altogether, I'd made some fifty jumps before being wounded. But just as a joke, I told him I'd only do the
event if Maine's first lady, Ann LePage, would make the jump
with me. I'd known her for some time, and we'd become good
friends. I would have done the jump anyway, but this made things
more interesting.

Shortly after that, to my surprise, I got a call saying that Mrs.
LePage was up for the jump. A few weeks later she and I found
ourselves falling from the sky. It was a bright sunny day, and we
both jumped tandem, separately, with instructors at our backs. It
felt pretty crazy to be jumping out of a perfectly good airplane
when I didn't have any arms or legs. But it felt good too, really
good, like I was back to my old self. Truly back for good.

■ ■ ■

I'D SO MUCH enjoyed the winter and summer sports I'd partici-
pated in when I went to Colorado that I started thinking of ways
to help other wounded veterans do the same. Maine is a beautiful state with four distinct seasons, so I established a nonprofit
organization called the Travis Mills Foundation, raised some
money, and secured the use of a campground to hold a retreat for
wounded warriors.

We brought five families out to the area the first year and
enjoyed tubing behind a powerboat, golfing, kayaking, and various other sports. We ate great lobster dinners together and talked
about how to succeed in various ways despite having disabilities.
When you're an amputee, you don't normally see other amputees
in daily life. But at the camp we had an opportunity to hang out
with other people with similar disabilities. Afterward, everybody
said the camp was really encouraging, so we held a camp the next
year too, and six families came to that. That camp was also a success, so Kelsey and I started dreaming of purchasing a property
for the foundation so we could hold regular events in both summer and winter.

Back when we were living with my in-laws in Texas, we'd met
a young attorney and his wife, Reece and Katie Norris, and they
quickly became two of our closest friends. Reece was instrumen-
tal in doing all the legal paperwork for my foundation. Katie ran
her own nonprofit organization called Fotolanthropy, where she
created documentaries about people who had overcome adversity.
As it turned out, Katie and her team made a documentary about
me. At first, it was just going to be a short ten-minute film. But
then the project grew into a full one-hour documentary. It won
awards, and it's been shown all over the country.

These sorts of things gradually became my new life. Motivational speaker. A celebrity of sorts. Head of a foundation. A national symbol of determination, of someone who believes in and lives by the motto *Never give up, never quit.*

PEOPLE ASK ME: If I could go back in time and change things, would I do it all over again? Would I join the army? Absolutely. I loved being in the army, and I'd go back to it in a heartbeat if I could. Would I want to be injured? Absolutely not. I wouldn't wish being injured on anybody. But being a quadruple amputee is my new reality. It's what happened, and there's nothing that can be done about it in hindsight.

Sure, even with as far as I've come in my rehabilitation, there are things I miss to this day.

I miss holding my wife's hand with my real hand. Having a prosthetic that senses pressure is good, but it's not the same as the real thing.

I miss the feeling of my bare feet on the grass in summertime. Maybe that sounds a bit weird, but I loved walking around barefoot when I was a kid.

I miss lifting weights to the degree I did before my injury. I can still lift weights a bit now, but it's not the same.

I miss picking my daughter up, tossing her in the air, and catching her. I don't do that now.

Truthfully, I miss every aspect of my old life. I would love to have come back from my third deployment and gone on with my original plan. But there's no point in living in the past, dwelling on what can't be changed.

I reminisce from time to time, and that's okay, but I never want to live in the past. When things frustrate me now, I laugh them off. Or I find new ways to get smarter. The other day there was a lamp turned on that I wanted to turn off. Kelsey was out of the house at the time. The switch was one of those twisty things and I couldn't grab the dial enough to turn the lamp off. I grew frustrated for a few minutes, then I chuckled to myself and unplugged the cord from the wall socket. That did the job.

I look forward to the medical advances that will come in the future. Researchers are so close to so many breakthroughs. Hopefully, in the next ten to twenty years, they'll be able to regrow and reconstruct limbs and repair severed nerve endings. But if nothing changes until I'm ninety-five and die, I'm fine with that too. What I have today works for me, and I keep working on new and innovative ways to tackle the world around me.

We live near Augusta, the capital of Maine, and there's been so much news coverage of me over the last few years that I'm recognized pretty much everywhere I go now. If I sit in a restaurant and have lunch with a friend, people come up to me during the meal and afterward and tell me thanks for my service. I love talking with people, and I'll crack jokes and even sign autographs from time to time. People tell me that my story encourages them. That if I can keep going forward then they can too. Often I'm called a hero, but I don't know about that. I didn't do anything special. I just had a bad day at work—you know what I mean? It was a normal day in Afghanistan that turned ugly. I just had a bad case of the Mondays.

Life at home isn't all easy, even as far as I've come. The other day I went to the barbershop and fell into a snowbank on the way out. The slush was deep and it was hard for me to get my footing. That was frustrating. People came along and offered to help me, and eventually I got out. Sure, I could go around with a chip on my shoulder, saying experiences like that suck. But having a negative perspective won't do me any good. I don't want to be in a miserable mood, and I don't want to be someone who's miserable to be around. I remind myself daily that I'm one of the lucky ones. I came home alive. I have a wonderfully supportive family. I have a community that respects what I've done. I have much. I truly do.

It sounds surprising to say it, but my initial thought when I was blown up and lying on the ground in Afghanistan was a thought of full confidence. One of our medics told me I was going to be okay, and I told him then to shut up, I knew I'd be okay. That was true then, and it's true now. If I had lived or died in that moment, that wasn't up to me ultimately. Maybe that's why I remained so calm when the injury happened. That's what faith looks like, I'd say.

Sometimes I feel like I'm not a very good Christian, because I don't know the answers to a lot of things. But my faith is more at play than I let on sometimes. It sucks that I got blown up, but I believe that God has a reason for everything, even that. I think His reason was that He wants me to help others. He wants me to help spread the message that when things get bad you can still keep going forward. Like I said, I'm not wounded anymore. There's nothing wrong with me. That's my message for anybody: you can keep going.

I don't think what I've gone through is particularly harder than what plenty of other people go through. Maybe your mom has gone through terminal cancer. Or maybe you lost your job. Or maybe you struggle with an addiction. I don't compare the degree of difficulty in my story to anybody else's. We all have our unique challenges to go through. The point is that you can keep going. You can choose to never give up. You can choose to never quit.

JUST A FEW months ago, my foundation was able to buy property for a camp. It's the historic Maine Chance Lodge previously owned by cosmetics pioneer Elizabeth Arden. We're working now to raise funds to transform the property into a fully accessible veterans family retreat center. I want it to be a gift to our nation's veterans, and I know that someday that goal will be accomplished.

It's good to set big goals like that, but it's also good to set smaller goals too. Sometimes they can be just as satisfying.

Chloe is three years old now, nearly four, and we love her more than anything. Someday Kelsey and I would love to have more children. It would be great to have a little Travis Mills Junior running around. Our daughter was such a bright spot in our lives during some really dark days in the hospital. She kept us going, reminding us that we had obligations greater than ourselves to think about. Whenever people ask her what happened to her daddy, she says, "Daddy got hurt at work in an explosion." She knows enough for now.

What does success mean for me? It's being able to do normal things again. How simple that seems—to live normally—yet you'd be surprised how important that becomes when you can't do it anymore. In fact, you'd be surprised how many people around the world don't ever get that opportunity. The ability to live in freedom might be taken away due to an injury, or it might be because of political oppression. To live a life in freedom is cherished, desired, worth fighting for, worth getting wounded for, and even worth dying for.

The other day I set the little goal of driving my family to the movies in my truck. It was a special day for Chloe, and we got popcorn and went and sat down, and we watched the silliest, squirmiest princess movie you could imagine. Chloe loved every moment of it. Afterward, we went out to dinner and then I drove us all home again. Kelsey had some time for herself in the early evening, and Chloe and I wrestled around, which is one of our favorite activities. She jumped on my back and bounced on my stomach and giggled and laughed. Later, I helped put Chloe to bed, and then Kelsey and I sat up late and had our time together and talked about the day.

That night I couldn't help but think that we slept "soundly in our beds because rough men stand ready in the night to visit violence on those who would do us harm," as the quote goes. When I was in the military, I'm proud to say those were *my* rough men doing their job. And I was proud to be counted as one of them. Today, other rough men do that for me and my family, just like they do for you.

The next morning, I got Chloe's waffles made and poured juice in a cup and set the waffles on her plate along with the butter and syrup. I poured cereal and made coffee for Kelsey, then let the dogs out. When breakfast was over, I drove Chloe to school. Simple things. Gold.

To live in freedom. To go forward. To love your family. To make something of your life. To never give up. To never quit.

That's success.

# ABOUT THE TRAVIS MILLS FOUNDATION

THE TRAVIS MILLS FOUNDATION is a 501(c)(3) nonprofit organization dedicated to helping wounded and disabled veterans and their families get a new chance at life.

During his recovery at Walter Reed, Travis discovered a passion for encouraging fellow wounded veterans when he traveled from room to room in the hospital and met others whose lives had been radically reshaped by the wars.

Today, Travis continues his mission by showing wounded veterans and their families that they can overcome their physical and emotional challenges and find purpose by staying the course through their recovery.

The foundation is actively involved with several dynamic veterans initiatives, in particular the newly purchased former Maine Chance Lodge once owned by cosmetics pioneer Elizabeth Arden (1878–1966). Travis's dream is to turn the historic lodge into a retreat center for wounded and disabled veterans and their families.

Once renovated, the retreat will fill a vital role in the recovery, camaraderie, spousal support, reconnection, and relaxation of our military heroes. Travis hopes the center will become a true and lasting symbol of a grateful nation.

Built in 1929, the lodge was once part of Arden's estate and served as Ms. Arden's private home. The Foundation purchased 17 acres of the estate, which includes the main house, stables, various outbuildings, and a lakefront cottage across the road.

From 1934 to 1970, the lodge was turned into the first elite destination spa in the United States. The spa served celebrity clients such as actress Ava Gardner, entertainer Judy Garland, author Edna Ferber, and former first lady Mamie Eisenhower.

Fundraising efforts have begun in earnest to renovate this iconic homestead. Upon completion of extensive rehabilitation, the property will become the nation's first fully accessible "smart home" facility dedicated to serving the reintegration needs of combat-wounded veterans and their families.

Travis is currently seeking your help to fulfill his mission. To sponsor or donate to the cause, please make checks out to Travis Mills Foundation and send to: 89 Water Street, Hallowell, ME 04347.

TravisMills.org
info@travismills.org
@ssgtravismills

# ACKNOWLEDGMENTS

KELSEY AND I HAVE so many people to thank.

We want to send enormous thanks to our parents, Dennis and Cheri Mills, and Craig and Tammy Buck. Thanks for always being there for us. Huge thanks also go to Zach Mills, Sarah Mills-Sliter, Josh and Deanna Buck, and Kaitlin Buck. To our daughter, Chloe, you are an absolute angel.

To all our friends, you mean the world to us.

To the doctors, nurses, hospital staff, medics, and rehabilitation therapists, thank you for your amazing dedication to helping people get better.

Thanks to Reece and Katie Norris, director Jon Link, and all the people who worked on the documentary.

Thanks to the board members of the Travis Mills Foundation.

Thanks to our agent, Rick Richter of Zachary Shuster Harmsworth, and to editor Mary Choteborsky and all the team at Crown Publishing. Special thanks to collaborative writer Marcus Brotherton.

Enormous thanks to my fellow soldiers at the 82nd Airborne Division.

## ABOUT THE AUTHOR

RETIRED U.S. ARMY STAFF SERGEANT TRAVIS MILLS of the 82nd Airborne Division is a motivational speaker and international advocate for veterans and amputees. He is one of only five servicemen from the wars in Iraq and Afghanistan ever to survive his injuries as a quadruple amputee. He started the Travis Mills Foundation, which benefits and assists wounded and injured veterans. www.travismills.org

## ABOUT THE COLLABORATOR

JOURNALIST MARCUS BROTHERTON has authored or co-authored more than twenty-five books, including *A Company of Heroes*, *Shifty's War*, and the *New York Times* bestseller *We Who Are Alive and Remain*, with twenty of the original Band of Brothers. www.marcusbrotherton.com